To my father with love and gratitude:
He planted in me a fascination with the human brain
and a passion to become an author, a doctor, and a professor—
ever since I was a child.

And to the families taking care of patients with
Alzheimer's disease:
I salute their dedication and admire their patience.

THE MEMORY CURE

HOW TO PROTECT YOUR BRAIN AGAINST MEMORY LOSS AND ALZHEIMER'S DISEASE

MAJID FOTUHI, M.D., PH.D.

McGraw-Hill

New York / Chicago / San Francisco / Lisbon / London
Madrid / Mexico City / Milan / New Delhi / San Juan
Seoul / Singapore / Sydney / Toronto

11 12 13 14 15   DOC/DOC   0 9 8 7

ISBN 0-07-143366-X (Paperback)

Medical illustrations by Wendy Beth Jackelow.

The purpose of this book is to educate. It is sold with the understanding that the publisher and author shall have neither liability nor responsibility for any injury caused or alleged to be caused directly or indirectly by the information contained in this book. While every effort has been made to ensure its accuracy, the book's contents should not be construed as medical advice. Each person's health needs are unique. To obtain recommendations appropriate to your particular situation, please consult a qualified health-care provider.

McGraw-Hill books are available at special quantity discounts to use as premiums and sales promotions, or for use in corporate training programs. For more information, please write to the Director of Special Sales, Professional Publishing, McGraw-Hill, Two Penn Plaza, New York, NY 10121-2298. Or contact your local bookstore.

 This book is printed on recycled, acid-free paper containing a minimum of 50% recycled, de-inked fiber.

Library of Congress Cataloging-in-Publication Data

Fotuhi, Majid.
    The memory cure : how to protect your brain against memory loss and Alzheimer's disease / Majid Fotuhi.
        p. ; cm.
Includes bibliographical references and index.
    ISBN 0-07-140924-6 (hardcover : alk. paper)
1. Alzheimer's disease—Prevention—Popular works. 2. Memory disorders—Prevention—Popular works.
    [DNLM: 1. Alzheimer Disease—prevention & control—Popular Works.
    2. Memory Disorders—prevention & control—Popular Works.
    WT 155 F761m 2003] I. Title.
RC523.2 .F68 2003
616.8'31—dc21
                                                          2002014316

CONTENTS

9

HEREDITY AND ALZHEIMER'S 159

AFTERWORD

EXCITING AND ENGAGING YOUR MEMORY 169

APPENDIX A

RESOURCES 179

APPENDIX B

CLINICAL TRIALS 201

APPENDIX C

ALZHEIMER'S DISEASE CENTERS 209

ENDNOTES 217

INDEX 229

FOREWORD

Scientists around the world are studying the causes of memory and cognitive impairment in late life, and they all agree that aging is not associated with significant memory loss. They also agree that significant decline is related to brain disease. Thanks to dramatic advances in research, scientists have a much better understanding of the molecular changes that occur in the brains of older people and believe that these discoveries will lead to better treatments, cures, and preventions in our lifetime.

In *The Memory Cure,* Dr. Fotuhi reviews recent discoveries in the field of memory research. He describes how memory works and what degree of forgetfulness can be expected with normal aging. He also describes the characteristic features of Alzheimer's disease and gives an up-to-date account of our current understanding of the brain changes that accompany the disease.

In the past two years, scientists have discovered a number of risk factors for developing memory loss and Alzheimer's disease. Dr. Fotuhi presents these recent discoveries and discusses the role of high blood pressure, high cholesterol, and other vascular risk factors in memory loss and the possibilities of developing Alzheimer's. He also discusses the role of diet, exercise, and vitamin E in prevention of the disease. Outlining the diagnosis process, he explains the kinds of tests used to distinguish Alzheimer's from other causes of memory loss, and he explains how heredity is connected to cognitive decline. Finally, he shares a memory protection plan that explains what individuals can do to keep their memory function at its maximum.

Dr. Fotuhi has performed a real service in pulling together this information, and he presents it in a way that is understandable, logical, and usable. This book epitomizes the phrase "user-friendly" and will benefit many people.

Peter V. Rabins, M.D.
Professor of Psychiatry
Johns Hopkins University School of Medicine

ACKNOWLEDGMENTS

I am grateful for the help of dozens of my friends, family, and colleagues who have inspired, guided, and assisted me in writing this book.

During the fifteen years of my postgraduate research and neurology training, I had the honor of working alongside some of the sharpest minds of our time; at Harvard, Doctors Michael Rosenblatt and Anne Young; at Hopkins, Doctors Solomon Snyder and David Zee. They inspired me to develop a deeper understanding of how the brain works.

The idea for writing this book arose from my conversations with my dear friend, Najeeb Khalid. I thank him for his intelligent questions, support, and assistance along the way. I also appreciate the kind support and love of Vijay Mathur and Elaine Newman, who always believed in me and in my future ever since I was an undergraduate student at Concordia University's Science College in Montreal, in 1983.

At Johns Hopkins Hospital, I have the privilege of working with and learning from outstanding Alzheimer's experts. They include Doctors Jason Brandt, Maria Corrada, Barbara Crain, Catherine Diaz-Asper, Barry Gordon, Argye Hillis, Claudia Kawas, Constantine Lyketsos, Lauren Moo, Cynthia Munro, Richard O'Brien, Donald Price, Peter Rabins, Ola Selnes, Juan Troncoso, and Sevil Yasar. I am particularly thankful to Doctors Jason Brandt, John Griffin, and Richard Johnson for their feedback and encouragement; to Dr. Ola Selnes for teaching me about neuropsychological testing; and to Carol Gogel, Helen Karagiozis, Mark Macek, Sean O'Donnell, and Erica Taylor for helping me with the evaluation of patients at the Alzheimer's Disease Research Center. Above all, I thank Dr. Peter Rabins for giving me considerate and thoughtful suggestions from the very initial stages of the manuscript. His book, *The 36-Hour Day,* has touched the lives of thousands and thousands of families around the world. He inspired me to write a book that would do the same.

I thank my friends Moona Alidoost, Barbara Crain, Anjali Deshmokh, Andy and Sheila Hofert, Amir Kashani, Saeed Tavazoie, Sohail Tavazoie, Hassan Velashjerdi, and Tanya Turner for their positive feedback. I also thank my friends Sandy Kilada, for her assistance in editing and preparing the initial draft of the manuscript, and Sevil Yasar for her expert and thorough review of the final manuscript.

I thank my very dear friend Dr. Alice Flaherty at Harvard Medical School for always helping me at every step of my career; she referred me to the best literary agent in New York, Ms. Anna Ghosh, at Scovil, Chichak, and Galen Literary Agency. I thank Ms. Ghosh for her intelligent recommendations, for working on this book even when she was on vacation, and for her continued interest in promoting it around the world. I was fortunate to have the opportunity to work with Ms. Nancy Hancock, Executive Editor at McGraw-Hill. She is extremely knowledgeable and experienced; her previous book, *The Wrinkle Cure*, remains a best-seller. I thank her for her passionate enthusiasm about my manuscript and for her patience as we improved it through a dozen revisions. I also very much enjoyed working with her assistant, Ms. Meg Leder, who also worked tirelessly with a personal interest and contributed a great deal to improving it. It was also a pleasure to work with the marketing and production teams at McGraw-Hill, especially Ms. Lynda Luppino and Ms. Jane Palmieri, and our illustrator, Ms. Wendy Jackelow.

I feel I have the most wonderful family in the world. The love I share with Hamid, Maryam, Vahid, Omid, Saeed, and my parents is the driving force for me to move forward in life. I especially thank my beautiful, brilliant, and charming wife, Bita, for giving me her full unconditional love and support every minute of every day.

Majid Fotuhi

INTRODUCTION

NEW DISCOVERIES, NEW HOPES

Memory is an integral part of all your daily activities. Everything you do requires either a memory of something you learned before or learning something new.

You may not appreciate the thousands of things you do remember every day. As you wake up, you remember simple things, such as how to brush your teeth, prepare breakfast, get dressed, drive to work, and park your car. You also remember more complex things, such as your goals for that day, the deadlines you have to meet in the next few weeks, and how you can improve your job performance. You remember a dozen phone numbers and Web sites by heart, and you keep track of news in politics or sports. On any given day, you remember the names of a dozen people, including family members, and a few things about each of them, such as their age, the color of their eyes, their interests in life, and what you do or do not like about them. You can name a dozen cities and say something about each one of them.

On a more philosophical level, you need your memories for your continued happiness and success. You use your memory of mistakes you've made in the past to achieve better results today. Remembering how you pleased your spouse and had a more satisfying relationship, you now do more of the same things that keep him or her happy. Remembering how you lost money on the stock market, you may now stay away from certain stocks. The more careful you are to learn from your daily experiences and try to improve on them, the more likely it is that you'll succeed in your personal and professional life.

Even your dog remembers the things that are important to him. He knows how to get your attention and convince you to take him out more or feed him better food. He too "learns" new things, especially if you "learn" how to train him well. Like humans, all animals have the brain capacity to acquire new information in order to improve their chances of survival in nature.

On a daily basis, you also forget a great deal. You may not remember what you had for lunch yesterday or what outfit you wore last Wednesday. This is indeed a blessing; most people don't appreciate how fortunate they are that they can forget all the daily trivial things in their lives. Imagine how cluttered your brain would be if you could store memories of every meal you ever ate, every person you ever called, and every piece of news you ever read. Your brain has a way of storing most of the information that matters to you in the long run and discarding all the rest.

If you're like most other people, you often complain about your memory. You recall vividly how you forgot the name of an acquaintance at a dinner party or how you sometimes blank out on where you parked your car in a garage. You remember the few occasions your memory failed and take for granted the thousands of times that it served you well. As you grow older, you have a tendency to forget things more often—and thus you may worry that your memory loss could be serious. In the back of your mind you may wonder if you're going to develop Alzheimer's disease. You are not alone. Millions of Americans share these concerns with you.

I have the opportunity to see many such individuals at Johns Hopkins Hospital. In the majority of cases, I determine that they do not have Alzheimer's disease. The mild forgetfulness they experience is often a normal part of aging. By the end of this book, you too will find that not all memory lapses are necessarily signs of serious brain disease. Many memory problems can be minimized through actions outlined in this book. You will also learn how to protect your brain against age-associated memory loss.

Over the past five years, we have witnessed an explosion of new discoveries in the fields of aging, memory, and Alzheimer's disease. The results are encouraging. They all point to the conclusion that normal aging is not associated with disabling memory loss and that you *can* reduce your risk of developing Alzheimer's, just as you can minimize your chance of developing a heart attack. These breakthroughs have also shed light on many of the popular misconceptions that surround aging and Alzheimer's disease. You can ease your fear of Alzheimer's by increasing your understanding of these concepts.

MISCONCEPTION 1: BECOMING SENILE IS A NORMAL PART OF AGING

Twenty years ago people thought it would be normal for those older than sixty-five to become senile and lose their mental faculties. This was attributed to loss of memory cells in the brains of older individuals. However, dozens of research studies have shown that although healthy older people may be slower to learn new things or may forget minor details, they don't lose their mental abilities to acquire new information, write, recognize friends, or plan a weekend. Scientists have also established that contrary to previous beliefs, you do not lose thousands of brain cells every day. With aging, there is some shrinkage of your brain, which is for the most part due to the thinning of some brain cells. As we will see in Chapter 2, this shrinkage translates into a slower processing ability—not an inability to form new memories.

The actual number of cells in your brain does not drop significantly as you grow older. Experimental research in animals has shown that parts of the brain involved in memory actually develop new cells. The exact role of these cells remains to be established, but the fact that new cells continue to sprout inside an adult brain is encouraging. The birth of new cells has also been shown in adult human brains and is an exciting area of research.

MISCONCEPTION 2: OLDER PEOPLE WITH MEMORY PROBLEMS MUST HAVE ALZHEIMER'S

Currently, many people, old or young, worry that the mild forgetfulness they experience must be a sign of Alzheimer's disease. However, research in this field has shown that patients with Alzheimer's do not have *just* memory problems. They lose many of their other mental faculties too. They can't balance their checkbook, they can't find their way in their own neighborhood, they can't recognize their grandchildren, and, toward the end of their disease, they can't even take care of their basic needs, such as showering or getting dressed. Forgetting a few things during the day and being disabled by the memory loss and confusion associated with Alzheimer's disease are completely separate entities. Some people develop a great deal of anxiety and stress over their risk of developing Alzheimer's disease and yet have no serious disease.

MISCONCEPTION 3: ALZHEIMER'S DISEASE IS VERY COMMON

Walter Rocca, M.D., Ph.D., professor of epidemiology and neurology at the Mayo Clinic in Minnesota, believes that Alzheimer's disease is not as widespread as people (and the media) think it is. "Only one in every one hundred individuals between the ages of sixty-five and sixty-nine has this disease," he reported at the third Aging of the Brain and Dementia Conference in November 2001. The numbers are much higher only for people in their eighties and beyond. However, these individuals may also have heart disease, poor vision, poor hearing, and limited exposure to the outside world—all of which contribute to their memory decline. In my experience, most people who worry about Alzheimer's disease don't have it. They often have mild forgetfulness that comes with aging (worried well), or they may have symptoms of depression.

MISCONCEPTION 4: THERE'S NO WAY TO PREVENT MEMORY LOSS AND ALZHEIMER'S

As recently as three or four years ago, everyone thought that Alzheimer's disease would strike people randomly. The discoveries of several research studies in different parts of the world now indicate that many factors can increase a person's risk for developing the symptoms of Alzheimer's—that the process is not quite random. For example, it has been established that many risk factors that double or triple your risk for developing a heart attack also increase your risk of memory loss and becoming demented. Those who take blood pressure or cholesterol-lowering medications regularly cut their risk of developing memory loss to less than half of what it would otherwise be.

As you'll see, there are many things you can do to substantially minimize your risk of developing memory loss or Alzheimer's disease as you approach the later decades of your life. With the memory protection plan, you'll learn to take steps to protect your brain against Alzheimer's in the same way that you can take measures to lessen your risk of incurring a stroke or heart attack. Fortunately, many of the lifestyle changes needed to help you lower your risk for one of these diseases also help you lower the risks for others.

MISCONCEPTION 5: THERE'S NO TREATMENT FOR ALZHEIMER'S DISEASE

Recently developed medications are revolutionizing the care for patients who suffer from Alzheimer's disease. And now, numerous new medications are in various stages of clinical trials for Alzheimer's, more so than for any other neurological disorder, such as epilepsy or migraine. Though these medications cannot yet stop or reverse the disease, they do reduce the symptoms. They help patients stay with their families and in their own homes for at least one to two more years, obviating the need to transfer them to a nursing home. There's hope that the newer medications will be even more effective in improving the memory so that these patients can stay at home longer, as well as engage in social and intellectual activities.

In the field of Alzheimer's research, there have been some welcome surprises too. One of them is the discovery that patients who are started on treatment earlier do better in the long run. Another is that medications for some other diseases have been found to help reduce the risk of Alzheimer's.

New vaccines for Alzheimer's are currently being tested in humans in clinical trials. In laboratory animals, these drugs clear some of the Alzheimer's-related proteins from the brain. The treated animals show lower traces of the disease and seem to perform better in memory tests. Such vaccines have the potential to ease the burden of Alzheimer's disease for the next generation of the elderly. If successful, Alzheimer's disease—like paralysis due to polio—could be eradicated. At a minimum, Alzheimer's may become more like diabetes or heart disease, for which effective medications exist to help patients lead meaningful and productive lives.

My Mission

Through my experience at Harvard Medical School and the Alzheimer's Disease Research Center at Johns Hopkins, I have seen many patients who suffer from severe strokes or Alzheimer's. I share the sadness they and their families experience. At times I feel frustrated, knowing that part of their tragic outcome could have been avoided if they knew and followed instructions to reduce the risk factors for these diseases during their mid-life. I have thus set a mission for myself: to make an impact by educating people on how to protect their brains against memory loss, Alzheimer's disease, and stroke.

I will be happy if I can delay the onset of memory loss by five years for some individuals with a high propensity to develop Alzheimer's disease. I also hope I can ease the fear of thousands of people who worry unnecessarily about memory loss or Alzheimer's. I believe I can achieve this by helping people understand the basics of this disease and by providing a plan to minimize their risks for developing it. I hope one of the people I get to help is you.

PART I

THE AGING BRAIN

PERFECT MEMORY
FOR LIFE

You probably can picture Neil Armstrong walking on the moon, John F. Kennedy's assassination, and the destruction of the World Trade Center towers on September 11, 2001. No doubt you remember where you were and exactly what you were doing on those days. Clearly, your brain has the capacity to store and recall detailed information from the distant past. What you might not know is that it's possible for you to have this kind of recall as you age: to have a perfect memory for life.

Understanding how your brain and your memory work is a necessary step to learning how to protect and stimulate your brain in order to achieve a lifetime of perfect memory. In this book, we will discuss how your brain and memory work and when they are at risk, and what you can do today that will improve your memory in the decades to come. We'll also explore "normal" memory and how and why it varies from person to person.

HOW MEMORY WORKS

Your memories are a reflection of your whole life. When you remember your child's first smile, you relive the joy you felt during that very special moment. Etched in hundreds of billions of cells in your brain, your memories come to the surface when you hear the voice of an old friend or see a picture of your childhood home. Cells in other parts of your body—such as your skin, stomach, and liver—slough off and get replaced, but for the most part, the cells in your brain are the same ones you were born with. They witness with you all that you experience over decades of your life. These brain cells are what mediate your sense of vision, hearing, and taste, as well as your experiences of joy, frustration, sadness, success, pride, and, of course, your memory. To do this, the cells in different parts of your brain have divided the responsibilities for making new and different forms of memory.

Let's begin our exploration with the three different types of memory and processes that occur in your brain when you encounter something new: long-term memory, short-term memory, and procedural memory.

LONG-TERM MEMORY

There are three stages in making a memory that lasts from hours to decades: acquisition, storage, and retrieval. To remember a name or an event, you first *acquire* that information in some parts of your brain, and then you *store* it in other parts. Once stored, you have access to that information and can *retrieve* it at any time. This process is analogous to operations in a large library. Books are first acquired from various sources, then stored in different places throughout the library. They can be retrieved easily by a call number.

Thanks to sophisticated new brain imaging techniques, as well as years of studies with animals and with patients who have memory problems, brain scientists can now pinpoint where most of the above processes in the brain take place. You acquire information from the world around you—mostly through your eyes and ears—in your hippocampus, and you store them in your cortex. Let's take a closer look by using an event you're likely to remember well.

Try and remember what you were doing on the morning of September 10, 2001. You probably don't remember much. Now think about what you were doing on the morning of September 11, 2001. No doubt you can provide accurate details on where you were, the people you were with, and how you were feeling. As you were watching the news on television with anxiety and stress, the sights of the World Trade Center towers crumbling down and the sounds of sirens in New York streets were pouring into your brain through your eyes and ears. All this information was funneled to your hippocampus, the part of your brain that is critical for making new memories.

In fact, you have one hippocampus on the left side of your brain and one on the right side. Each looks like a small banana and sits near your ears. In the hippocampus, a subset of information—pieces that are relevant to you—gets etched more firmly and is then sent to other parts of your brain for long-term storage. To continue our library metaphor, you can think of the hippocampus as a librarian (in the acquisition section) who throws out the junk mail and keeps the important publications.

The part of your brain that receives the information from the hippocampus is the *cortex*. We'll discuss this further in the next chapter, but for now, suffice it to say that the cortex is a sheet of cells sitting on top of the brain, and each part of it has a specific function, such as vision, hearing, or smelling. On September 11, the "sight" of the towers crumbling down was shipped for long-term storage to the "vision" parts of your cortex, and the "sound" of sirens was shipped for long-term storage to "hearing" parts of the cortex. Thanks to your hippocampus and cortex, all this information sits vividly in your brain, and you can instantly retrieve it.

In contrast, you forgot the events of September 10 because they were not too crucial to you. Your hippocampus did receive a great deal of information that day, as it does every day, but it was not worthy of long-term storage. On a daily basis, you encounter thousands of pieces of information, but only the pieces that are meaningful and significant are likely to make an impression on your hippocampus and get shifted to other parts of your brain for storage in long-term memory. As you'll see in the Afterword, we'll discuss ways you can heighten your attention and senses in order to memorize things that are not that important but which you'll want to remember anyway, like the names of acquaintances you see once or twice a year.

SHORT-TERM MEMORY

Often, you need to keep some information in your brain for only a few minutes. This is what a waiter does when he takes your lunch order without writing it down and remembers it until he goes to the kitchen. The information about your order reaches his hippocampus but does not get stored in his cortex; unless you were his only customer or if you ordered something unusual, the waiter will not remember your order the next day. This is called *short-term memory*.

Another example of short-term memory is momentarily committing to memory a telephone number provided by directory assistance. You keep this information in your hippocampus for only a few minutes, perhaps until after you dial the number. You quickly forget this phone number since your hippocampus does not consider it worthy of long-term memory. Still another short-term example occurs when you listen to the morning news on radio or TV. Within minutes of hearing it, you can list most of what you learned.

Once you leave the house, however, you probably forget most of the news and remember only the stories that you consider relevant. You subconsciously erase all the information that is not meaningful to you.

Hippocampus: Gateway for New Memories

You might be wondering how scientists discovered that learning new names and phone numbers happens in the hippocampus, and not some other corner of the brain. The important discoveries in this field have come from studies of patients who had surgery in the memory portions of their brain as well as studies with animals.[1]

In the 1940s, Wilder Penfield, M.D., a neurosurgeon at the Montreal Neurological Institute in Canada, placed a small electrode on the surface of the brain during brain tumor surgeries. In this way, he could record the electrical activity of those brain cells so he wouldn't remove any of the normal cells along with the tumor. Since the brain itself cannot feel pain, he could perform this type of surgery under local anesthesia.

Dr. Penfield was able to also deliver small electrical shocks and see if the patient's arm twitched. After recording and stimulating the surface of the brain—the cortex—in more than one thousand patients, he was able to map where different functions for control of arm movements, vision, and sensation in the hands were located on the cortex. In some patients, the stimulation of areas around the hippocampus led to a coherent recollection and description of an earlier experience. These memorylike responses could not be elicited elsewhere in the brain. Thus, it appeared that the hippocampus and its neighboring structures were important for memory.

In some rare patients, the hippocampus on both sides had to be removed to relieve severe seizures that could not be treated with medications. Brenda Milner, Ph.D., professor of psychology at McGill University in Montreal, worked with Dr. Penfield and studied the memory of these patients before and after surgery. She discovered that though they had completely lost their ability to make new memories, they could still recall old memories. One of her patients was Mr. H. M. She would talk to him for ten minutes, leave the room, and when she returned half an hour later, he would greet her as if he had never seen her before. If she left the room and returned a third time, he was just as surprised when she told him her name. These patients would listen to the same joke three or four times and laugh each time as if they'd never heard the joke before. Without a functioning hippocampus, they were unable to "acquire" and learn new information. And yet, they could tell stories from childhood, high school, or any time period before the surgery, which meant that even without their hippocampus they could still recall old memories.

Carol Barnes, Ph.D., professor of psychology at the University of Arizona, has recently performed studies in rats that show how cells in the hippocampus are important for remembering the location of food in their environment.[2] She placed small recording electrodes in the brains of the rats to track the activity of cells in the hippocampus as the rats looked for food pellets in a maze. When the rat was not searching, the cells showed no activity. When the rat approached the location where it thought the food should be, based on previous experience, the neurons would start responding. This study showed that certain cells in the hippocampus had learned the location of the food in the maze and would show increased activity when the rat went to that location.

Other researchers have performed similar experiments with monkeys. They found cells in parts of the cortex that show increased activity if the animal saw a familiar face, but not other faces. These cells are parts of a network devoted to remembering faces.[3]

The hippocampus is the gateway for the formation of new memories. In a simplified computer analogy, it works as RAM (Random Access Memory), where information is kept for a brief period of time. In this analogy, the cortex serves as the hard disk where permanent memories are kept.[4]

PROCEDURAL MEMORY

You learn how to ride a bicycle by trial and error. You fall a few times and then you gradually discover how to keep your balance without falling. When you first learn how to play tennis, you hit the ball all over the court (and get frustrated) until you figure out the best way to hold the racket and hit the ball so it will go over the net and land inside the other person's court. You "get a feel" for the racket, the ball, and the court. Similarly, when you first learn how to peel a cucumber, tie your shoelaces, or learn to dance, you acquire new skills by physically performing the same movement over and over again. *Procedural memory* is operating whenever you have to repeat certain hand or leg movements to learn something new. You could never perform these movements well just by reading about them or watching them on television; you must physically do them.

Dr. Brenda Milner discovered that procedural memory does not depend on the hippocampus. She saw that patients who had selective damage to their hippocampi could still perform and learn new skilled hand movements, even though they could not learn any new names, phone numbers, or dates. For example, you could teach them how to trace the edges of a star by having them look at their hand indirectly in a mirror. They initially found it difficult and spent a great deal of time on the task, but they improved with practice. However, when told that they were getting better with daily exercise, they might say, "What are you talking about? I've never seen this task before."[5]

If not in the hippocampus, then where does the procedural memory take place in the brain? Learning new dance steps or learning how to use chopsticks to eat Chinese food takes place, at least in part, in the *cerebellum* and the *basal ganglia*. The cerebellum is an apple-sized structure sitting at the back of the brain, near the neck. Basal ganglia are a constellation of brain areas located at the base of the brain. As you'll see in the later chapters, these areas are less prone to damage with aging or in Alzheimer's disease.

The fact that a different part of the brain is involved for learning new movements than the part used for learning new names and facts is good news for patients with Alzheimer's disease. It means we can enhance the quality of their lives by teaching them exercises that involve the arms and legs—at a time when their ability to learn and understand written and spoken language is limited. Learning a new fun game brings smiles not only to the faces of these patients, but also to the faces of their families and caregivers.

PERFECT BUT SLOWER MEMORY SKILLS

As you grow older, some degree of wear and tear in your body is inevitable. You may walk slower, find that your bowel and bladder don't work as regularly as they used to, and need glasses or hearing aids. It would be reasonable to expect that your memory would show some mild slowing too. However, while most people don't mind walking slower, having a weaker grip, or seeing things less clearly, they very much mind having difficulty with their memory. People attach more meaning to their mental slowing than they do to their physical slowing.

Several research studies have indicated that it is only the speed of the learning process that slows down with aging and that the elderly maintain their baseline ability to learn and remember. In Denver, Colorado, at the April 2002 meeting of the directors of the Alzheimer's Disease Research Centers in the United States, Tim Salthouse, Ph.D., drew on his research in discussing memory in people from age eighteen to eighty. Part of his data was collected from vocational companies that test employees who ask for promotions. The subjects were of course motivated to do well since their managers could use their test results in deciding if they deserved to be promoted.

Examining the memory performance of this research group through advancing decades of life, Dr. Salthouse found, perhaps not surprisingly, that the older a person was, the slower his performance was.[6] Thus, the thirty-year-olds were slower than the twenty-year-olds but faster than the forty-year-olds. A similar decline across ages was noted with respect to their visual acuity and grip strength. However, the subjects maintained their ability to learn new things—though at a slower pace—way into their eighties.

Though it would be great to be able to learn new things as quickly as when you were a child, it is not essential for success. In today's society, people over age sixty-five rule the country. The most outstanding senators, judges, doctors, lawyers, economists, and CEOs are not the men and women in their thirties, but are the individuals who carry with them several decades of experience and know-how. Their brains and memories work quite well. Such individuals have the advantage of having both knowledge and wisdom. The main disadvantage for them lies in their speed of processing information: They are indeed slower than they once were. Contrary to the proverb that says "You can't teach an old dog new tricks," you *can*. It just takes longer.

Mr. and Mrs. Gonzales attend tango lessons in a dance studio in Texas almost three nights a week. They are in their seventies. They find it difficult to perform many of the complicated steps and need more time to master them. They keep practicing—and are having fun doing it. They dance much better than some of the younger couples in the class.

The good news is that as you can improve your physical health and minimize age-associated decline with respect to strength and stamina, you can also strengthen your memory muscles and become better at learning and remembering—regardless of your age. Researchers at the University of Texas at Austin have developed an eight-session cognitive enhancement program entitled, "Memories, Memories, Can We Improve Ours?" Before and after presenting this program, they tested 19 older adults whose average age was eighty-three. The subjects showed a significant improvement in prospective memory items, such as asking for an appointment, asking for a belonging, and delivering a message.[7]

This illustrates an important point: *It is never too late to start improving your memory.* You can get better at remembering things even if you are in your eighties. Most people stop trying to challenge their memory as they grow older because they assume they've lost their mental strength. They are often surprised with their own performance after making an effort. To be successful in shaping up your memory muscles, you need to concentrate, be motivated, and be determined. There's no reason why you cannot maximize your mental fitness—just as you can maximize your physical fitness—at any age. In future chapters, you'll discover the specific steps you can take to achieve this goal.

SIGHT, SOUNDS, AND MEMORY

At the beginning of the chapter we discussed the three stages of memory: acquisition, storage, and retrieval. The acquisition step involves the entry of information from the world around you—through mostly your eyes and ears—to your brain. If you only can absorb half the material you're exposed to, you cannot expect yourself to remember all of it. If you have poor vision or hearing, which is common among the elderly, your ability to remember it all will be limited.

As an older person, you may need glasses and/or hearing aids, or you may need to adjust the glasses or hearing aids you already have. Unfortunately, most older individuals do not adjust these important sensory devices on a regular basis. In a study of people of advanced years with hearing aids, scientists found that a quarter of the group had hearing aids that were not functioning properly. When they tuned the hearing aids, patients appreciated how much better they could hear. This may sound trivial, but it's very important because the acquisition of information relies on the sensory stimulation by sight, sound, taste, touch, and smell. If your brain cannot fully hear the name of a person you are meeting for the first time, you can hardly expect yourself to remember that person's name when you see them at a later time. Sometimes people confuse difficulty with hearing and communication with early Alzheimer's disease.

Mr. White, a delightful eighty-six-year-old retired schoolteacher, came to my office accompanied by his wife. She was concerned that he was exhibiting early signs of Alzheimer's disease. He did not like answering the phone or listening to the news on the radio, and he would forget the names of acquaintances. After talking with him, I learned that he had not checked his hearing aids in a long time and could barely hear me. He explained that he continued to handle their household finances, did crossword puzzles daily, and kept up with current affairs through read-

ing the newspaper. He did not like answering the phone because he felt that "people speak too fast these days." His formal tests showed some mild memory problems and an outstanding score for his math and language skills. I felt that given his level of functioning at the age of eighty-six, he did not have Alzheimer's disease. He had some mild forgetfulness that was acceptable and would most likely show improvement with better sensory input (hearing). Prescription: He needed a good pair of hearing aids.

Mr. White's case contains an important point regarding memory and old age in our society. *Life moves faster today than it did forty years ago.* Newscasters and reporters on the evening news speak rapidly and often in truncated sentences. Even animated TV shows like *The Simpsons* and cartoons roll in a much quicker pace than did the *Flintstones* or *Bugs Bunny*. People swamped by deadlines and appointments sometimes speak at the speed of light. Elderly people find it difficult to keep up with the fast tempo of information presented to them. Once they have the opportunity to register the information at their own pace, they can remember it just as well as a younger person, if not better. In the example above, Mr. White had read most of the news in the newspapers at his own pace, rather than getting news from TV programs, and was up-to-date on events around the world.

One of the most memorable classes I attended at Harvard Medical School was a small group session about evaluating the elderly. To appreciate what they might experience on a daily basis, we were given goggles, earplugs, and gloves and were asked to thread a needle. We realized how frustrating it was not to see, hear, and feel our hands well. We learned how difficult it must be to keep up with the fast pace of modern life as we age. This exercise helped us realize that we need to slow down when we interact with our elderly patients.

TEENAGERS VERSUS RETIREES

Memory problems are not limited to older adults. Even teenagers and people in their twenties forget things. The difference is in *how* younger and older adults view lapses in their memory. When a teenager forgets the name of a classmate or where he left his books, he'll probably ignore it or think it's funny. He most likely moves on to other things and does not dwell on his memory failure. Later, while eating dinner or talking on the phone, he may remember the information.

Older people may have the same frequency of memory lapses, and they too will remember what they had momentarily forgotten. However, when these "senior moments" happen, they become alarmed. They lack confidence in their memory and fear that they may be starting to show the first signs of aging or Alzheimer's disease. The best approach for everyone is not to dwell on these moments, to realize that they are normal throughout everyone's life, regardless of your age.

MEMORY LAPSES AND LAUGHTER

In his book *Memory,* Barry Gordon, M.D., Ph.D., professor of neurology at Johns Hopkins Hospital, suggests that if you can laugh about your memory lapses, other people will laugh with you and tell you about their own experiences. Dr. Gordon describes a story that illustrates this point:

> *A hostess was introducing her old and dear friend at a party and suddenly forgot her name. She looked at her friend and laughed. Her friend noticed that she had blocked on her name and went on to introduce herself. She could relate to similar experiences in her own life. At the end, everyone laughed and no one was embarrassed.*[8]

VARIATION IN MEMORY PERFORMANCE

According to Marilyn Albert, Ph.D., professor of psychiatry and neurology at Harvard Medical School, there is a great deal of individual variability in learning and memory among the elderly, much more so than among a group of young adults.[9] People have different color eyes, height, level of intelligence, and not surprisingly, different capability for learning and memory.

Starting from high school, some individuals have inherently better memories and seem to know everyone's name at a party and do well in memory puzzles. This variability among people increases throughout the advancing decades of life, in part because of each person's educational experience, physical health, and occupational achievements. You could either have a photographic memory or struggle to remember a grocery list, and yet in either case be considered "normal" as long as it's how you've been all along. In other words, each person is different, and "normal" for that person is based on what he or she was able to do a few years earlier, not necessarily on what other people his or her age can do.

Mr. Lewis, a handsome ninety-one-year-old gentleman, was a retired engineer. He had a very active lifestyle, and he showed me a list of 20 things he had to do the day he came to my clinic. During the week, he was busy taking care of his stocks, attending to his family, and reading technical journals. Recently, he was concerned by the fluctuations in the stock market, and he decided to sell some of his shares and invest in mutual funds. On weekends, he worked on repairing the wings of his airplane. He loved to fly by himself. His physical and mental health were comparable to most sixty-year-olds. He had a propensity to forgetfulness, so he made a habit of using "to do" lists. Despite his old age, Mr. Lewis showed no signs of slowing down. When I asked about the secret for his longevity, he laughed and said, "A positive attitude and a smile."

A great deal of the differences among people with regard to their mental faculties is a reflection of their early childhood education and their habit of learning new things throughout life. Concerning physical fitness, there are similar variations among people. Some of the elderly participate in triathlons, while others take long walks. Here, too, past experiences contribute to variability among the elderly; those who exercise regularly are less likely to develop physical disabilities.

THERE'S HOPE

The fact that you have vivid memories of Neil Armstrong's landing on the moon or the events of September 11 shows that you *can* have perfect memory for life. As you grow older, you do experience some slowing in the process of making new memories and remembering old ones. However, according to Dr. Marilyn Albert of the Harvard Medical School, once you give yourself enough time to learn the material well, you do not forget what you've learned any more rapidly than younger people.[10] You need to be realistic with your expectations and realize that your brain memory system is designed for you to remember things that are relevant and important—not all the details of everyday life. As you will see in future chapters, you can maximize your learning ability by improving your brain function—through reducing the risk factors that slow down your brain and increasing those factors that enhance your brain.

2

UNDERSTANDING
THE AGING BRAIN

YOUR BRAIN AND YOUR BEHAVIOR

Your brain makes you who you are. Your personality, your worries, your joys, and your plans for the future all arise as a result of activity among the more than 100 billion cells in your brain. Even the excitement you feel when you kiss someone you love originates from the firing activity of certain brain cells. These cells are activated when your lips send strong sensory messages to your brain. In response, your brain cells trigger the release of excitatory hormones that quicken your heart rate, something you do notice. You attribute the "love" you feel to your heart, since it is there that you feel the palpitation, but the true source of the feeling is in the firing activity of your brain cells.

Though you can't observe the operation of your brain at work the way you can touch your chest and feel the beating of your heart, you can get a feel for the link between your brain and your behavior by paying attention to how beverages, food, or drugs that change the activity of your brain cells change your behavior. Consider the following examples:

• The caffeine molecules in your morning coffee reach certain brain cells that mediate your sense of attention and mood. After a few sips, you start feeling more energetic, and your outlook on life and how much responsibility you can handle improves. You feel good. After about an hour the effects start to wear off, those cells return to their baseline level of activity, and you miss that extra energy.

- If you skip breakfast, you may experience a drop in your blood glucose levels right before lunch. With less glucose available to your brain cells, you may become more irritable or have difficulty concentrating. After you eat, you become yourself again.

- In the evening, if you drink a glass of wine with dinner, you feel more relaxed; unlike caffeine, alcohol molecules slow down the firing activity of your brain cells.

- Prescription drugs can alter your mood and behavior. Antidepressant medications make a person who is depressed feel better and able to cope with his or her problems in a more positive way. Such drugs don't make the problems vanish, but they do restore the imbalance in the brain chemicals that led to the depression. Recreational drug abuse can change a person's mood and behavior in a more rapid and dramatic way. These changes include hyperactivity, somnolence, delusions, or hallucinations. Both of these examples illustrate how your behavior can fluctuate as a result of changes in the cellular activity of your brain.

For centuries, scientists have been trying to find out which areas of the brain are linked with the control of behavior. Their discoveries from experiments with animals, the treatment of soldiers with brain injuries, and modern imaging techniques point to areas in front of the brain, right behind your forehead, called *frontal lobes*. One interesting example involves a railroad worker who had parts of his left frontal lobe destroyed from an accident.

Mr. Phineas Gage, a young foreman on a railroad blasting crew in the United States in 1848, was a polite, proper, and considerate man. One day, while manipulating a mine with his tamping metal rod, the mine exploded. The one inch, thirteen pound rod flew through his left cheek and left eye, penetrated his forehead, and came out of the top of his head. He was taken to the hospital immediately. To everyone's surprise, he had a rapid recovery. However, he was not quite the same person he used to be. His friends and family noted that his personality and behavior had deteriorated dramatically. With his frontal lobes damaged, he had turned into an obstinate, childish, crude, and aggressive man prone to uttering gross profanities. He ended up divorcing his wife and quitting his job. He later worked as a stable hand, a coach driver, and a sideshow freak (with P. T. Barnum's circus).[1]

BRAIN EVOLUTION

A simple story of how the brain has evolved illustrates how it works.

Simple organisms like bacteria did not have any nerves. They could only detect the levels of chemical nutrients or toxins in their surroundings and chose to wiggle toward or away from them. The fish in the ocean were the first to have a simple spinal cord and a primitive brain. They could move more freely and chase prey. Birds and mammals developed more sophisticated nervous systems. Their brains had an elaborate layer of cells on top, called the cortex. As a result, these animals were able to hunt more successfully, build nests, and protect their young more effectively.

The cortex became increasingly larger in cats, dogs, and monkeys. It enabled them to not only take care of their instinctive needs, but to experience and express feelings like joy and jealousy. They still could not speak. Human brains grew to have the largest amount of cortex. As a result, humans are capable of performing complex tasks such as speaking, writing poetry, playing an instrument, and flying to the moon.

The role of the frontal lobe in human behavior was also evidenced by surgeries in the 1940s on patients with excessive aggressive behavior who had failed to improve with available medications. In these "frontal lobotomies," surgeons would carefully remove parts of the frontal lobes. Many patients would lose their aggression and become calm and quiet. Of course, as better medications became available, this crude procedure was no longer appropriate.

Antonio Damasio, M.D., Ph.D., chairman of the Department of Neurology at the University of Iowa and an international leader in the field of brain and behavioral sciences, recently studied human emotions with the use of modern PET imaging techniques.[2] In these experiments, Dr. Damasio and his colleagues asked 41 volunteers to recall events that brought about feelings of anger, happiness, sadness, and fear while lying still and being monitored by PET scan. The level of brain activity was measured, showing that different emotions activated different parts of the brain. In other words, it appears that your *experience* of different emotions takes place throughout many regions of the brain, while your ability to *control* your emotions and behavior depend to a great extent on your frontal lobes.

LOOKING INTO YOUR BRAIN

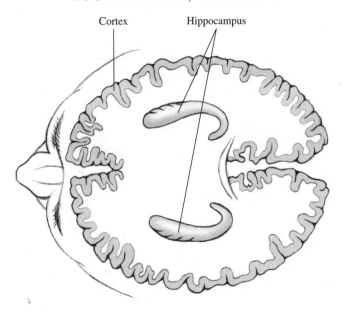

Cortex   Hippocampus

The part of your brain essential for making new memories is called the hippocampus. Without it, you may remember your childhood memories, but you would not be able to learn new phone numbers. There is one hippocampus in the left side of your brain and one in the right side. Each looks like a banana, lying deep in your brain near your ears.

The part of your brain essential for hearing, seeing, thinking, speaking, writing, solving problems, and making plans is called the cortex. This is also where the sights and sounds of old memories are stored. The cortex is like a watermelon rind that surrounds the other brain structures, including hippocampus. You can see that these are all interconnected.

YOUR BRAIN AT WORK

Your brain does a lot more than mediating your ability to experience emotions and making sure that you smile appropriately with your friends and family. You can walk, read, drive, cook, solve mathematical problems, travel, make plans for your week, and play sports. You can understand abstract thoughts (such as the meaning of proverbs), appreciate the complexity of world political crises, or read poetry. But where do these different functions of the brain take place?

Scientists believe that the most important part of your brain for the functions described above is the cortex. It is a thick sheet of cells sitting on top of the brain and extending all the way from the front—behind your forehead—to the back (see Looking into your Brain on page 18). This layer of cells has tight interconnections with other parts of your brain. It constantly receives information from them and sends out commands.

The cortex is perhaps the most sophisticated part of the brain, and its complexity is what distinguishes humans from animals. The human cortex has expanded greatly, compared to even monkeys, and is folded tightly on itself in order to fit inside the skull. The cortex on the right side of your brain controls the left side of your body, and the cortex on the left side of your brain controls your body's right side.

Each segment of the cortex seems to be more directly linked with one of the functions of the brain. For example, areas in the back of the cortex are more important for your vision. This area is called the "visual cortex." If a patient develops a stroke in the visual cortex (left and right), he becomes blind. The auditory cortex enables you to hear sounds, the olfactory cortex is for your sense of smell, the somatosensory cortex enables you to distinguish different tactile sensations, and the motor cortex gives you the ability to control your arm and leg movements. There are also cortical areas devoted to understanding language, producing speech, and recognizing faces. The hippocampus, which helps you form new memories, is also an extension of your cortex.

If you had special glasses and could look at the cortex through the skull, you could not differentiate between these different cortical areas. There are some differences between cortical areas—between the visual cortex and motor cortex, for instance—but they are apparent only after a brain is sectioned and viewed under a microscope. However, by simply looking at the brain, you can see that some of the folds of the cortex are more prominent. The spaces between the larger folds are roughly in the same location from one person to the next. They serve as landmarks for scientists to divide the *visible* surface of the cortex into four subdivisions: the frontal, temporal, parietal, and occipital "lobes." A fifth lobe that lies deeper in the brain, called the limbic lobe, cannot be easily distinguished by looking at the outside surface of the cortex. Each lobe consists of three to five different "functional" cortical areas. For example, the temporal lobe contains the cortical areas for hearing, understanding language, and memory.[3]

─────

NAVIGATING THROUGH YOUR BRAIN

Let's navigate through your brain as your spouse asks you to set the dinner table (see Setting the Table on page 21). Her voice enters through your ears, reaching the parts of your cortex for hearing and then to those parts that enable you to understand language. If you were asked to set the table in Chinese, you wouldn't know what to do (assuming you don't know Chinese). The language part of your brain is centered mostly in the left temporal lobe, near your left ear.

Once you comprehend what you need to do, you need to remember what goes on the table and in what order. The memory of typical items for a dinner table resides in cortical areas near the language areas in the *temporal lobes*. Planning how to first put the plates, then glasses and silverware, and finally the food dishes happens in the *frontal lobes*—the vicinity of cortical areas that enable you to decide how to plan your behavior later at the dinner table. The information about the memory of the items on the table is therefore sent from the temporal lobes to the frontal lobes. As you carry things to the table, the cells in your motor cortex, which is also a part of your frontal lobe, control the movement of your arms and legs. They send commands to the cells in your spinal cord, which in turn activate your muscles.

As you walk back and forth, you don't bump into the table or the walls because you know—in your own mind—where things are. This sense of "orientation to space" is mediated by a part of the cortex called the *parietal lobe*. This is another large part of the cortex. The parietal lobe sits between the temporal lobe and front lobe on each side of your brain, and is in continuous communication with them as you complete your task.

If you watch TV, listen to music, or talk with a friend while you set the table, you're engaging multiple parts of your brain at the same time. The parts of the cortex responsible for your ability to watch TV—in the visual cortex—sit in the back of your brain, in the *occipital lobe*. If you experience a sense of satisfaction or joy for having set the table well, other parts of your brain—parts of the *limbic lobe*—are activated too.

What happens to various parts of your brain when you're simply lying down on your bed and reading a book? Are the cortical areas for your leg movement, facial expression, or hearing silent during this period? The answer is no. All your cortical areas maintain a baseline level of activity, which increases as needed. So even if you are only reading a book, you still move your legs once in a while, have an expression on your face (even if it's not happy or sad), and hear some noise in the background.

SETTING THE TABLE

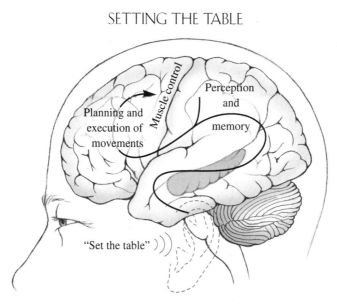

The information from the world around you—the sounds, sights, and other sensations—is processed by your brain. After you hear and comprehend a request—for example, set the table—the information flows to the back half of your cortex, the area for perception and memory. When you decide to take action, the information then moves to the front half of your cortex, the part for the planning and execution of movements. This information then flows to the motor cortex, which controls the muscles of your arms and legs.

This is an oversimplified view of the brain; in reality, things are a lot more complicated.

These are gross generalizations. The actual processes that take place in your brain are far more complex. However, these examples do demonstrate how different parts of your brain focus on different aspects of your daily actions. As you can see, your brain performs myriad functions, most of which happen subconsciously.

To summarize, each main lobe in the cortex is a part of a network of brain cells with specific functions:

1. Frontal lobes are the part of the cortex sitting in front of your brain, just behind your forehead. The cortex here serves your ability to plan your

A JOURNEY INSIDE THE BRAIN OF A FATHER PLAYING BASEBALL WITH HIS SON

Imagine watching the father's brain in action as he prepares to hit the ball. But first let's take a tour of his brain. The main part that can be seen from the outside is the *cortex*. It looks like a sheet of cells with many small and large folds that hides the deeper brain structures. The larger folds on the cortex are in about the same places in all people and can be used as landmarks on the brain. They divide the cortex into subdivisions, or *lobes*. The cortex in each lobe is linked with specific functions of the brain. The left and right cortical areas serve similar functions, though with some variation. Now let's look at what goes on in the father's brain as he is about to hit the ball that his son throws. We'll focus on the cortex and its different lobes, which are the areas that show the greatest degree of change with aging and with Alzheimer's disease. The cerebellum, other brain structures, and the spinal cord remain largely intact.

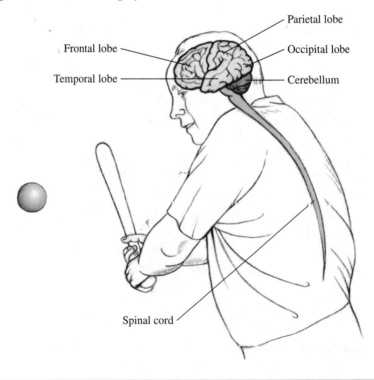

Parietal lobe

Frontal lobe

Occipital lobe

Temporal lobe

Cerebellum

Spinal cord

- *Frontal lobes.* Parts of these large cortical areas are linked with planning, execution, and control of movements. Thus, as the father looks at the ball, these areas are extremely active. They're anticipating how fast the ball will be hitting the bat and how hard he needs to hit it. Brain cells in these areas send messages to his spinal cord in order to control his arm swing.

  Other cortical areas in the frontal lobe are linked with abstract thinking and making long-term plans. At the moment, they're less active. They would become more active later if he considers buying a bigger house or if they should have another baby. Still other cortical areas within the frontal lobes, and especially those on the left side, are linked with the ability to speak. They're active as he tells his son to throw him the ball.

- *Parietal lobes.* These cortical areas are located farther back behind the frontal lobes. They're linked with the sense of touch, feeling weight and motion, proprioception (the sense of knowing where your hands are without looking at them), and self-orientation. These areas are highly active as he senses the weight of the bat and the texture inside his batting gloves, and feels that he's standing in the best spot to hit the ball.

  Some cortical areas of the parietal lobes, especially those on the right side, are linked with the sense of art and music appreciation. Other areas, on the left, mediate the ability to solve mathematical problems. These areas are less active at this time.

- *Temporal lobes.* Some of the cortex in the temporal lobe mediates the sense of hearing and of understanding language. They would become active only if his son told him something. Other parts of the temporal lobe are folded (hemmed) inward and would not be visible from the outside. These include the hippocampus, which is essential for learning and memory. Since he's about to hit the ball, there probably wouldn't be much firing in these brain cells.

- *Occipital lobes.* These cortical areas mediate his sense of vision. They are active as he sees the ball coming at him.

- *Cerebellum.* The cerebellum, about the size of an apple, is tucked under the cortex in the back of the brain. It's linked with the ability to fine-tune movements so they become more accurate with practice. It's also important for balance and coordination. The cerebellum would be highly active as the batter maintains a stable posture in order to optimize his ability to hit the ball and swing his arms.

- *Spinal cord.* Some cells in the spinal cord extend their output branches to muscles in arms and legs. They receive commands from the frontal lobes and the cerebellum about how fast and when to activate muscles. They are highly active as the batter balances his legs and moves his arms. Other cells in the spinal cord are important for breathing, heart rate, sweating, bowel movements, and sensation from the skin.

day, organize your work, type a letter, pay attention to details, and control the movements of your arms and legs. It also contributes to your personality and your behavior.

2. Temporal lobes are the part of the cortex sitting on the sides of your brain, just between your ears and temples. The cortex here serves your ability to hear, understand language, and form memories. The hippocampus sits deep inside your brain, but it is still a part of the temporal lobe.

3. Parietal lobes are the parts of the cortex sitting between the frontal and temporal lobes. The cortex here serves your ability to distinguish between the texture of a piece of wood from a piece of fruit by touching it (your sense of touch), and your ability to orient yourself in the city in order to know how to get from your house to your work. It also helps you balance your checkbook or appreciate arts and music.

4. Occipital lobes are the part of the cortex in the back of your brain. The cortex here serves your ability to see the world around you and to recognize the faces and pictures you have seen before.

5. Limbic lobes are the parts of the cortex that cannot be seen on the exposed surface of the brain. Each limbic lobe consists of parts of other lobes that lie deep in the brain or on the medial aspects where the two halves of the brain face each other (like two halves of a cut apple touching each other). These cortical areas mediate your ability to experience emotions such as joy, sadness, fear, or satisfaction. They are the parts of your brain that influence your feelings and behavior.

BRAIN CELLS TALKING

There are two main types of cells in your brain, *neurons* and *glia*. Neurons are the main cells that send and receive signals. The glia cells support neurons and ensure that they can function without interruption. Some glia form a protective sheet around the branches of neurons, while others soak up the excess ions or toxic metabolites that could be harmful to neurons.

Each neuron is shaped like an octopus with thousands of branches extending from it. One of these branches, the *axon*, is thin and long and serves as the output of the neuron. The other branches, *dendrites*, are often shorter and thicker and serve as input segments of the cell. The extensive combination of different-sized cell bodies and branching patterns results in

BRAIN CELLS HAVE LONG BRANCHES

Each neuron looks like a microscopic octopus, with a central nucleus and long branches floating around it. One of these branches—the axon—is usually thinner and longer than the others, like a string on a balloon. The axon is usually the output branch that sends signals to other neurons. The thicker branches—dendrites—act as recipient docks and receive signals from other neurons. The junction point where the end of an axon comes to almost touch the dendrite is called a synapse.

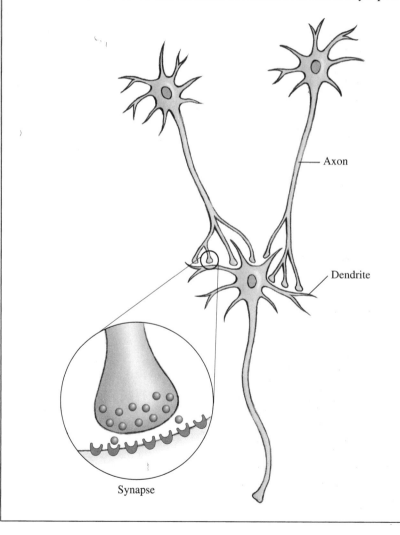

Axon

Dendrite

Synapse

a thousand different shapes and types of neurons in your brain. This is in contrast to your liver, heart, or kidney, where there are only a dozen different cell types working together to make that organ work.

Neurons in different parts of the brain "talk" to each other by sending and receiving (electrochemical) signals through these branches.[4] For example, some neurons from the motor cortex—such as those responsible for moving your leg—have a long thin axon that travels all the way to the lower part of your spinal cord. The cell body of this neuron is microscopic—one thousand times smaller than the tip of a needle—but its axon is two feet long! Neurons that communicate with their counterparts on the opposite side of the brain have branches that are two to six inches long (see Brain Cells Have Long Branches on page 25).

BRAIN POTENTIAL

There is far more potential in your brain than you can imagine. Just look at the accomplished people in sports, arts, science, or medicine to see how an individual can produce amazing results. If motivated, you too can run faster, jump higher, read more, create artistic masterpieces, and do just about anything you wish to accomplish. The secret for your potential lies in the unique way your brain is assembled.

The brain has evolved to improve our chances of survival in nature. The cells in your brain have the capability to undergo microscopic changes that enhance their overall function. Each individual neuron receives thousands to millions of input (synapses) from other neurons and itself can send out thousands to millions of synapses. Extrapolating from animal studies, the number of these synapses increases when you learn something new or when you experience something dramatic.

If you were to learn how to play the guitar for the first time, new synapses would form in your brain as you practiced. The existing synapses also would become stronger, and as a result you have a more efficient connection in the chain of neurons involved in the control of your fingers to play the strings. The concept of your brain's ability to undergo remodeling (at a molecular level) is called *brain plasticity* and takes place primarily in the cortex.

Brain plasticity is most evident in children. Kids who undergo heroic brain surgeries for removal of large tumors manage to recover well and become like their classmates in a few years. In such patients, the healthy part of the brain takes over and performs functions for the parts that were removed. Even in adults, as in the cases of patients who suffer strokes, the brain generates millions (if not billions) of new synapses to compensate for the loss of dead neurons. The majority of patients who have had strokes show some degree of improvement, and many return to their baseline level of functioning. The current research in the field of rehabilitation medicine focuses on ways to accelerate the rate of synapse formation to expedite recovery.

BRAIN RESERVE

Brain researchers used to believe that the neurons in adult brains didn't have the ability to expand with practice or stimulation. However, Gerald Kempermann, Ph.D., and his colleagues shattered this dogma in the 1990s. They showed that adult mice playing in colorful and enriched cage boxes formed new neurons and synapses in their brains (hippocampus), as compared to other mice living in the typical, simple (and boring) cage boxes.[5] Learning more in a stimulating environment was associated with the birth of new cells and synapses in the brains, something most people thought would not be possible beyond the childhood years.

A new concept of "brain reserve" is now emerging. It refers to the idea that throughout your life you accumulate more and more synapses as you challenge your brain and learn new things. This pool of synapses serves as a reserve for your retirement years. The more synapses you have formed throughout your life, the better you can handle damages to your brain. Much like accumulating more money for retirement during your working years prepares you for more financial challenges later in life, stimulating your brain to form more synapses enables you to resist adversities such as Alzheimer's disease.[6]

In my own experience with patients in their sixties to nineties, I consistently find that those interested in learning new things and in exploring the world around them are far less likely to develop memory loss or the signs and symptoms of Alzheimer's disease. In fact, I can reliably predict which of my patients are more likely to become demented within five years after talking with them for thirty minutes and learning about their daily activities, hobbies, and the diversity of their interests. My clinical observations were recently confirmed in two large studies in which elderly individuals who participated in more leisure and intellectual activities significantly decreased their risk of developing Alzheimer's disease. We will discuss these studies and the role of synapses in more detail in Chapter 6.

BRAIN RESERVE

The diagrams on the facing page illustrate what may happen in the hippocampus with education, aging, and Alzheimer's disease. Each of us has an average number of neurons and synapses (middle panel). Some scientists believe that childhood education, and perhaps continued cognitive stimulation throughout life, causes more synapses to form in the hippocampus and other cortical areas (more dots, as shown in the top panel). This would enhance communication between neurons and improve cognitive abilities.

With aging, there is some loss of synapses for everyone, though the number of neurons for the most part does not change (fewer dots, as shown in the lower left panel).

With late stages of Alzheimer's disease, there is a profound loss of neurons and synapses (as shown in the lower right panel).

It could be that the more synapses you form during childhood and mid-life, the more your brain is able to resist adversities, such as Alzheimer's disease, in late life.[7]

Some scientists believe the more synapses you accumulate during your lifetime, the more you have to draw from during your later years. This concept is called *brain reserve*. Much like accumulating money for retirement during your working years prepares you for financial challenges later in life, stimulating your brain to form more synapses enables you to resist adversities such as Alzheimer's disease (in which you lose synapses). By engaging in challenging activities such as working on crossword puzzles, playing bridge, learning a new dance step or how to play an instrument, or mastering a foreign language, you can increase your brain reserve.

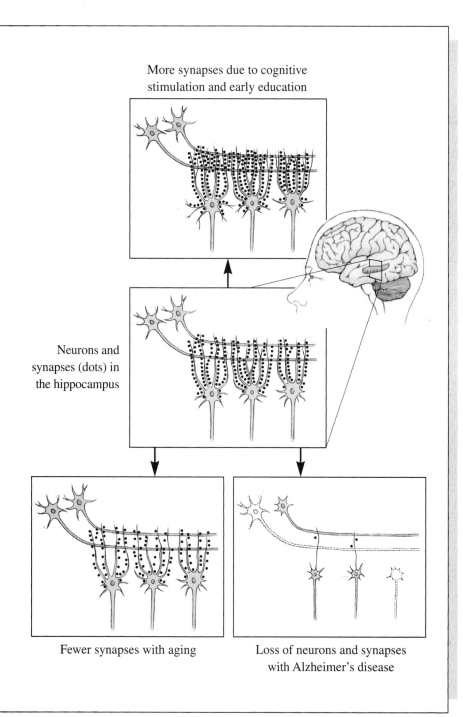

More synapses due to cognitive
stimulation and early education

Neurons and
synapses (dots) in
the hippocampus

Fewer synapses with aging

Loss of neurons and synapses
with Alzheimer's disease

AGING AND YOUR BRAIN

There is some wear and tear in your body as you age. Scientists have been trying to pinpoint the cause of this decay in order to reverse the aging process. Their discoveries have shed light on what happens inside the cells in your body, and how they can be remedied, at least in part.

Free radicals play a central role in the aging process. These are nasty little molecules that are generated as a normal by-product of the chemical reactions inside cells. Often they are oxygen molecules that lack one electron on their outer surface. To be stable, oxygen molecules need a pair of electrons on their surface. As a result, oxygen free radical molecules tend to latch onto any nearby molecule to steal an electron and settle down. They can attack the surface membrane of other cells or even their DNA, the genetic blueprint inside the nucleus of the cells.

When free radicals attack the surface membrane of cells, they can cause pores that result in the drainage of water. Dehydrated cells cannot function well and are prone to injury and death. When free radicals attack the DNA inside the cells, they interfere with the cell's ability to make new proteins. There is usually some spontaneous low-level damage to the DNA that gets repaired on a regular basis, but DNA attacked by loads of free radicals cannot repair itself effectively.

Some of the proteins in the membranes of damaged cells can trigger the production of inflammatory molecules. Inflammation, of course, is a phenomenon you can see as a swelling and reddening of the skin, such as over an injured knee. This is your body's way of sending immune cells to the site of an injury to clear damage and restore normal tissue. One of these molecules is called *arachidonic acid*. When free radicals latch onto the arachidonic acid on the cell membrane, the inflammatory process begins. The end result is that the cell gets injured, first directly by the free radicals, and then indirectly by the immune cells that are recruited as a part of cellular inflammation.

Fortunately, there is a protective mechanism against free radicals. Throughout life, antioxidant molecules, such as *gluthathione*, neutralize and detoxify free radicals almost as fast as they're generated. However, with advancing age it seems that the balance tips slightly, favoring free radicals, and thus can cause wear and tear in the body's cells. This is the logic behind the recommendations to take antioxidants or anti-inflammatory medications to slow the aging process.

Your brain is not exempt from the normal wear and tear process of aging. There is a degree of dehydration, and the brain does shrink slightly with each decade of life. Each individual neuron loses some of its rich dendritic branches and becomes somewhat more simplified. The density of synapses diminishes.[8] The protective covering of axons becomes thinner and leads to slower signal transmission from one neuron to the next. These changes, however, are modest compared to the enormous pool of neurons, dendrites, and synapses. Contrary to common misconceptions, you do not lose 10,000 neurons a day, and the brain does not shrink considerably. In summary, the loss of dendritic branches and fewer synapses result in slower processing between neurons in the temporal, frontal, or parietal lobes, but not in loss of their function. This explains why you may become slower as you age yet still retain all of your mental abilities.

A BALANCING ACT

Throughout life, you increase the number of synapses in your brain as you learn, read, take on challenging tasks, and exercise. Toward the last third of your life the normal aging process takes away some of these synapses. Clearly, the more synapses you have to begin with, the more you can tip the balance in your favor. You also have many opportunities to reverse the changes that come with aging through changes in your lifestyle.

3

A LIFETIME OF MEMORY

You may have witnessed how a loved one or someone else you know started having memory problems and within five years could no longer recognize anyone. You may wonder if the occasional memory lapses you experience are going to lead to Alzheimer's disease in a few years as well. In this chapter we'll discuss the difference between normal forgetfulness and Alzheimer's disease. Once you understand this difference, you'll worry less about having this disease yourself.

MEMORY PROBLEMS ACROSS AGES

Most people in their third and fourth decades of life complain of some mild memory problems, especially with regard to remembering names. They are best described as "worried well," since they rarely have a real disease.

People in the fifth and sixth decades start focusing more on the occasions when their memories fail. Their concerns are usually out of proportion to the actual degree of their memory decline. However, some individuals in this age group may indeed have memory loss that is more pronounced than that of their neighbors and coworkers. They often turn out to have depression.

People in their seventh and eighth decades forget things more frequently. This is in part because of the quality of the information they receive, as we discussed earlier. Problems with hearing, seeing, and focusing on information contribute to perceived memory loss. Many people learn to adjust, adhere to an active lifestyle, and manage to overcome their memory decline by taking notes and making reminders. Those who are physically fit have higher expectations regarding memory performance, and they experience a great deal of frustration with themselves when they find any slowing in learning and remembering.

Some individuals in this eldest age group do indeed have profound memory loss, even after adjusting for the expected age-associated memory impairment. Some not only have memory issues that begin to interfere with their ability to carry on with daily routines, but soon become dependent on others to aid them with the simplest activities of daily living.

People in their ninth decade of life and beyond have the highest prevalence of memory decline and Alzheimer's disease, though a minority still work and keep busy lifestyles. Many people in this age group have multiple medical problems that dull their senses and curtail their ability to interact with others.

Brain specialists who evaluate patients with memory complaints first establish the severity and rapidity of their memory decline. Based on this information, they identify their patients in one of the three following categories:

1. Age-Associated Memory Impairment (worried well)

2. Mild Cognitive Impairment

3. Dementia/Alzheimer's Disease

They then use this classification to determine the appropriate treatment plan for their patient.

COGNITION

Understanding what cognition is will help you understand the three different types of memory loss. The term cognition refers to your higher brain functions, such as:

Learning and memory. The ability to remember what you ate for breakfast and what year you finished high school, and to learn how to operate your new computer or microwave.

Language. The ability to comprehend the news on TV, name items around your kitchen, read a novel, write a letter, or tell your friends about your summer vacation.

Orientation to time and place. The ability to approximate what time it is right now, know the day of the week, determine how to walk home from different areas in your neighborhood, or give directions to a friend (correctly) on how they can drive to your house.

Calculations. The ability to figure out the tip for a waiter, mentally tabulate your total grocery bill before the cashier tells you, or figure out if you can afford to buy a new car based on your salary.

Recognizing familiar faces or objects. The ability to find your brother's face in a high school graduation group picture, recognize the faces (not necessarily the names) of old friends you see again at a party, and identify your car in a crowded parking lot of a shopping mall.

Executive functions and abstract thinking. The ability to follow the sequence of steps to cook a meal, put gas in your car, or set the table for dinner; plan your day, your weekend, and your vacation; organize a picnic; interpret proverbs; decide how to interact with your family members and your boss.

AGE-ASSOCIATED MEMORY IMPAIRMENT
(WORRIED WELL)

Age-Associated Memory Impairment (AAMI) refers to the mild forgetfulness that happens with aging. You experience this when you lose your keys or forget some appointments. Such memory lapses are entirely normal. And it is the normal course of human aging when you discover that you're slower in learning new things when you're in your fifties. Forgetting why you walked in a room, blocking on a friend's name, or forgetting where you parked your car happens to millions of people every day and by itself does not represent a disease.

Recall our earlier comparison to a slowing in your physical abilities as you age. As long as you do not have other "cognitive" problems and your occasional memory lapses do not interfere with your daily responsibilities, you have normal "age-associated memory impairment."

Can a person with mild memory problems now develop Alzheimer's disease ten years later? The answer is maybe. Memory problems are indeed the first signs of Alzheimer's. But in fact, the vast majority of people with mild memory problems do not develop the disease. As you age, you're also at risk for developing stroke, heart attack, and disabling arthritis, not to mention the risk of having a car accident or cancer. There's no point worrying about Alzheimer's disease while your brain is still working well. The smart thing to do is to learn how to protect your brain against memory loss with aging and Alzheimer's, which is what you're doing by reading this book.

Recently, Dr. Donald Connor and his colleagues at the Sun Health Research Institute in Arizona carried out a memory study with a group of healthy elderly. They first asked these volunteers if they had significant memory problems. Two-thirds said yes. Then they asked if they had significant memory problems compared to others their age. Nine out of ten respondents who'd said yes changed their answers to no. They felt that their memory problems were not that different from other people in their age group. The researchers then asked the same study participants if their memory problems had worsened within the last couple of years. Again, eight out of ten changed their yes answers to no.[1] These results reflected how most elderly individuals do appreciate that their mild memory decline is within normal limits for their age. It's unfortunate that this realization does not seem to alleviate people from worrying about their memory and the risk of developing Alzheimer's disease.

MILD COGNITIVE IMPAIRMENT

Mild Cognitive Impairment (MCI) refers to memory loss that falls outside normal limits for each age group.[2] A person with MCI has impairment mainly in one area of cognition—learning and memory—and not in the other areas mentioned earlier. An example is when a person has increasing difficulty remembering phone numbers and the names of acquaintances, and needs frequent daily reminders for events and appointments. He may occasionally ask the same question multiple times. However, he would not have difficulty performing his job duties, driving home, or making plans for the weekend. A person with MCI continues to function at home and at work. Once he loses his ability to take care of his responsibilities, however, his cognitive impairment is no longer "mild."

> *Mr. Hamilton was a retired postal worker. He was enjoying his retirement years but was becoming more forgetful. He had to keep checking the calendar, and he found himself taking many notes to remember simple things. When he went to a restaurant with his wife, he had difficulty figuring out the 15 percent tip for the waiter—something he used to do easily. Despite these minor inconveniences, he continued to play cards with his friends, travel with his wife, pay his bills, and balance his checkbook. When I tested his memory, he could remember only one of the four items I asked him to remember, but he did very well*

in all other tests, such as drawing, simple calculations, and writing. I diagnosed him with mild cognitive impairment and suggested that he start taking vitamin E. I also encouraged him to walk more, to partici-pate in activities that are both intellectually stimulating and fun, and to improve his diet in order to receive more vitamins and antioxidants (see Chapter 6).

MCI is a controversial topic among Alzheimer's researchers. There are no clear-cut borders between MCI and normal forgetfulness or dementia. Ronald Petersen, M.D., Ph.D., professor of neurology at the Mayo Clinic in Rochester, Minnesota, has pioneered the concept of MCI and believes that a person with MCI needs to have four criteria:

1. He must have memory problems, as demonstrated by a formal memory test.

2. He must continue to have "largely" normal cognition.

3. He must be "essentially" independent in his routine activities of daily living.

4. He must not be demented.[3]

At the 2002 Alzheimer meetings around the world, there were a dozen reports on the new imaging techniques that may help doctors distinguish MCI patients from those who have normal age-associated memory impair-ment or those with Alzheimer's disease or other forms of dementia. Using this new technology in research performed independently in various coun-tries, it appears that the hippocampus and its neighboring structure—the entorhinal cortex—get smaller and have less blood flow in patients with MCI, more severe than in normal elderly and less severe than in patients with Alzheimer's disease. Some studies showed that the shrinkage of the hippocampus is more pronounced on the left side of the brain, while oth-ers showed that the entorhinal cortex shows changes even before the hip-pocampus does, and thus may be a better area to focus on for diagnosing this disease.

All these researchers face a major challenge. There are many patients who have MCI but whose brains appear normal, with no shrinkage of the hippocampus. Yet more challenging is the fact that some have no signifi-cant memory problems, though their brain images show smaller hip-pocampi and entorhinal cortex. While the advances in imaging techniques move us toward discovering new answers, they are not perfect and cannot be used alone to help doctors diagnose MCI or Alzheimer's disease; however, they may prove helpful as a part of a combination of various tests plus memory questionnaires.

Do people with MCI need to take medications? Drug companies are conducting large-scale clinical trials to see if their medications for Alzheimer's disease would also help people with MCI. Vitamin E, Motrin, Aleve, Celebrex, Vioxx, and cholesterol-lowering medications such as Lipitor are other drugs in various stages of clinical trials for MCI patients. Everyone in the field of Alzheimer's research is anxiously awaiting the outcome of these trials, which should become available in the next two to three years. The results could have a major impact on the health of our society, since preventing mild cognitive impairment would offer increased productivity later in life by those who would have been affected by MCI. The results could also have major financial rewards for pharmaceutical companies, since such drugs have the potential to become more popular than Viagra.

DEMENTIA AND ALZHEIMER'S DISEASE

Dementia refers to a profound and progressive decline in memory accompanied by problems in one or more additional areas of cognition. A demented person usually starts by having frequent short-term memory problems. He would ask the same question ("Are we going to see our dentist tomorrow?") five to ten times in the same afternoon, each time forgetting the answer. He may then appear confused, not knowing the month or the location of the neighborhood grocery store. He would gradually lose his ability to function independently at home or at work, and limit his daily activities. He might get lost in his own neighborhood, put the clock in the refrigerator, cry for no clear reason, and be unable to even button his shirt or take a shower alone. These symptoms can progress rapidly within two to three years. Dementia is not a mere loss of memory, but the loss of a person's mind as a whole. A dozen different ailments, including cancer, stroke, major depression, hypothyroidism, vitamin deficiency, Parkinson's disease, and AIDS, can all lead to dementia.

Alzheimer's disease is a form of dementia diagnosed only when all other causes have been eliminated. It accounts for approximately 70 percent of dementia cases. A man with Alzheimer's may appear completely healthy and normal at first; you might not detect anything abnormal when you meet him. But then you realize that he does not know his wife's name, his home address, and cannot count to ten. Such a patient would not have any physical signs that make him stand out from other people in a crowd.

He might also have no insight into his profound memory loss. Instead he might smile and laugh as if nothing was wrong.

> *Mr. Danlof was a retired businessman. He was diagnosed with Alzheimer's disease three years earlier. His wife took him for his annual medical exam. While in the waiting room, he asked if he could go to the bathroom. She agreed, and waited for him to return. After half an hour she went to the men's bathroom and found him sitting on the toilet bowl with his pants still on. He was unable to unzip his pants and had ended up soiling himself. His wife asked the security guard to watch him, then went to a nearby shopping mall, found him a pair of pants, and quickly went back to the doctor's office, where she washed him, gave him the new pants, and brought him home. At dinner that night he had no recollection about what had happened. He asked his wife why he wasn't wearing any underwear.*

CHARACTERISTICS OF ALZHEIMER'S DISEASE

Neurologists, along with psychiatrists and clinical psychologists, have developed tests to distinguish among the different types of memory problems. Many of these tests are simple paper-and-pencil questionnaires and are based on the current understanding of how the brain works and how Alzheimer's disease affects the brain. These tests, which we'll go into in more detail in Chapter 8, check for memory and other cognitive functions. In the majority of cases, listening to the patient and her family is enough to discover if she has Alzheimer's disease. Here are some characteristic features of patients developing Alzheimer's or other forms of dementia:

1. ***Changes in personality and behavior.*** The first symptom may be apathy, a lack of interest in participating in the enjoyable activities of daily living. The person may lose interest in playing with grandchildren, dancing, having dinner with friends, or working in the garage. He may forget the etiquette of appropriate social behavior; for example, he may tell a couple that they have an ugly child. Another person may become paranoid about his spouse, thinking that his 80-year-old wife is having an affair with the neighbor's son. He may become combative and lose the ability to control his anger. He may shout for no apparent reason, then smile as if nothing had happened. Occasionally, a person changes his personality and becomes sweeter, kinder, and gentler.

Mr. Jackson, a retired engineer, came to my clinic accompanied by his wife. She recalled that she first became alarmed six years ago when he no longer spent his Saturdays fixing things in the garage. He had lost his passionate interest in carpentry. He would also ask the same question ten times in the same day. He would get frustrated with operating the dishwasher or washing machine. Per his wife's request, he agreed to see a doctor, and was diagnosed with early stage Alzheimer's disease. His symptoms stopped getting worse with drug treatment, and he was able to live with his wife at home instead of moving into a nursing home. Interestingly, his family felt that his personality had changed for the better. "He used to be a rough and aggressive man, but now has turned into a sweet gentleman," his wife said with a smile.

2. ***Difficulty with language.*** A woman with dementia may gradually lose her ability to read, understand, or write. She will use the term "thing" to refer to common objects she cannot name. When asked, she may not be able to name even ten items around her kitchen. In late stages of the disease, she may lose her ability to speak and only utter meaningless sounds.

3. ***Difficulty with skilled movements.*** A grandmother with dementia may gradually lose her ability to button her shirt, zip up her pants, pour tea in a cup, or tie her shoelaces. She may lose hand coordination for sewing, cooking, or gardening. Later in the disease, she may even lose her ability to walk, and have frequent falls.

4. ***Difficulty with recognizing familiar faces and places.*** A grandfather with dementia may not recognize his own children or grandchildren. He may not even recognize the difference between salt and pepper. He might walk past his own house and not realize that he has lived there for decades.

5. ***Difficulty with "executive" functions.*** This refers to higher brain functions that require planning, thinking, and understanding difficult concepts. A demented person cannot set the table or cook a meal, as she no longer knows the proper order of steps involved to do them. She may have difficulty with driving, as she gets frustrated with her inability to pay attention to multiple things at the same time. She may even have problems operating the microwave. She will have trouble making decisions or understanding what goes on around her or in the country.

TEN WARNING SIGNS OF ALZHEIMER'S DISEASE

1. Memory loss that affects job skills
2. Difficulty performing familiar tasks
3. Problems with language
4. Disorientation to time and place
5. Poor or decreased judgment
6. Problems with abstract thinking
7. Misplacing things
8. Changes in mood and behavior
9. Changes in personality
10. Loss of initiative

Sample examples:
- Putting the iron in the fridge
- Difficulty reading and understanding the newspaper
- Forgetting the month or the year
- Getting lost in one's own neighborhood
- Confusion with simple numbers and daily calculations
- Rapid changes in mood from laughing to unjustified crying

Based on the understanding of what goes wrong in the brains of patients with Alzheimer's disease, in 2001 the American Academy of Neurology set forth a set of early warning signs for this disease.[4] (See the Ten Warning Signs of Alzheimer's Disease above.)

People with Alzheimer's differ with regard to the combination of symptoms they manifest; no two patients with Alzheimer's disease are identical. Some may have more problems with language or recognizing familiar faces, while others may have more difficulty with orientation to time or place. Below are some examples of the kinds of problems you might see in a person at each stage of the disease.

EARLY STAGE

- Spends all day preparing dinner, but forgets to serve it
- Has difficulty setting the table
- Pays the same bill three times
- Forgets how to type, even if she's been typing for 20 years

WHO HAS ALZHEIMER'S DISEASE?

Patients with Alzheimer's disease get worse rapidly, usually over two to five years. In contrast, healthy older people may have the same degree of mild memory problems for twenty years. The diagram below shows how the memory of two individuals has grown worse over the years:

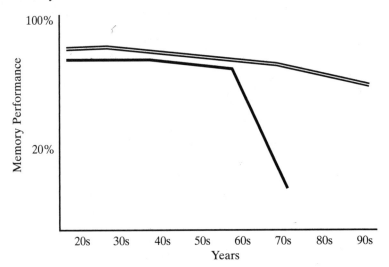

Which of the two patients may have Alzheimer's disease?

A. ____ Patient shown on top, with double lines

B. ____ Patient shown on the bottom, with a thick line

(Answer: B)

- Confuses dates, constantly rechecks the calendar
- Appears more withdrawn, less interested in playing with grandchildren

At age sixty-five, Mr. Jackson was a pleasant man at work and at home. His coworkers noted that he hadn't been able to keep up with his work for about a year. He would forget about appointments frequently, show up confused at the office on Sunday, get lost in the hallways, and appeared more apathetic about his job. His wife also noted that he was more confused when they were driving together. She took him to their primary physician, who then referred him to a memory clinic. A set of laboratory tests and a brain MRI were all normal, and he was diagnosed with Alzheimer's disease. His family kept him in his own home environment and cared for him as he continued to get worse.

MIDDLE STAGES

- Does not recognize nephew or cousin
- Repeats the same question three times within an hour, forgets the answer each time
- Becomes restless, irritable, and fidgety
- Is easily agitated, especially in the evenings
- Accuses spouse or neighbor of cheating or stealing
- Develops hallucinations (sees and hears things that are not there)
- Wakes up in the middle of the night, wanders through the rooms or into the street
- Has difficulty reading signs or following written directions
- Develops sloppy table manners
- Undresses in public for no clear reason
- Cannot easily get in and out of the car
- Is unaware of his or her memory problems
- Forgets having had lunch, keeps eating

Mrs. Hunter was a pleasant seventy-year-old woman. She was tall, strong, and appeared to be happy. Her husband, on the other hand, appeared exhausted and frustrated. He reported that she had "lost her mind" but kept her energy and strength. Most days, she chased the dog all day, wandered aimlessly in her own house, and acted like a misbehaving child. She was always eating something, to the extent that her husband had to lock the refrigerator door. She used to be her family's center of attention and invited friends and family for dinner all the time. Now she could no longer cook a simple dinner, set the table, or even put things in the dishwasher. Her friends stopped coming to her house and the dog was afraid of her. Her family members had frequent arguments as to whether she should be taken to a nursing home. She was not aware that there were any problems.

LATE STAGES

- Cannot recognize spouse
- Develops worsening bowel and bladder incontinence
- Puts everything in mouth
- Cannot speak normally, screams, and vocalizes strange grunting sounds
- Has difficulty swallowing
- Needs help with shower, dressing, eating, and toileting
- Requires full-time supervision

Mrs. Hendrick had Alzheimer's disease for five years. She was eighty-five years old. She could not feed herself, take a shower, or get dressed. She would often look at her husband of forty years and cry. She was unable to speak and could only utter sounds. She lost her ability to walk and was bedridden.

AAMI, MCI, OR ALZHEIMER'S?

Most people with AAMI do not get worse rapidly. They complain of the same degree of memory problems for twenty years. This is not the case for individuals with MCI, almost half of whom go on to develop Alzheimer's disease within three years. The other half of patients with MCI continue to have memory problems but may not get worse rapidly. Occasionally, some people with MCI may actually get better. There is a great deal of research to find out why some people with MCI develop Alzheimer's disease or stay the same, while others improve. The answer may prove to be the steps you can take to protect your brain against Alzheimer's disease, which we'll discuss in Chapter 6.

The important point to stress here is that the dementia in those who have Alzheimer's disease does not look anything like the mild forgetfulness in people who lose their keys, forget the location of their car, or miss occasional appointments. Alzheimer's is a disease that cripples not only a person's memory, but also most aspects of cognition. I am often surprised to find young professionals who think they may have Alzheimer's disease.

Miss Raxer was a dental student. She did not particularly enjoy studying. She always complained that when she read her anatomy textbooks the information didn't stick in her brain. Since she knew that I saw patients with Alzheimer's, she came to me and said, "I'm pretty sure I have

AAMI, MCI, OR ALZHEIMER'S?

More than 90 percent of people who complain of memory problems do not have Alzheimer's disease (AD). They may have age-associated memory impairment (AAMI), the common forgetfulness that occurs with aging. Some who may have more profound memory problems, but still manage to do their jobs and take care of their daily responsibilities, are labeled as having "mild cognitive impairment" (MCI). They are, however, at high risk for developing Alzheimer's disease in the future.

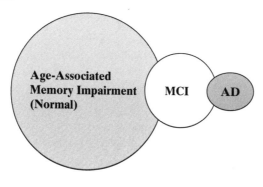

Alzheimer's disease. Is there any medication you can give me to save my memory?" I explained to her the differences in memory performance and assured her that the very fact that she'd passed her exams so far demonstrated that she didn't have Alzheimer's disease. She needed reassurance, not medications.

Ms. Harrington was a twenty-seven-year-old executive of a financial company in New York. She was convinced that she had Alzheimer's disease. She could provide many examples that proved to her that her memory had been failing her ever since she was a child. Once, in fifth grade, she forgot to show up for a final art exam. She would always forget the names of her friends when she was in high school or college. Meanwhile, within four years of graduating from Harvard University she managed to move from a position as an intern to become the vice president in a large financial firm. At work she could recount the names of 50 different companies in her field and their performance in the stock market for the past few months. She was in charge of multiple projects and constantly traveled around the world. After I explained the concept of MCI and Alzheimer's disease, she laughed and said, "I've been so crazy; I don't have Alzheimer's disease."

Asking certain questions can help doctors determine if the person who complains of memory problems has AAMI, MCI, or AD. When I see patients who are in their thirties to fifties who complain of memory deficits, I ask them questions regarding their fields of interest. I might ask an accountant to tell me about the new tax laws, and ask a taxi driver how he would drive from one end of town to the airport. I often suspect depression as the cause of memory problems in younger individuals, and so I ask them about their diet, energy, sex life, and sleep. I adjust my expectations about the patient after I ask about their prior education and career accomplishments. When I suspect that a patient may have Alzheimer's disease, I simplify my questions and may ask about a birthday party he or she attended last (see chart below). All patients, young or old, undergo a full set of standardized tests as well. Their test results are interpreted as compared to their

	AGE-ASSOCIATED MEMORY IMPAIRMENT	MILD COGNITIVE IMPAIRMENT	DEMENTIA/ ALZHEIMER'S DISEASE
Do you remember what happened at the party?	Yes, most of the events	Yes, only some of the events	"What birthday party?"
Do you remember the name of the birthday person?	Yes, may need prompting	Maybe, even with prompting	No
Could you follow driving directions to get there?	Yes	Yes, with mild degree of difficulty	No
Could you stop to buy a gift on the way there?	Yes	Yes, may need some help	No

WHAT TO DO FOR PEOPLE WITH MEMORY PROBLEMS

Everyone who complains of memory problems needs to be evaluated in order to identify the cause of the problem. Once a patient's memory problem is diagnosed to be in one of the following three categories, specific management strategies are suggested. Memory problems, like any other health concern, requires regular interval follow-up evaluation with a qualified health professional.

AAMI (Worried Well)

1. Reassurance and encouragement
2. Reduce your negative risk factors (Chapter 6)
3. Consider lifestyle changes to protect your brain against memory loss (Chapter 6)
4. Memory exercises (Afterword)

MCI

1. Consider taking vitamin E
2. Consider taking other protective medications or participate in clinical trials (Chapter 7)
3. Reduce your negative risk factors (Chapter 6)
4. Consider lifestyle changes to protect your brain against memory loss (Chapter 6)
5. Memory exercises (Afterword)

Dementia/AD

1. Take vitamin E
2. Take Alzheimer's medications (Chapter 7)
3. Supervision for the patient
4. Education and support for the family
5. Participation in trials for new drugs

prior level of functioning and to other people in that age group. I will explain the process of making a diagnosis of Alzheimer's disease in detail in Chapter 8.

4

A JOURNEY INSIDE AN ALZHEIMER'S BRAIN

As the number of older Americans rises, and estimates for the number of patients with Alzheimer's disease skyrocket, the need for a cure is becoming more urgent. The number of eighty-year-olds is expected to double by 2030 and to triple by 2040. One out of every five Americans will be over sixty-five by 2050. There are approximately 4 million patients with Alzheimer's disease in the United States now, and this number is expected to at least triple in the next fifty years.[1] Clearly, the potential financial and emotional impact of Alzheimer's disease will be enormous in upcoming decades.

Scientists, armed with millions of dollars in research funds from the government and the pharmaceutical industry, are in a race to find a cure for the disease. For this to happen, however, doctors first need to establish what goes wrong inside the brains of people who develop Alzheimer's.

Unfortunately, this is an especially difficult challenge, since a definitive diagnosis of Alzheimer's disease can be made only after examining thin brain sections under a microscope and looking for *plaques* and *tangles* (see pages 52 and 53), the hallmarks of the disease.[2] And this can only be done after a person dies.

THE DISCOVERY OF PLAQUES AND TANGLES

Dr. Alois Alzheimer was a physician in Germany during the 1890s. One of his patients, a woman in her forties, had completely lost her memory and developed strange behaviors. When she died, at the age of fifty-one, Dr. Alzheimer decided to examiner her brain at autopsy.

He had discovered a way of staining brain sections that would clearly show the individual neurons, and added a silver stain that allowed him to visualize them even better. Under his microscope, he saw many neurons in various parts of the deceased woman's brain that appeared normal. However, he also noticed something that no one had reported before: gum-like clumps outside some cells, and an abnormal collection of proteins inside other cells. He dubbed these plaques and tangles, respectively.

A decade later, Dr. Alzheimer's students and colleagues saw other patients who had lost their memories and the ability to care for themselves. Interestingly, at autopsy these patients also had plaques and tangles in their brains. Out of respect for their mentor, doctors decided to call this form of dementia *Alzheimer's disease*.

PLAQUES

In the 1970s, scientists determined that plaques consisted mostly of a protein called *beta-amyloid*. They discovered that under normal conditions, a larger protein—the amyloid precursor protein—gets scissored into three small pieces, the alpha-amyloid, beta-amyloid, and gamma-amyloid. In the brains of patients with Alzheimer's disease, too much beta-amyloid is produced—a lot more than the other two forms. This overwhelms the brain's mechanism of clearing excess proteins. As a result, beta-amyloid accumulates and forms insoluble gumlike plaques.

Amyloid plaques damage the connection points between neurons (synapses) and interfere with their ability to communicate with one another (see pages 52 and 53). Plaques seem to develop initially in the cortical areas in the temporal lobes, which explains why Alzheimer's patients first develop profound memory loss. As the disease progresses, additional plaques develop in the frontal lobes of the brain. Patients who suffer from a more severe form of the disease have far more plaques than those with mild forms. The brains of individuals unaffected by Alzheimer's can have a few scattered plaques. Scientists are now trying to find out why millions of plaques form in the brains of patients with Alzheimer's disease while very few form in the brains of healthy older individuals.

TANGLES

Neurons have a fairly large cell body and many hundreds to thousands of long branches—the dendrites and axons—protruding from them. The nutrients from the cell body need to be transported to nerve endings. Inside healthy brain cells, long threads of proteins serve as tracks for this transport of nutrients.

When scientists examined the brains of patients with Alzheimer's disease who had died, they discovered that some of these transport proteins were tangled. It became clear that neurons with "tangles" in their branches could not send nutrient molecules to their nerve endings, and therefore they couldn't communicate with other neurons. Tangles also initially develop in temporal lobes and later appear in other cortical areas. Patients who experience a more severe form of the disease have far more tangles than those who suffer from a mild form. Cells with tangles die sooner than other neurons. As with plaques, scattered tangles can also be detected in the brains of healthy elderly people.

WHAT HAPPENS AFTER PLAQUES AND TANGLES FORM?

Amyloid plaques seem to trigger an inflammatory response. As we discussed in Chapter 2, inflammation occurs throughout your body when there's an injury; it's your body's way of healing itself. For example, if you hurt your knee in a football game, you'll notice swelling later, in and around the injured knee. This is part of the inflammatory response to maintain blood flow and the delivery of nutrients and repair proteins to the injured area, to promote rapid recovery.

A mild degree of inflammation also occurs in the body and the brain with normal aging. In some situations the inflammatory response itself becomes a problem. An example is arthritis, where excess inflammation in the joints results in unnecessary pain and discomfort for patients.

In the brain, the inflammatory cells may cause injury simply by their arrival in and around the plaques. Part of the inflammatory process involves the formation of highly reactive molecules called oxygen free radicals, which were mentioned in Chapter 2. If you recall, these vicious molecules can bind and destroy everything that comes within their vicinity. They can disrupt the membrane of cells by inserting holes in them, or they can bind to the cell's DNA—the genetic blueprint for production of proteins—and interfere with its survival.[3]

The inflammatory process appears to destroy large numbers of brain cells in Alzheimer's patients. This is a hypothesis supported by examination

WHAT GOES WRONG
IN THE BRAINS OF PATIENTS
WITH ALZHEIMER'S DISEASE?

A slice through the hippocampus in the temporal lobe would show the invasion of plaques and tangles in the hippocampus and its neighboring areas. Some neurons are filled with tangles and die. Other neurons are plagued by a collection of plaques around them.

Amyloid plaques, made up of a core of beta-amyloid protein cluster, form gumlike blockage between neurons and prevent them from communicating with one another.

The immune system in the body perceives the plaques as invasive, and inflammatory cells arrive to dissolve them. Since the plaques are insoluble, they're hard to remove, and more inflammatory agents are recruited. However, the plaques remain despite the efforts of the inflammatory cells, and the activity of the inflammatory cells ends up killing other healthy synapses and cells around the plaques.

Neurofibrillary tangles block the flow of nutrients from the cell body to the nerve endings, interrupting the communication inside the cell and eventually destroying it.

Since plaques and tangles initially interfere with the functions of the temporal lobe, the patient may first experience memory loss or difficulty reading. As the frontal lobes are affected, a person may become disorganized or engage in inappropriate behavior. When the parietal lobes are affected, the patient may lose his orientation skills. Eventually, all lobes are affected, and the person is unable to perform such routine tasks as brushing teeth or changing clothes.

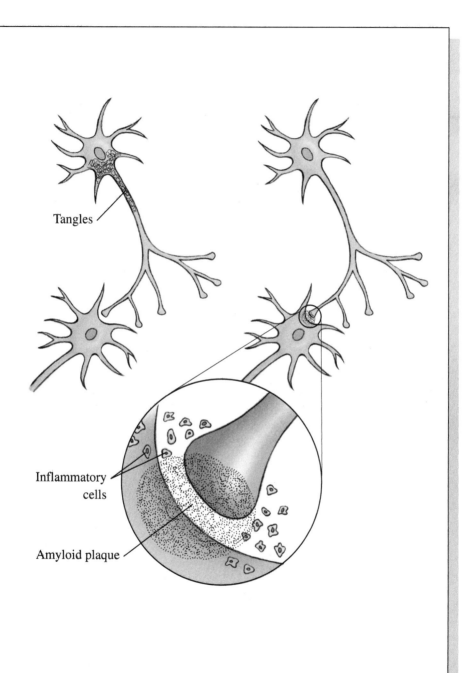

Tangles

Inflammatory
cells

Amyloid plaque

of the stained brain sections of patients who died with Alzheimer's disease, which reveal inflammation in and around the plaques. Clinical observation suggests that taking anti-inflammatory drugs for other health issues, such as arthritis, reduces your chance of developing Alzheimer's disease. However, anti-inflammatory drugs, which are currently being vigorously studied for memory-saving applications, have many serious side effects, including gastrointestinal bleeding.

Another contributor to Alzheimer's disease may be that the natural repair mechanisms that rid the body of free radicals are faulty. The protein Apolipoprotein E, for one, which has the potential to protect the lipid membranes of cells against free radical injury, might be a less efficient

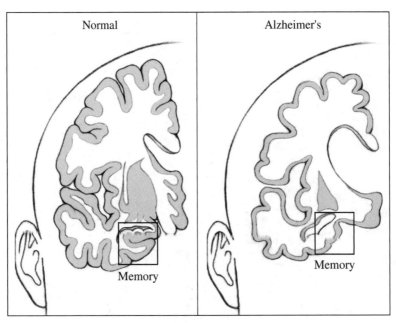

COMPARING THE BRAIN IN AN ALZHEIMER'S PATIENT WITH THE BRAIN IN A HEALTHY INDIVIDUAL

Normal

Alzheimer's

Memory

Memory

A cross section of a brain of a person with early Alzheimer's disease shows more shrinkage in memory and language parts compared to the brain of an unaffected person. As the disease advances, other cortical areas degenerate too.

variant in the brain of an Alzheimer's patient; less efficient, that is, in repairing the damage. Without an adequate repair system, the free radicals that are brought in from the bloodstream to the inflammation sites around a plaque can kill nearby innocent neurons too. Antioxidants such as vitamin E, which aid in the absorption of free radicals, seem to ease the burden of Alzheimer's disease in some patients. (For more information on the role of vitamin E in preventing memory loss, see Chapter 6.)

Plaques and tangles initially interfere with the functions of the temporal lobe[4] (see Comparing the Brain in an Alzheimer's Patient with the Brain in a Healthy Individual on page 54). The resulting symptoms include memory loss and having difficulty reading and writing. As the plaques and tangles appear in frontal lobes, the other functions of the brain deteriorate as well. A person experiencing this deterioration may develop apathy, disorganization, have problems concentrating, and exhibit inappropriate behavior. Next involved are the parietal lobes, interference with which can create difficulty with orientation skills; for example, those who get lost in a familiar shopping mall or even at home. Eventually, all the lobes are overridden with these plaques and tangles, and the patient loses the ability to perform simple daily tasks such as brushing teeth, going to the bathroom, or changing clothes.

ACETYLCHOLINE

Scientists at Johns Hopkins Hospital, studying the brains of patients who died with Alzheimer's disease, were surprised to find that certain neurons died without any evidence of plaques or tangles in or around them. A group of such neurons, with the fancy name of Nucleus Basalis of Meynert, can be found at the base of the brain. They usually make acetylcholine, a chemical messenger for communication between neurons. The acetylcholine-producing neurons send their long branches to the hippocampus and cortex. It's thought that they are important for learning and memory. Thus, if they die, it means less acetylcholine in the hippocampus (and other cortical areas), and less memory. These cells remain intact in healthy people.

ALZHEIMER'S DISEASE AND STROKES

Alzheimer's disease and strokes are two completely different diseases, but sometimes they happen together in the same patient (see Comparing the Brain in Alzheimer's Disease with Mini-Strokes and One Large Stroke on pages 56 and 57). And multiple mini-strokes can accelerate the development of symptoms in a patient with a mild form of Alzheimer's disease.

COMPARING THE BRAIN
IN ALZHEIMER'S DISEASE
WITH MINI-STROKES AND
ONE LARGE STROKE

In mini-strokes, sometimes referred to as "silent strokes," small blood vessels are blocked due to atherosclerosis (about the size of a grain of rice), and the brain areas around each of them dies. Initially mini-strokes do not cause symptoms, but as thousands of them pile up over decades, a person may experience a slowness in his thinking and a gradual loss of his ability to remember things.

In strokes that affect large blood vessels, chunks of the brain become deprived of oxygen and nutrients. They may cause a sudden loss of control on one side of the body, or the patient may lose his ability to speak or walk. Large strokes rarely affect the hippocampus, and when they do, the patient loses his memory suddenly.

In Alzheimer's disease, plaques and tangles set off a slow degeneration in the brain that begins in the hippocampus and its neighboring cortical areas. As plaques and tangles develop in other temporal, frontal, and parietal lobes, the patient loses his memory and other cognitive abilities and the hippocampus shrinks dramatically.

Patients who have both mini-strokes and Alzheimer's plaques and tangles lose their memory and cognition earlier than patients who have only one of these conditions. You can prevent developing strokes, large or small, through lifestyle modifications (see Chapter 6).

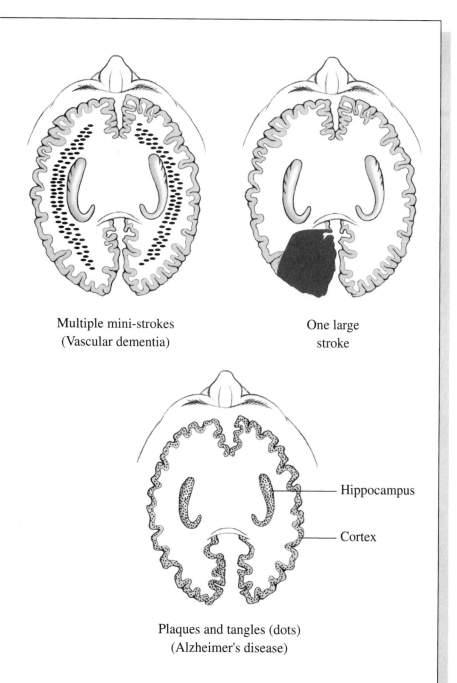

Multiple mini-strokes
(Vascular dementia)

One large
stroke

Hippocampus

Cortex

Plaques and tangles (dots)
(Alzheimer's disease)

When a large blood vessel in the brain is blocked, the part of the brain that is deprived of oxygen and nutrients dies. This is called a stroke, or a brain attack. Like a heart attack, it happens in an instant. Depending on which part of the brain was affected by the stroke, a patient may suddenly become paralyzed in one arm, lose the ability to speak, and/or fall with dizziness.

In mini-strokes, small blood vessels are affected. Because each of them nourishes only small areas of the brain (the size of a grain of rice), the person may not notice any sudden problems. Over time, however, these mini-strokes accumulate and slow his thinking and problem-solving ability. He may experience memory loss and be diagnosed with vascular dementia. The symptoms in this form of dementia are very similar to Alzheimer's disease. MRI images of the brain show mini-strokes as bright spots and help distinguish vascular dementia from Alzheimer's.

In Alzheimer's disease, the blood vessels do not seem to be the primary problem. The MRI of a patient with Alzheimer's would not show a significant number of bright mini-strokes. It may show shrinkage as a result of the thinning of the cortex in temporal, frontal, and parietal lobes. The plaques and tangles that form in the temporal lobes and later spread to the rest of the cortex are too small to be seen on regular MRI images of the brain.

The latest imaging techniques with PET (Positron Emission Tomography) scans now in development use radioactively labeled markers to show a reduced level of cellular activity and the tiny plaques in the brains of living Alzheimer's patients (see Chapter 8). These scans are a very expensive addition to current medical technology for evaluation of Alzheimer's disease, so patients may have limited access. However, PET scans are becoming useful in distinguishing patients with Alzheimer's disease from those with vascular dementia or MCI.

Both mini-strokes (vascular dementia) and Alzheimer's disease damage the cortex and impair a patient's memory and cognition. However, just a few mini-strokes or a few plaques and tangles are not sufficient to make a person lose his mental ability. Only when they occur in excess or together does the patient show a sharp mental decline. Fortunately, strokes, like heart attacks, can be prevented by changing your lifestyle (see Chapter 6).

PIECE OF A PUZZLE

The exact nature of the relationship between plaques, tangles, and the death of acetylcholine-producing neurons is at this time unclear. A few plaques and tangles are seen in the brains of healthy elderly people. Research indicates that too many amyloid plaques set the initial stage for slowing of memory and thinking. When tangles are added, and especially in the presence of risk factors, more profound memory loss and cognitive decline ensues and the patient shows signs of Alzheimer's disease. In other words, a patient can have amyloid plaques in her brain but may not show any overt difficulty with her thinking.

One would think that the plaques and tangles would be somehow related. However, a clear interaction between these two abnormal processes has eluded scientists for more than two decades. Some cells have plaques while other cells have tangles. Some scientists believe that plaques may indirectly trigger the formation of tangles. Much work is needed before these questions are resolved. The unfortunate reality remains that plaques and tangles destroy the brain, and no one has found a way to stop them.

As if the problem of plaques and tangles in the hippocampus and cortex was not puzzling enough, we're also unclear as to why separate groups of neurons in the base of the brain also die in the brains of patients with Alzheimer's.

Scientists continue to look for a connection between these three processes. The puzzle is complex, but progress is being made and hopefully some day scientists will piece together the larger Alzheimer's picture.

5

IF IT'S NOT ALZHEIMER'S DISEASE, WHAT IS IT?

At the Alzheimer's Disease Research Center at Johns Hopkins Hospital many patients complain about their memory. After performing various tests, we often find a specific cause for these memory problems. In some cases, we learn that the reason for their memory decline is depression. In other cases, we find low thyroid levels or that the patients are taking too much of a medication that is known to slow cognition. In still other cases, we diagnose them with Alzheimer's disease.

Due to public misconceptions and the way the disease is depicted in the media, many people believe that memory loss and Alzheimer's disease are synonymous. The truth is that more than 90 percent of those who complain about poor memory and worry they may be developing Alzheimer's do not have it.

Just as a headache is a symptom that can be due to a variety of causes, ranging from the flu to a brain tumor, memory loss is a symptom that can be due to a number of different illnesses, among them alcoholism, or from medication side effects. Alzheimer's is only one explanation of why a person can't remember things. While it is not as rare as brain tumors, it's not as widespread as either heart disease or cancer.

The majority of people concerned about Alzheimer's disease actually have mild to moderate depression. In contrast, most patients who have Alzheimer's may not be aware of their total memory loss and are brought to our clinic by their family members.

COMMON CAUSES OF MEMORY LOSS

In this chapter we'll explore the common contributors to memory loss.[1] These include

- Depression
- Mini-strokes
- Alcoholism and vitamin deficiency
- Low thyroid levels
- Medication side effects
- Hearing and vision problems
- Sleep problems
- Delirium

DEPRESSION

When you're depressed, you don't have energy or any interest in getting together with friends. You feel unattractive and sad, and you blame yourself for whatever goes wrong around you. You may sleep too much or not enough, eat too much or lose your appetite. You may also have no motivation to learn new things. The depression may crawl inside you so slowly that you don't even realize when it began. All you notice is that things are falling apart, you're missing your deadlines, and you don't seem to remember anything at all.

Depression paralyzes your memory and thinking in many different ways. Lack of energy and low motivation prevents you from paying attention to what you read: Since you don't absorb that information well in the first place, you forget it easily. Sleeping problems and feeling groggy during the day dull your intellect. Feelings of guilt leave you preoccupied with a sense of being inadequate and with a poor self-image. You may believe you're incapable of learning anything new, which could lead to more failures at work, and that in turn might convince you that you are indeed not smart enough. Such thought cycles can leave you wondering if you have the beginnings of Alzheimer's disease.

The first step to stop the cycle of more depression and more memory problems is to realize that you have an illness. Most people are so drawn into their sadness that they forget their problems might be due to a brain disease that can be treated. Those who do receive antidepressants regain their motivation, sleep better, have a better self-image, and can remember more. Unfortunately, depression often goes untreated in many people. And in some cases depressed patients are mistakenly labeled as having Alzheimer's disease.

From a biological point of view, depression is the result of imbalance in chemical neurotransmitters in the brain, namely norepinephrine and serotonin. Like acetylcholine-producing neurons, which we discussed in the previous chapter, the cells that produce these neurotransmitters sit at the base of the brain. They send out long projections to the cortex and usually provide a background level of excitation.

The more alert and interested you are, the more these neurons are stimulated and the more they activate the cortex. With enhanced excitation, the cortex functions better; as a result, you can think more creatively, solve problems more effectively, and remember more. When you're depressed, however, the opposite happens. The neurons release less of their neurotransmitters, the cortex does not get adequately activated, and you can't think clearly. Antidepressants can help restore the balance.

Understanding the biology of depression helps explain why it may produce symptoms similar to those of Alzheimer's disease. In both conditions the cortex in the temporal and frontal lobes are affected. In depression, the cortex is temporarily less active because it does not receive its usual stimulation from the norepinephrine- and serotonin-producing neurons. In Alzheimer's disease, the cortex is permanently damaged with plaques and tangles, and it receives less stimulation from acetylcholine-producing neurons.

Can Depression Be a Sign of Alzheimer's?

If your grandmother appears withdrawn and has no interest in playing with her grandchildren, it doesn't mean she has Alzheimer's disease. She might be depressed.[2] Or her particular depression might indicate that she's beginning to develop Alzheimer's.

Experienced doctors can distinguish between the depression that precedes Alzheimer's disease and other forms of depression, which often occur for no clear reason. One way is to see how patients respond to treatments. A patient with Alzheimer's may feel better with antidepressant medications but will continue to lose her cognitive abilities over the next one to three years. A patient with regular depression often regains her previous level of functioning.

Another indicator is to assess how well the rest of the brain works. In contrast to a patient who has Alzheimer's disease, a depressed patient can still read, write, solve simple math questions, drive, work, and have insight into his problem. Doctors can also diagnose a patient from his performance on paper-and-pencil memory tests, which will be described in Chapter 8. Depressed patients often take longer to answer the questions, but most of their answers are usually correct. Patients with Alzheimer's may not be able to answer the same questions, regardless of how much time they have.

As we said before, and it bears repeating: The majority of people who have memory problems and fear that they have Alzheimer's disease may be experiencing the symptoms of depression. They're frequently surprised to learn that depression is a brain disease. Many people are unaware that there are a number of effective medications to help treat their depression, and that they can regain both their memory and their confidence with these medications.

MINI-STROKES

When blood cannot reach brain cells, they die. As we mentioned in the previous chapter, this is what we call a "stroke." There are two types of strokes: large vessel strokes and mini-strokes.

Blockage of a large blood vessel leads to the destruction of a large section of the brain. A man who experiences a stroke in the left side of his brain may suddenly lose the ability to speak, move his right arm, or walk. If only his left temporal lobe is affected, he would lose his ability to understand language or learn new things.

Blockage of small blood vessels leads to mini-strokes, sometimes called "silent strokes." Since people who suffer mini-strokes continue to walk and talk normally, their strokes can go undetected. However, when thousands of these mini-strokes pile up in different parts of the brain, memory loss sets in. Common in people with hypertension, diabetes, or those who have high cholesterol levels and are smokers, mini-strokes can lead to *vascular dementia*. Occasionally, one single large stroke impairs a person's memory without causing many other symptoms.

Mr. Salkovac was a seventy-year-old retired construction worker in good overall health. He lived with his daughter and son-in-law. His wife had died two years earlier. He enjoyed playing with his grandchildren, taking them to the playground, and helping them with their homework. However, the family had noted that for about a month he hadn't been as sharp as usual. He would repeat the same question many times, each time forgetting the answer. Once, he could not find his way to the playground and was brought home by neighbors. They were worried that he'd developed Alzheimer's disease.

His family brought him to the E.R. at our hospital. The CT scan of his brain showed that Mr. Salkovac had had a large stroke in his left temporal lobe, depriving his hippocampus of blood, which caused his memory loss. He probably had his stroke a month earlier, but since he didn't have the typical one-sided paralysis so common in stroke patients, nobody realized that he might need medical care. He had high blood pressure and high cholesterol levels. We started him on blood pressure medications, cholesterol-lowering medications ("statins"), and aspirin. He improved over the ensuing months. He did not have Alzheimer's disease.

You can prevent developing a large stroke or mini-stroke by making changes in your lifestyle and seeing your physician regularly. Exercise, eating a healthy diet, quitting smoking, and minimizing stress all help improve circulation to your heart and brain, and in so doing lower your risk of strokes. If you have high blood pressure or a high cholesterol level, you need to discuss it with your doctor and receive proper treatment. We will discuss these issues in more detail in Chapter 6.

EXAMPLES OF MEDICAL TESTS FOR EVALUATION OF ALZHEIMER'S

1. Complete blood test screening for health issues such as anemia, high cholesterol, excessive inflammation, diabetes, liver disease, thyroid function, vitamin B12, folate, Lyme, or syphilis

2. Urine analysis to check for kidney problems or diabetes

3. Chest X ray to check for lung cancer or evidence of heart disease

4. EKG to check for heart problems and EEG to check for subtle seizures

5. Brain imaging, with CT scan or MRI, to check for stroke, tumor, infections, or brain problems other than Alzheimer's disease

6. Spinal tap done occasionally to obtain cerebrospinal fluid and to test for specific brain diseases such as hydrocephalus

ALCOHOLISM AND VITAMIN DEFICIENCY

Alcoholism is a disease that causes memory decline for life. A person who drinks ten alcoholic beverages a day ends up consuming one ton of alcohol over thirty years, enough to fill a large swimming pool. Such enormous amounts can directly damage the brain, and especially those parts necessary for hand-eye coordination, walking, and memory. If you were to see a drunken person stagger out of a bar and then speak to him the following day, you'd know that it's possible he would not remember what happened to him. The term *alcohol dementia* refers to loss of cognition in alcoholics, and it's different from vascular dementia or Alzheimer's disease.

In addition to excessive drinking, most alcoholics have a poor diet. Many don't get enough vitamins like thiamine, folate, or B12. Thiamine deficiency by itself can affect some of the memory parts of the brain; even laboratory animals lose their memory if their diet does not include thiamine. Folate and B12 vitamins are also needed if the memory parts of the brain are to work properly. One reason alcoholics develop poor memory is because of the direct damage done by alcohol and another is the scarcity of essential vitamins in their diet.

Sometimes people feel ashamed of their alcohol habit and, as a result, aren't forthcoming about this habit when they see a memory specialist. However, experts know that the memory problems in alcoholics differ somewhat from those who have Alzheimer's disease. For example, alcoholics maintain their ability to read and speak, are aware that their memory is failing, and can live alone and take care of themselves. Alzheimer's patients, in contrast, often lack insight into their problems, can't communicate their needs well, and end up becoming dependent on others to accomplish the ordinary activities of daily living. Experts can also use memory tests to distinguish between dementias due to alcoholism and those due to Alzheimer's disease.

Mr. Brown was a sixty-five-year-old gentleman who was brought to our Alzheimer's center because his family felt he was developing Alzheimer's disease. He was short and thin, had a nice smile, and did not talk much. After I performed the memory tests on him, I realized that his cognitive deficits were not characteristic of Alzheimer's disease. I asked about his drinking habits, and initially he and his family said that he used to drink, but only one to two glasses of vodka at night. Later, family members mentioned that he also used to drink a dozen beers during the day. It turned out that his drinking problem had led to liver disease, stomach ulcers, and severe bleeding in the past. He did not have Alzheimer's disease. He had alcoholism.

Drinking one or two glasses of wine with dinner is quite different from alcoholism and, in fact, can markedly protect your brain against ministrokes and Alzheimer's disease. We will discuss this in detail in Chapter 6.

LOW THYROID LEVELS

Thyroid is a hormone that regulates many of the functions in the body, from blood pressure, bowel movements, and mood, to the texture of your skin, the rhythm of your heart, and the speed of your memory.

Many people have low thyroid levels in their blood and don't know about it. They tend to develop fatigue, obesity, constipation, dry skin, and depression. As their overall level of functioning declines, so does their memory. These symptoms accumulate gradually, so no one suspects a hormone problem. Fortunately, a simple blood test can show the imbalance in thyroid levels, and low levels can easily be treated by thyroid medications. Checking for thyroid levels is a routine part of medical evaluation of all patients who have a poor memory.

MEDICATION SIDE EFFECTS

Most elderly people take multiple medications. And many people of all ages take some form of prescription drug. A number of common drugs are known to dull the memory, including medications for blood pressure, sleep, pain, and some intended for allergies. If the start of a person's memory problems coincides with the use of a new medication, chances are the two are related. Primary physicians pay particular attention to patients who develop new symptoms after a new medication is initiated. Changing or stopping the offending medication often stops the memory problems, *but this must be done under the supervision of a physician.*

HEARING AND VISION PROBLEMS

As we saw in Chapter 1, sometimes the supposed problem with memory is in fact due to poor vision or poor hearing. A person who cannot hear what people say and can't read instructions may easily be mistaken for someone who has Alzheimer's disease. Imagine yourself reading a newspaper while wearing foggy glasses. How much do you think you'd remember about what you were reading? Simply adjusting reading glasses or hearing aids improves the quality of life for the elderly, whether or not they have a disease. Every older individual needs to have routine hearing and vision tests.

SOME MEDICATIONS THAT MAY SLOW YOUR MEMORY

Type of Drug	Generic Name	Brand Name
Antianxiety drugs	alprazolam	Xanax
	diazepam	Valium
	lorazepam	Ativan
Antibiotics	cephalexin	Keflex
	ciprofloxacin	Cipro
	metronidazole	Flagyl
Antidepressants	amitriptyline	Elavil
	imipramine	Tofranil
Antihistamines	diphenhydramine	Benadryl
	pseudophedrine	Sudafed
Antinausea drugs	hydroxyzine	Atarax
	meclizine	Antivert
	metoclopramide	Reglan
	prochlorperazine	Compazine
Antiulcer drugs	ranitidine	Zantac
	cimetidine	Tagamet
Cardiac drugs	propranolol	Inderal
Pain medications	hydrocodone	Vicodin
	meperidine	Demerol
Seizure medications	carbamazepine	Tegretol
	gabapentin	Neurontin
	valproic acid	Depakote

SLEEP PROBLEMS

Unfortunately, sleep problems often accompany the normal aging process. The elderly are more likely to wake up due to a slight noise, and they might need to go to the bathroom frequently at night, which interrupts their sleep. Not just old people, but young people too may have difficulty with learning and memory without adequate sleep. Scientists believe that inadequate sleep results in production of excess stress hormones that interfere with the normal functioning of the hippocampus. We'll come back to this in Chapter 6.

DELIRIUM

Confusion and memory loss are quite common in elderly individuals who develop urinary tract infections or pneumonia. Sometimes the disorientation a person experiences is the first manifestation of her infection. In a majority of cases, fever, malaise, and specific symptoms such as burning with urination or a severe cough follow within days, which make it easy for doctors to pinpoint the source of the bacteria. Examination of urine and sputum as well as a chest X ray remain the primary tests in the E.R. for evaluation of confusion in an elderly patient. Fortunately, a few days of antibiotic treatment kills the bacteria, and the patient returns to her prior level of functioning.

LESS OBVIOUS CAUSES OF MEMORY LOSS

In evaluating a patient with serious memory decline, neurologists look for evidence of a dozen diseases, including Down's syndrome, cancer, anemia (low blood count), Huntington's disease, Mad Cow disease, seizures, head trauma, Lewy body dementia, frontotemporal dementia, posterior cortical atrophy, and normal pressure hydrocephalus, which is a specific type of hydrocephalus. We also check for liver, kidney, heart, and lung diseases. These are less common causes of memory loss, but they do occasionally occur. Fortunately, each has obvious features that distinguish it from Alzheimer's disease. Let's examine several.

CANCER

A brain tumor growing in the memory area of the brain can cause dementia. As the tumor grows, patients often develop other symptoms, such as arm weakness or double vision. When they seek medical attention, the tumor is discovered on MRI pictures of the brain. Occasionally, memory loss is a secondary consequence of breast, ovarian, and testicular cancers. Again, MRIs and blood tests can pinpoint the location of the cancer.

PARKINSON'S DISEASE

In some cases, forgetfulness may be related to Parkinson's disease. This is a neurological disorder that impairs a patient's ability to move his or her body spontaneously. Without treatment, patients lose the ability to make facial expressions; develop a stooped, bent posture; write in very small letters; speak in a soft voice; walk with a shuffling gait; fall frequently; and can't get in and out of cars and chairs easily. Later in the disease their memory declines. This type of memory loss differs from the dementia seen in patients suffering from Alzheimer's disease, who often move around without much difficulty.

Brain experts can easily determine if a patient has Parkinson's disease by taking note of clinical symptoms such as hand tremor, stooped posture, and masklike facial expressions. A patient's family members unfamiliar with this disease may believe that their loved one is developing Alzheimer's.

Some patients have features of both Alzheimer's and Parkinson's diseases. They're forgetful, get lost in their own neighborhood, walk with a shuffling gait, and have trouble getting out of chairs. Their symptoms often fluctuate from day to day. They have frequent hallucinations and major sleeping problems. These are symptoms of diffuse Lewy body disease. These patients have an abnormal accumulation of *Lewy bodies*, made up of synuclein proteins, inside the brain cells.

INFECTIONS

Infections such as syphilis, lyme disease, and HIV also can contribute to memory loss.

Syphilis is a sexually transmitted disease caused by the bacteria *Treponema pallidum*. More common in the 1950s and 1960s than it has been since, some of those infected in their youth have heart or memory problems in their senior years. This is called "tertiary" syphilis. Medical tests for evaluating memory loss reveal that the bacteria is still present in their blood, and treatment with antibiotics can kill the bacteria and cure the disease. The memories of these people usually improve, if only somewhat. Fortunately, fewer and fewer cases of syphilis are present in the general public. Checking for evidence of syphilis in the blood, as in checking for thyroid levels, is a routine part of evaluation of patients who have poor memory.

Lyme disease is an infection caused by a bacteria similar to the one causing syphilis. It starts with a tick bite that transmits bacteria from the host animal into the human recipient, usually creating a skin lesion. Like syphilis, it can later cause problems in almost every organ in the body. Skin lesions, as well as joint and heart problems, are common. In some rare cases a person with a Lyme infection may develop memory loss and dementia a few years later. A simple blood test can determine if someone is infected. Antibiotics can kill the bacteria and cure the disease. Lyme infection is not common enough to warrant routine screening for all the patients who complain of poor memory. However, since the ticks, and thus the disease, are more common in New England, patients in those states are tested more frequently.

HIV infection is another epidemic around the world. Since HIV occurs mostly in young people and often damages so many other organs, it is not difficult to distinguish AIDS dementia from Alzheimer's disease. In any case, most AIDS patients develop dementia at some point in the course of the disease.

LOOKING FOR ANSWERS

Determining the cause of any mental decline is a necessary first step to improving your memory. Now that we have explored the brain and many of the factors that impact your memory, we can move on to discuss the ten steps you can take to protect your brain against memory loss with aging and Alzheimer's disease.

PART II

THE MEMORY PROTECTION PLAN

6

PROTECT YOUR BRAIN AGAINST MEMORY LOSS AND ALZHEIMER'S DISEASE

Nobody knows for certain why some elderly are afflicted with Alzheimer's disease. However, there is some good news. Extensive research in the field of aging and the brain has established a number of risk factors for developing memory loss and Alzheimer's. By increasing your awareness of these risk factors and taking active steps to modify your exposure to them, you can dramatically reduce the risk of developing memory decline as you grow older. You have the opportunity to take control of your health, improve your cognitive abilities, protect your memory, and possibly reverse or delay the onset of memory loss during the second half of your life.

RISK FACTORS

Some diseases have a clear cause. Pneumonia, for instance, can develop from a bacterial infection. Yet you might be surprised to learn that the cause of many of the diseases that affect your body and brain remain unknown. Doctors are still struggling to find out why so many people in our society have high blood pressure, diabetes, or cancer. In trying to identify the underlying etiology for these diseases, they study thousands of people who suffer from any one of them to see what they may have in common. When it was discovered that most people who develop diabetes in their adult life are overweight, it followed that by controlling their weight, they have more control of their diabetes. Another example: High cholesterol, smoking, and obesity seem to be more common in individuals with high blood pressure. Thus, obesity and smoking are "risk factors" for hypertension. And of course it's now common knowledge that smoking increases the risk of lung cancer. Most risk factors are modifiable. You have the ability to lower your cholesterol, stop smoking, and lose weight. In doing so, you can lower your chance of having high blood pressure. Similarly, if you stop smoking, you diminish the chances of developing lung cancer. Unfortunately, however, some risk factors cannot be modified. Being a man, being over the age of sixty-five, or being African American are some of the risk factors for developing a heart attack—and they cannot be changed. People with these factors need to concentrate instead on risk factors that can be modified.

Scientists are constantly conducting research to find the cause and risk factors for common diseases. Doctors are eager to convey this information to their patients so that patients can minimize their risk factors and stay healthier longer. The same process is occurring now for Alzheimer's disease. For decades, people thought that Alzheimer's and memory loss would hit elderly individuals at random and that there was nothing they could do about it. In the past two years, a number of risk factors have been discovered for memory loss and Alzheimer's disease.[1] These include factors that can be modified, such as:

- High blood pressure
- High cholesterol levels
- High homocysteine levels
- Poor diet
- Smoking
- Diabetes mellitus
- Chronic stress
- Depression
- Head trauma

- Obesity
- Isolated and passive lifestyle

There are also factors that can't be modified, such as:

- Aging, especially being over eighty years old
- Having a family member with Alzheimer's disease
- Having the E4 version of the Apo-E gene (see Chapter 9)
- Lack of childhood education

LONGITUDINAL STUDIES

The identification of risk factors for memory loss and Alzheimer's disease has provided an exciting opportunity for protecting your brain against them. Many of these discoveries have come about through painstaking and lengthy (and expensive) research projects called *longitudinal studies,* a research protocol in which scientists usually invite thousands of individuals to enroll in a long-term study. Blood pressure, cholesterol levels, or other factors that may be related to the disease being investigated are examined, and the participants are asked about their life habits, occupation, and other issues that may be related to the disease in question. Scientists at first gather this information from volunteers who take part in the research, and these volunteers are questioned again once or twice a year. In fact, they're monitored anywhere from two to fifty years, or until they die. In some studies, their brains are examined after death.

The scientists then see which subjects develop diseases such as lung cancer or heart attack and so on, and which ones don't. They perform statistical analysis to find a correlation between each person's individual characteristics and his or her chance of developing the disease. This is how smoking was confirmed as a risk factor for developing lung cancer, and how high cholesterol was confirmed as a risk factor for heart attacks.

Many longitudinal studies for memory decline with aging and Alzheimer's disease have been in progress for the past two to three decades. The results are just now becoming available. While some of the identified risk factors were expected, others have been surprising. Fortunately, the majority of the risk factors can be modified. Many of these modifiable factors also happen to be the same ones associated with heart attacks and strokes. In North America, stroke is the third leading cause of death and the number one cause of disability. So by addressing these risk factors, you can make great strides in protecting your brain and improving your quality of life for decades to come.

AVOIDING MULTIPLE RISK FACTORS

Discoveries announced over the past two years indicate that lifestyle choices have a major impact on the chance of developing memory loss and Alzheimer's disease. Choices you make concerning diet and activity, or taking up or continuing habits like smoking, can contribute to high blood pres-

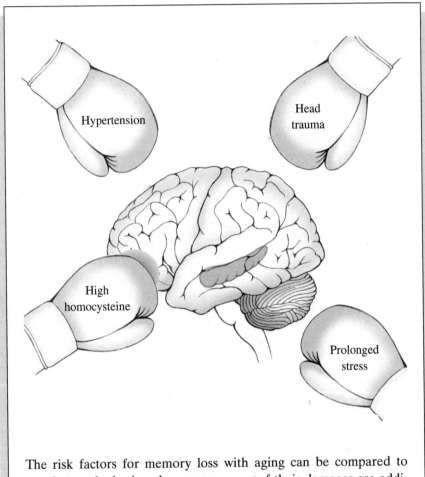

The risk factors for memory loss with aging can be compared to punches to the brain—the consequences of their damages are additive. A person whose brain is exposed to multiple risk factors throughout life and is then hit by Alzheimer's disease late in life is more likely to become symptomatic at a younger age.

sure or elevated cholesterol. These might not make a noticeable difference on how well your memory works today, but they may impact your brain in the long run, making it more or less vulnerable to the effects of aging and to the degeneration caused by Alzheimer's disease. By learning about these risk factors, you can take the necessary steps to keep your brain in good condition.

The cumulative effect of multiple risk factors is analogous to punches to the brain in an imaginary boxing game. Mini-strokes and depression are like two blows to the brain. The negative effects of high blood pressure, high cholesterol, or low vitamin levels are like repeated smaller punches to the brain. Overeating and a stressful lifestyle further exhaust the brain. Finally, Alzheimer's disease is like one big punch coming late in the game. By itself, Alzheimer's may not knock out the brain at once, but after a dozen previous punches, it can.

LEARNING FROM THE NUNS

Is Alzheimer's a disease that strikes people at random? To learn more about what determines who is more likely to develop the disease, David Snowdon, Ph.D., and his colleagues began to study the life habits, overall health, and memories of 678 nuns in the Midwest in the 1980s. The nuns had given the researchers their consent to have their brains examined after they died.[2]

The results were surprising. One-third of the 251 nuns who died during the period of the study had clear evidence of Alzheimer's disease, as determined by the presence of a multitude of plaques and tangles in their brains. But they hadn't displayed any signs of Alzheimer's while they were alive. In contrast, some of the nuns had very few plaques and tangles and yet were diagnosed with Alzheimer's disease years before they died. The brains of this second group of nuns also had evidence of mini-strokes. Could it be that they had lost their memory due to a combination of mild Alzheimer's disease and mini-strokes? These results raised the possibility that a person can have mild Alzheimer's and show no symptoms of dementia.

Other research groups have come to the same conclusion: If you protect your brain against factors that lead to mini-strokes during mid-life, you can protect yourself against memory loss with aging. Now it appears that you can delay or minimize the symptoms of Alzheimer's disease, even if you already have some plaques and tangles in your brain. In other words, you can protect your brain and have a direct impact on your cognitive ability by following certain steps to modify your lifestyle and health habits.

MEMORY PROTECTION PLAN: TEN STEPS TO BETTER MEMORY IN YOUR SEVENTIES

In general terms, since the primary cause of Alzheimer's disease remains unknown, there is no one thing you can do to prevent it. The best approach to aging with a healthy memory is to keep your brain in good shape, just as you would take measures to keep your heart or knees in good condition. The good news is that the sooner you start taking good care of your brain, the longer you'll maintain your mental faculties. Even better news is that many of the lifestyle changes needed to protect your brain against memory decline will also protect your skin, joints, and heart against aging.

Here are ten suggestions toward maintaining your ability to remember well in your last decades of life and protecting your brain against Alzheimer's disease. **Please discuss them with your physician first. Every person is different and needs individual attention. It's never a good idea to start taking over-the-counter medications, change medications, or make significant changes in your activity level without first consulting your physician.**

These suggestions are based on more than 1000 articles in the field and my eighteen years of involvement with brain research, as well as my experience with patients at Johns Hopkins Hospital.

As noted before, scientists continue to explore what happens in Alzheimer's disease and how you can protect your brain against memory loss. Some studies have focused on memory decline, while others have addressed the question of dementia more specifically. A handful of studies have concentrated on the link between particular factors and Alzheimer's disease. Your goal is to reduce the risk of losing your memory and to improve your cognitive abilities into your eighties and nineties. As such, I have included all factors that lower your risk of memory loss and dementia, whether it is called memory loss with aging, Alzheimer's disease, or vascular dementia.

STEP 1:
TAKE CONTROL OF YOUR BLOOD PRESSURE

Normal blood pressure is around 120/80. When it's higher than 140/90, it is called *hypertension*, which is one of the most common health problems in our society. Hypertension is the main risk factor for two major causes of death and disability in North America: heart attacks and strokes. Dozens of drugs are available to treat it successfully. Unfortunately, most people fail to take their high blood pressure seriously and do not take the appropriate medications.[3]

About 42 million Americans have hypertension. Only 10 million have their hypertension under control. The other 32 million are either unaware of their high blood pressure, are aware but do not take measures to lower it, or are aware but do not take their medications regularly. In Canada, there are 5 million people with hypertension, and only 1 million have their blood pressure under control.

Chronic moderate to high blood pressure reduces the amount of blood flow to most organs in your body, including your heart, eyes, genitals, and your brain. It impedes blood flow by making the walls of blood vessels thicker and their lumen narrower. This in turn limits the amount of nutrient-rich blood that can flow through them. Less blood translates into less oxygen and nutrients for the cells in your body. When this happens every day for several decades, the organs in your body start showing signs of damage. The less nutrients and oxygen that are available to your brain cells, for instance, the more the cells may become vulnerable to damage caused by Alzheimer's disease.

Hypertension can also damage the brain and cause dementia through the development of mini-strokes or large strokes affecting the hippocampus. When a dozen such silent mini-strokes occur, a person will show no symptoms. But when thousands of mini-strokes accumulate in the brain, the person will start showing symptoms, ranging from apathy or slowing in thinking to forgetfulness and dementia. Only when an MRI is performed on the brain are these mini-strokes discovered. The best way to avoid strokes, large or small, is to detect high blood pressure early and to treat it aggressively.[4]

Alzheimer's disease and stroke injure the brain in different ways, but the consequences of their damages are additive.[5] If a person has mild brain degeneration typical of Alzheimer's disease, he may not show any symptoms for a couple of years. In fact, he may be able to continue routine social activities. Similarly, if a person has hypertension and multiple mini-strokes, he may be free of any obvious symptoms; he could still hold a job, take care of his family, and read the newspaper. However, if a person has both of these diseases, he would become symptomatic much sooner than if he had only one or the other. Alzheimer's and mini-strokes become two separate punches that knock out the brain quickly when they happen at the same time. (See the illustration on page 78.)

Evidence Links High Blood Pressure with Poor Memory

Several recent studies support the idea that mid-life high blood pressure leads to poor brain function later in life.[6] One example of such a study was published in the *Neurobiology of Aging*.[7] In this longitudinal, "Honolulu-Asia Aging Study," of Japanese-American men born between 1900 and 1919 and living in Hawaii, investigators measured the blood pressure of 4678 volunteers in 1965, 1968, and 1971. Thus, it was known who had normal blood pressure and hypertension, and which men had been treated. The participants were contacted again approximately twenty-five years later, between 1991 and 1993. Some had moved and some had died, but 3734 were available for further testing.

This time, in addition to measuring blood pressure, researchers administered a cognitive test. It was found that men who'd had hypertension in mid-life were much more likely to perform poorly in these tests. In fact, those with hypertension (systolic blood pressure higher than 160) were 4.8 times more likely to be demented than those with normal blood pressure.

Further, the brains of those who had died and agreed to have their brains analyzed after they passed away were examined. Researchers discovered that the volunteers who had high blood pressure during mid-life had smaller brains that showed evidence of having experienced multiple mini-strokes.[8]

The Link Between Mid-Life Hypertension and Alzheimer's

Parallel with the longitudinal study in Hawaii, a group of Scandinavian researchers were performing similar research in Finland. They published their results in the *British Medical Journal* in June 2001.[9] These scientists gathered blood pressure data and other information from approximately 2000 volunteers in 1972, 1977, 1982, and 1987. They invited them back for continuation of the study in 1998, more than twenty years later, to see who had developed Alzheimer's. The 1449 volunteers who completed the study ranged in age from sixty-five to seventy-nine. The scientists found that 49 had developed Alzheimer's disease.

People with higher blood pressure in mid-life were more likely to be among those with Alzheimer's disease in their late life. The risk was 2.1 times higher for those who had borderline hypertension (140 to 159) and 2.8 times for those who had marked hypertension (higher than 160). These findings raised the possibility that high blood pressure could damage the brain in more ways than just narrowing the blood vessels; it may be directly linked with causing Alzheimer's disease.

A half dozen other studies are providing evidence that untreated high blood pressure for decades contributes to the development of memory loss and symptoms of Alzheimer's disease later in life. The elderly individuals who have additional medical problems, such as diabetes or heart failure, have an even higher risk of becoming demented. Fortunately, regular treatment with effective medications can minimize the deleterious effects of hypertension.

Treatment of Hypertension Can Lower the Risk of Dementia

In a large-scale research trial in Europe, scientists recruited 2418 volunteers whose average age was seventy and who had hypertension.[10] They gave placebo pills to half the group and active medication to the other half. Researchers then monitored the cognitive function and blood pressure of the participants over a two-year period. By the end of the study, those who were treated with medications had cut their risk of developing dementia by half; there were fifteen patients with Alzheimer's disease in the placebo group, but only eight in the treated group.

In another study, scientists studied a group of 1373 elderly volunteers, whose average age was sixty-five, in Napes, France, to see if people with hypertension who receive effective treatment do better than those who do not control high blood pressure.[11] Some of the subjects were taking medications and some were not. The volunteers' memory and cognition were measured with standard tests. After four years, those who had hypertension and weren't taking medications were 4.3 times more likely to have memory decline than those without high blood pressure. The risk was 1.9 times higher if they were taking medications but their blood pressure was still high. It was 1.2 times higher if their blood pressure had come down under good control. In other words, controlling blood pressure minimized the risk of experiencing cognitive decline.

While some scientists are continuing to show that treatment of hypertension in mid-life lowers the risk of dementia in late life,[12] others have not been able to see the same link in their study populations.[13] These latter researchers emphasize that hypertension leads to dementia mainly when it is combined with other risk factors, such as heart failure or diabetes. In any case, all neurologists and cardiologists agree that high blood pressure is deleterious to your heart and brain and should be treated promptly.

Mr. Harrison, a seventy-five-year-old retired postal worker, had diabetes, hypertension, and high cholesterol. Despite these illnesses, he appeared to be in very good physical condition and he'd had no obvious sign of decline with aging. His memory and cognition were also intact. Throughout his mid-life, he'd made an extra effort to take all his med-

ication regularly, exercise, and eat well. His wife would also check to make sure he didn't miss any of his medications. I felt that his good health was mostly due to his ability to take control of his medical illnesses and conquer them. Had he not done so, he would have been suffering from multiple complications of his hypertension and diabetes, such as heart attack, stroke, and dementia. I was pleased to see that primary prevention can work well if people take it seriously.

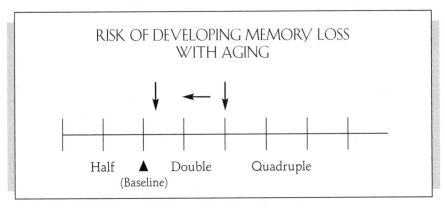

TAKING AN AVERAGE OF RESULTS FROM SEVERAL STUDIES, UNCONTROLLED HYPERTENSION IN MID-LIFE CAN TRIPLE YOUR RISK OF DEVELOPING COGNITIVE DECLINE LATER IN LIFE (ARROW ON THE RIGHT). IN CONTRAST, TAKING CONTROL OF HYPERTENSION CAN SIGNIFICANTLY LOWER THIS RISK (ARROW ON THE LEFT).

BLOOD PRESSURE MEDICATIONS FOR MILD COGNITIVE IMPAIRMENT

In a study of different blood pressure medications on the treatment of hypertension, Edwin Jacobson, M.D., and his colleagues at UCLA noted that before treatment, some patients with hypertension complained about pronounced memory problems. Though they were not demented, they had mild cognitive impairment. Dr. Jacobson's group decided to check the memory performance of these patients before treatment and for three to six months afterward to see which of the two types of medications was superior: a beta blocker or a calcium–channel blocker. The age range of the sixty-six men and women who participated in this study was sixty-five to eighty.

Researchers measured the patients' blood pressure at each visit and gave them memory tests. The results were reported at the sixteenth annual meeting of the American Society for Hypertension in 2001. By the end of the study, both groups had better memory, regardless of the type of medication used to lower their blood pressure. As long as their blood pressure was treated successfully—to fall below 140/90—their memory had improved.

One of the subjects was a physics professor who had stopped teaching because he believed he'd developed Alzheimer's disease. After his blood pressure was brought under control with these medications, his memory improved. He was able to return to his job on a part-time basis and teach again.

Several longitudinal placebo-controlled trials around the globe are investigating which of the dozen different blood pressure medications are more effective for the elderly population. Some of these trials include Hypertension in the Very Elderly (HYVET), Omapatrilat in Persons with Enhanced Risk of Atherosclerotic Events (OPERA), and Dementia Prevention in Hypertension (DEPHY). The results of these trials should become available within the next three years.[14]

Why People Don't Take Hypertension Seriously

If high blood pressure contributes so much to the development of memory problems, strokes, and heart attacks, and if it can be easily treated, why don't most people take care of it? The answer, I think, is because mildly elevated blood pressure does not produce pain or discomfort. Even people with very high blood pressure may only have vague symptoms of mild headache, blurred vision, or discomfort in their chest. Most people whose blood pressure runs above normal levels are not aware of it.

Due to the lack of acute pain or symptoms, even those who know they have high blood pressure often neglect to take medications on a regular basis. They don't realize that over time this "silent" disease with its widespread deleterious effects infers damage to their heart, kidney, and brain. A recent study in the *New England Journal of Medicine* showed that even those with normal blood pressure, but with readings at the higher limits, experience long-term negative effects, such as heart attacks.[15] The current guideline for physicians is to encourage patients to maintain a blood pressure around 120/80.

On a cautionary note, there may be exceptions to this guideline. For example, the elderly with heart failure need to adjust their blood pressure very carefully; for these patients, lower blood pressure may be an indication of worsening heart failure and is usually associated with a poor outcome.

Also, an eighty-year-old person may not need aggressive treatment of a borderline high blood pressure. Primary physicians have a great deal of experience with management of hypertension and take into account all factors before prescribing any medications.

Have your physician measure your blood pressure soon. You can also check your pressure with machines available in most large pharmacies or drugstores. These machines are less accurate, but they do give an approximate indication if your blood pressure runs high. If you discover that your blood pressure is above normal limits, take it seriously. Discuss it with your doctor—sooner rather than later. If you're in your mid-life, it's the single best investment you can make for your long-term health.

Lifestyle modifications are the first steps toward controlling your hypertension (unless it is dangerously high). Here are some of the more important things your doctor may suggest:

- *Lower the amount of salt in your diet.*   Even a mild modification, such as not adding extra salt to your regularly cooked meal, can make a noticeable difference in your blood pressure over time. Avoid salty French fries.
- *Lose some weight (if you're overweight).*   For every ten pounds you lose, you drop your blood pressure by 2.5 points. In my view, the best way to lose weight is to eat less; consider eating half the amount of food on your plate for a few months, and you'll see a difference both in your weight and in your blood pressure.
- *Quit smoking (if you're still smoking).*   Smoking is the worst thing you can do to your lungs, heart, and brain.
- *Exercise.*   Even if you don't lose weight, exercise can help you lower your blood pressure. If you can, measure your blood pressure before and after an exercise session; you'll see that even one hour of playing tennis can lower your blood pressure. (Later, we'll discuss the importance of exercise for preventing memory decline.)

STEP 2:
LOWER YOUR CHOLESTEROL

The link between high cholesterol and deleterious health effects is well established. High cholesterol is a risk factor for heart attacks around the world, so it's not surprising that statins—cholesterol-lowering medications such as Pfizer's Lipitor (atorvastatin) and Merck's Zocor (simvastatin)—have become the leading prescription drugs in the United States and England. The new discoveries showing that lowering cholesterol appears to also considerably lower the risk of Alzheimer's disease promise to make statins even more popular.

Atherosclerosis Can Cause Cognitive Decline

High levels of cholesterol damage the inside lining of the blood vessels, and atherosclerotic plaques form at the sites where those blood vessels are injured. With continued high levels of cholesterol, these plaques grow in size and trigger inflammation, which builds on and around them. The lumen of the blood vessels narrows gradually, as the plaques grow larger and larger. When this happens in the vessels that supply nutrients and oxygen to the heart muscles, a person may experience pain or "tightness" in his chest when he exerts himself. If the lumen gets blocked completely, the person will develop a heart attack.

High cholesterol levels, especially when combined with high blood pressure, can narrow the lumen of the small blood vessels in the brain too. If the inside lumen gets completely blocked, a patient develops mini-strokes (or mini–brain attacks). As mentioned several times before, a few of these go unnoticed. When thousands of these mini-strokes spread throughout the brain, the patient develops memory and thinking problems. With the blockage of bigger vessels in the brain, the strokes are more obvious and the patient may develop weakness in one side of the body or completely lose the ability to speak or understand language. Sometimes the large blood vessels linking the heart and the brain, the internal carotid arteries, are affected.

You can feel your carotid arteries pulsating by placing your finger over the left or right side of your neck. These vessels carry the blood to the left and right side of the brain and are equally prone to atherosclerosis and blockage. The left and right sides of the brain are specialized for different functions. The left side is more involved with the ability to speak, read, and remember. The right side appears to be more closely linked with the ability to appreciate art, write poetry, and orientation to time and direction.

Scientists at the University of California in San Francisco recently studied 4019 patients over the age of sixty-five who were enrolled in a cardiovascular research project.[16] They discovered that those with significant blockage of the left carotid artery were six times more likely to have memory problems than those with right-sided blockage. A person with a narrowed left carotid artery may have no clear physical symptoms, except memory loss or difficulty thinking clearly. To family members around him, these symptoms might appear worrisome for Alzheimer's disease.

However, if his left carotid artery were surgically fixed, he might regain his memory and intellectual functions.

> *Professor Smith, an endocrinologist in a medical institution in California, enjoyed teaching students how to perform a physical examination on patients. In one of his small group classes, he was showing students how to use a stethoscope to listen for a special whooshing sound in the neck, a sound usually associated with a partially blocked internal carotid artery. One of the students asked if he could practice on the professor's neck, and to everyone's surprise, the student heard that characteristic sound on his left carotid artery. The professor's physician ordered an ultrasound of his neck that confirmed that he had a tightly blocked left carotid artery. Professor Smith underwent surgery for the removal of that atherosclerotic plaque and recovered within a few days. Following the operation, the former slowness in his thinking, which he'd attributed to working too much and getting old, had been alleviated. The professor knew he was lucky, since most blocked arteries are discovered only after people experience a stroke.*

High Cholesterol and the Risk of Alzheimer's

In the same Scandinavian research study that tracked the blood pressure of 1449 volunteers for more than twenty years, cholesterol levels were also measured and recorded at regular intervals.[17] The results were again surprising. Individuals with high cholesterol levels (more than 250 mg/deciliter) in mid-life were 2.2 times more likely to develop Alzheimer's disease in their late life, as compared to those with normal levels in mid-life. In this study, those with both high cholesterol and high blood pressure were worse off. High cholesterol plus borderline hypertension meant a 2.8 times higher risk of Alzheimer's disease, and the combination with a marked hypertension (higher than 160) meant a risk that was 3.5 times higher.

High cholesterol may directly contribute to the formation of amyloid plaques.[18] In 1992, Larry Sparks, M.D., senior scientist and head of the Ralph and Muriel Roberts Laboratory for Neurodegenerative Disease Research Center at the Sun Health Research Institute in Sun City, Arizona, put forward this idea. To test his hypothesis, he gave rabbits a very high fat diet for eight weeks. He found that the brains of cholesterol-fed rabbits had higher levels of amyloid, as well as a significant quantity of markers for free radicals and inflammation. When he put them back on a regular diet for two weeks, the amyloid load dropped by 50 percent, establishing a link between cholesterol and amyloid plaques.

Similar results were replicated in experimental mice genetically engineered to have Alzheimer's-type amyloid plaques. Mice on a high-cholesterol diet had more amyloid in their brain. When they received cholesterol-lowering medications, the amyloid levels dropped.

Observations of this kind have led to the idea that excess cholesterol in the brain may serve as a seed around which the amyloid plaques build up. High cholesterol levels may also favor the formation of beta amyloid (found in Alzheimer's plaques) in lieu of other forms of amyloid, which don't pile up as gumlike plaques. Whatever the explanation, there is general agreement among neurologists that mid-life untreated high cholesterol is deleterious to your health and should be treated.

Good or Bad Cholesterol and Poor Cognition

Special proteins, called lipoproteins, carry the cholesterol in the blood. Some of these proteins are called low density lipoproteins (or LDL), and others are called high density lipoproteins (or HDL). LDL is commonly referred to as "bad cholesterol" since it's associated with hypertension and heart attacks. HDL, on the other hand, appears to have beneficial effects and is referred to as the "good cholesterol." Does this distinction also apply to the role of lipoproteins in cognitive impairment?

Kristine Yaffe, M.D., and her colleagues at the University of California in San Francisco studied 1037 postmenopausal women to answer this question.[19] They monitored their total cholesterol, LDL, and HDL, and gave them cognitive tests over a four-year period. These women had coronary heart disease and were a part of the "Heart and Estrogen/Progestin Replacement Study." Women with the highest level of total cholesterol were 1.76 times more likely to have mild cognitive impairment, as compared to those with the lowest levels. Moreover, it was the high LDL that correlated with poor memory, not differences in HDL levels. Claudia Kawas, M.D., and Maria Corrada, Ph.D., also found a link between a higher ratio of LDL to HDL and the risk of dementia in their "Baltimore Longitudinal Study of Aging." They presented these results at the American Academy of Neurology in April 2002 in Denver, Colorado.

Are the polyunsaturated fats better than saturated fats? Several exciting studies presented at the Eighth International Conference on Alzheimer's Disease and Related Disorders in July 2002, in Stockholm, Sweden, showed that regular consumption of polyunsaturated fats in fish was associated with a significantly lower risk of memory loss or Alzheimer's disease. For example, researchers from France monitored the dietary habits of 1674 participants over ten years and discovered that those who consumed seafood at least once a week had cut their risk of developing Alzheimer's disease by 40 percent.[20]

Statins May Lower the Risk of Alzheimer's

Researchers have discovered that people who take cholesterol-lowering medications dramatically reduce their risk of Alzheimer's disease. David Drachman, M.D., chairman of the neurology department at the University of Massachusetts in Worcester, together with colleagues in England, reviewed computerized medical information of 60,000 patients over the age of fifty. The data was from the British General Practice Research Database. It was found that 25,000 people had normal lipid values, 25,000 had high levels and were taking medications to lower it, and 10,000 had high levels and were on no medications. Over a six-year period, 284 individuals developed dementia. The majority of these patients were from the group with high cholesterol and were on no medications. Researchers found that those taking statins had a 70 percent lower risk of developing dementia.[21]

In another epidemiological study, Benjamin Wolozin, M.D., and his colleagues at Loyola University Medical Center in Maywood, Illinois, gathered data from 56,000 people treated at military hospitals. They discovered that patients taking statins had a 60 to 73 percent lower risk of developing Alzheimer's disease, as compared to patients who were taking medications for their blood pressure. This study suggested that statins had beneficial effects of their own, and were not working only by reducing the cardiovascular risk factors.[22]

Most recently, Robert Green, M.D., M.P.H., and colleagues from Boston University studied 2581 participants enrolled at fifteen medical centers in the United States, Canada, and Germany. They found similar results. Statins dropped the risk of Alzheimer's disease by 79 percent in those who were taking them for at least six months. This protective effect was present independent of people's ethnicity and genetic risk for Alzheimer's disease.[23]

Researchers are still trying to establish with confidence that statins prevent Alzheimer's disease or cognitive decline before they can be recommended to everyone. Such confidence requires more long-term longitudinal and placebo-control clinical trials involving thousands of people with different backgrounds. Meanwhile, their role in reducing the risk of heart attacks is well-accepted and established in the medical literature. Even if further research proves that statins are not the magic drugs for protecting your brain against Alzheimer's disease, you still need to lower your cholesterol to prevent your chance of developing heart attacks.

Moreover, statin drugs seem to have beneficial effects above and beyond their ability to correct cholesterol levels. Some researchers believe that they may act as antioxidants and reduce the damage produced by free radicals. Clinical trials are now underway to establish if statins can prove effective for preventing dementia or treating Alzheimer's disease.

Testing for Cholesterol

Cholesterol levels rise with a high fat/low fiber diet. Some people have high LDL or low HDL because of the type of genes they inherit from their parents. Either way, they wouldn't know their cholesterol level was high unless they had a blood test, since high cholesterol levels do not produce any symptoms by themselves. We discover high levels in some of the patients who come to the hospital with heart attacks or strokes as we look for the cause of their disease.

Some people do know about their elevated cholesterol level but fail to take care of it; they're too busy with other problems in their daily life. As long as they don't feel any direct pain and discomfort, they postpone addressing their high cholesterol level. Often this later date can be too late.

How Can You Lower Your Cholesterol Levels?

Have your physician check your cholesterol levels. If they are mildly elevated, diet and exercise may be all you need to bring them back to normal levels. If they're excessively high, you'll need medications. Current statin drugs work well and can lower your cholesterol levels within a month.

Here are some specific suggestions on how to lower your cholesterol:

- Learn about the cholesterol contents of foods from their labels. You should try to keep your cholesterol intake to less than 300 mg per day.
- Increase the amount of fiber in your diet by eating high fiber breads.
- Eat fish at least once or twice a week.
- Quit smoking.
- Exercise. In addition to a dozen other beneficial health effects, exercise decreases your LDL and increases your HDL.
- Drink a glass of wine with dinner. One glass of wine with dinner can lower LDL and increase HDL too. Excess alcohol (more than three glasses a night) is deleterious to your heart and brain.
- Take statin medications. These are wonder drugs that have beneficiary effects on your heart and your brain.

STATINS THAT PREVENT COGNITIVE DECLINE AND ALZHEIMER'S

Which of the dozen different statins would work best in the prevention of cognitive decline and Alzheimer's disease? There are two types of statins: those that can enter the brain and gain access to neurons, and those that cannot. There is no obvious reason to expect that one would be superior to the other with respect to prevention or treatment of Alzheimer's disease. With the elderly becoming the fastest growing segment of the population, any drug that is proven to be more beneficial in this regard will be highly popular. At least three drug trials are now underway to answer these questions.[24]

- *ADCS (Alzheimer's Disease Cooperative Study).* ADCS is a trial sponsored by the National Institutes of Health to see which of the statins is more effective for patients with mild to moderate Alzheimer's disease. Three hundred patients with normal lipid levels are enrolled in twenty centers across the United States.
- *PROSPER (Prospective Study of Pravastatin in Elderly Risk).* Started in 1998, PROSPER will be completed soon. Its 5804 participants are receiving either pravastatin or sugar placebo tablets. Researchers want to know if patients taking this statin will have better cognition by the end of this four-year study, and if they will have experienced fewer heart attacks and strokes.
- *ADAPT (Alzheimer Disease Anti-inflammatory Prevention Trial).* The focus of this trial, which involves 2625 people, is to establish whether anti-inflammatory drugs (Aleve and Celebrex) are effective in preventing Alzheimer's disease. The participants are over seventy years old, have normal cognition at baseline, and also have a first-degree relative with Alzheimer's disease or other forms of dementia. The trial is being conducted in numerous centers around the country, including Johns Hopkins Hospital. Some of the participants also take statins on their own. Dr. Larry Sparks is checking the statin use in these individuals in order to establish which one is more protective against developing Alzheimer's disease.

For now, you need to take statins only if you have high cholesterol levels that put you at risk for heart disease. Your physician should check your cholesterol levels periodically to make sure you're taking the appropriate dose.

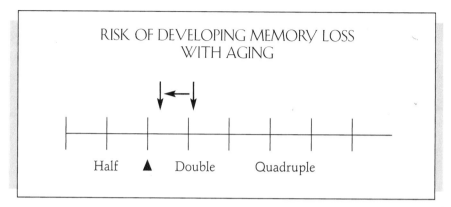

HIGH CHOLESTEROL LEVELS ARE ASSOCIATED WITH A HIGHER RISK OF MEM-
ORY LOSS (ARROW ON THE RIGHT). CHOLESTEROL-LOWERING STATINS CAN
LOWER YOUR RISK OF MEMORY DECLINE AND ALZHEIMER'S DISEASE (ARROW
ON THE LEFT).

STEP 3:
CHECK YOUR B12 AND HOMOCYSTEINE LEVELS

Physicians and scientists have been interested in the role of cholesterol in
all areas of health and disease for decades. They know how it causes heart
attacks, how it can be measured in the blood, and how it can be treated
effectively in weeks. But they're just beginning to explore the role of homocysteine, a small natural molecule that, like cholesterol, is an important part
of the cells in your body.

Homocysteine seems to have deleterious effects at high levels. The latest breakthrough has been the discovery that there's a link between high
homocysteine levels and the development of Alzheimer's disease—those
with higher homocysteine levels seem to be at a higher risk of getting this
disease.[25]

Who Has High Homocysteine Levels?

Homocysteine is an amino acid molecule that floats in your blood. Like
other amino acids, it serves as building blocks of proteins in your body. It
usually gets converted, in a chain of reactions (analogous to an assembly
line), to yet another amino acid (called Methionine). This conversion
requires vitamin B12 and folate. If for some reason you have low levels of
these vitamins, the homocysteine gets backed up, since it cannot get converted to the next amino acid in the assembly line. This is the most common

reason for developing high homocysteine levels.[26] A small minority of people inherit genes that cause high homocysteine levels. Much like high cholesterol, the elevated blood levels of homocysteine do not produce any symptoms. The next question is: Why would some people have low B12 or folate levels?

With normal aging, there's some slowing in the process of the absorption of vitamins in the gastrointestinal tract. Older individuals (especially those above seventy or eighty) may absorb only part of the vitamins they eat in their diet. Some people, especially women, lack the protein in the stomach that ordinarily helps with the absorption process. This usually happens due to an immunological disease that may occur along with low thyroid levels. Other people may simply not eat enough vitamin-rich vegetables. A simple blood test can show if you have normal levels of homocysteine, B12, and folate.

Why High Homocysteine Levels Cause Problems

Scientists have now established with certainty that high homocysteine levels account for thousands of heart attacks and strokes every day. Homocysteine, like cholesterol, can irritate the inside linings of your blood vessels and set off inflammation. This in turn contributes to the hardening of the vessels with atherosclerotic plaques and to the formation of small blood clots at the injury sites. The clots in turn block the blood flow in the vessels in your heart and brain, which leads to heart attacks and strokes.

Homocysteine also may directly contribute to formation of amyloid plaques. Scientists are still working to pinpoint the exact reason why high homocysteine levels would be associated with slowing of memory and thinking, or the development of Alzheimer's disease. In reality, it may be the culprit in all the above processes.[27]

The Link Between High Homocysteine and Alzheimer's

For almost a decade, researchers knew that people with high homocysteine had a higher risk of developing heart attacks, strokes, and having a poor memory.[28] However, the question remained as to whether high homocysteine was associated with Alzheimer's disease. In February 2002, the long-awaited answer appeared in an article in the prestigious *New England Journal of Medicine*.[29]

In this longitudinal study, Sudha Seshadri, M.D., and his colleagues at Boston University monitored 1092 elderly people living in Framingham, just outside Boston, for an average of eight years. These individuals were part of several long-term studies by researchers at Harvard Medical School since 1948. Their blood pressure, cholesterol levels, and lifestyle habits had been recorded on a regular basis for decades.

The subjects were nondemented men and women with an average age of seventy-six. Over the study's eight-year period, 111 developed dementia. Dr. Seshadri's team studied the link between their blood homocysteine results at baseline and their risk of developing Alzheimer's disease. They found that those with high homocysteine levels were twice as likely to have this disease than those who had normal levels (below 14 micromoles per liter). For every five-point increase in homocysteine levels, there was a 40 percent increased risk of Alzheimer's disease. These results were striking, since no one expected such a dramatic association between an amino acid in the blood and risk of dementia.

These researchers also found that people's homocysteine rose with advancing age. The average homocysteine level was 11.5 for those between ages of sixty-five and sixty-nine, and was 22.3 for those between ages of ninety and ninety-four. This observation suggests that homocysteine may be partly responsible for the higher prevalence of dementia among the elderly. Most people in their seventies and eighties may not even know that they have high homocysteine levels.

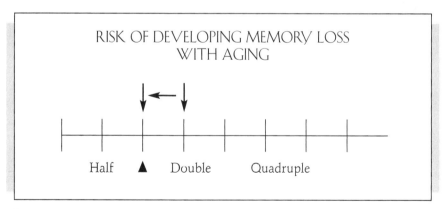

HIGH HOMOCYSTEINE LEVELS, ASSOCIATED WITH LOW B12 AND FOLATE VITAMINS, CAN DOUBLE YOUR RISK OF DEVELOPING COGNITIVE DECLINE WITH AGING (ARROW ON THE RIGHT). TAKING VITAMINS BRINGS DOWN THE HOMOCYSTEINE TO NORMAL LEVELS WITHIN WEEKS (ARROW ON THE LEFT).

How Treating High Homocysteine Improves Cognition

Several longitudinal studies are trying to answer this question, and the result will probably be available in the next three to five years. However, a small study in Sweden suggests that treating high homocysteine in the elderly can improve their cognition.[30]

The cognitive performance of thirty-three patients with dementia, whose average age was seventy-four to seventy-nine, was monitored before and after treatment. At baseline, patients who had very high homocysteine levels (above 19.9) were more demented than those with lower levels. Patients with mild to moderate dementia showed improvement, while those with severe dementia did not get better. This was a very small study, and the results await confirmation from the large clinical trials now under way.

Can Low B12 and Folate Lead to Dementia?

High homocysteine levels are due in part to low levels of B12 and folate. However, these two vitamins also have other roles for the cells in your body. For example, vitamin B12 is a major component of the linings that insulate the branches of the nerves and protect them (from exposure to other chemicals in your brain). These coverings are like the plastic wrappings around the wires in your house. They're particularly important for the long and thin branches of neurons, insulating them and ensuring that the information flows rapidly and efficiently from one neuron to the next. Patients who have low B12 levels are more likely to develop fatigue, depression, memory loss, or slowness in their thinking and dementia.[31] In severe cases of B12 deficiency, the result can be permanent damage to the nervous system.

Ms. Smith was a calm and delightful twenty-seven-year-old woman in Baltimore. She lived with her husband and two children, and worked as a cashier. She gradually began to have serious memory problems and confusion with numbers, to the point that she lost her job. She saw her physician, who thought she might be depressed. Ms. Smith continued to get worse and exhibited strange behavior: screaming for no reason, neglecting to take care of her children or pay attention to her own hygiene. She was transferred to Johns Hopkins Hospital.

We performed a set of routine blood tests for common causes of memory loss, and discovered that Ms. Smith had almost no vitamin

B12 in her blood. It turned out that she had a form of autoimmune disease that affects the gastrointestinal lining and prevents the absorption of B12 into the body. Her brain and spinal cord MRIs showed extensive damage to her nerves. Immediately she started receiving injections of B12, and she gradually improved, though the damage to her nervous system was so extensive that she never fully recovered. This could have been avoided if her B12 levels had been checked initially.

Ms. Dashmore was a brilliant pharmacy student with a history of epilepsy. She was free of seizures with effective medications and had come to see me for a regular follow-up visit. She reported doing well at school, though she felt tired most of the time, had difficulty concentrating, and lacked her usual zest for life. I was concerned she may have depression; low thyroid, B12, or folate levels; anemia; or may be experiencing side effects from the seizure medications. Her blood tests showed that her B12 level was below normal. After taking daily B12 supplements for several months, she regained her usual level of energy and joie de vivre. It turned out she was a vegetarian and was not careful about eating enough dairy products to make sure she had adequate levels of B12.

Testing and Treating B12, Folate, and Homocysteine Levels

The elderly are at a higher risk of having low levels of B12 and folate vitamins and high levels of homocysteine. Certainly, they should be tested if they have significant memory loss. Vegetarians who are not careful about their diet may also need to check their blood, especially if they feel fatigued, have diabetes, or have a sore tongue that has a red "beefy" appearance. People who have surgery in their gastrointestinal tract may also have difficulty absorbing vitamin B12, and they need to check it if they have unexplained symptoms of lack of energy and slower thinking.

Treating high homocysteine is as easy as lowering high cholesterol levels. Patients need to take high doses of vitamins B12, B6, and folate. They can see positive results in less than a month. People who have difficulty with absorbing vitamin B12 in their gastrointestinal tract need to take vitamin B12 injections once a month.

STEP 4:
EAT A DIET RICH IN FRUITS AND VEGETABLES, AND ADD SOME WINE

There's a great deal of evidence that the wear and tear that comes with aging and leads to skin wrinkles, joint pain, and blurred vision may be due in part to inflammation. As mentioned earlier, when there's injury in any parts of your body, your immune system sends inflammatory cells to that area. These cells chew away the bacteria or whatever else is causing the damage. They produce toxic free radical oxygen molecules to break down and digest the offending chemicals in a process called oxidation. With aging, some low level of inflammation and oxidation takes place without any apparent reason. This is why antioxidants, such as vitamin E, and anti-inflammatory medications may be used to help combat the effects of aging.

Do Foods Rich in Vitamins Improve Cognition?

James Joseph, M.D., chief of the Human Nutrition Research Center on Aging at Tufts University, and his colleagues designed an experiment to test the hypothesis that adding blueberries, which are rich in antioxidants, to a diet can improve memory.[32]

They compared the performance of middle-aged rats to young rats, with and without a diet supplemented by blueberries. They put each group of young and middle-aged rats in a large box with two toy pigs, then removed the rats from the box for one hour, switched one of the toys with a new pig toy, and put the rats back in the box. The young rats noticed that there was a new toy around and spent 64 percent of their time exploring it. The middle-aged rats on a regular diet were not as eager to explore the new toy, and only spent 44 percent of their time on it. Similar middle-aged rats fed with blueberry supplements, however, acted more like the young rats, and spent 70 percent of the time playing with the new toy pig. In summary, it appeared that adding a fruit rich in antioxidants to a diet enabled a middle-aged animal to perform more like a young animal.

Another rich source of antioxidants is spinach, and scientists have begun to formally test the effects of spinach in a diet.[33] In a study presented by Paula Bickford, Ph.D., at the Society for Neuroscience meeting in San Diego in 2001, rats were fed with spinach supplements and their performance was compared with other rats on a regular diet. They found that the animals that received the additional spinach were able to learn faster than those on a regular diet. This research provided further support that antioxidants can make a measurable difference in memory performance. Some researchers are now trying to determine if diets supplemented with blueberries or spinach could prevent the formation of plaques in the brains of older animals.

Some scientists have examined the role of curcumin, found in curry spice. Like vitamin E and other antioxidants, curcumin can absorb free radical molecules and prevent them from damaging the brain. It was reported in the *Journal of Neuroscience* in November 2001 that in test tubes and in animal models of Alzheimer's disease, curcumin seems to reduce the toxicity due to amyloid proteins.[34] The much lower incidence of Alzheimer's disease in India—4.4 times less than in the United States—may in part be related to a diet rich in curcumin or other spices. Pharmaceutical companies in search of magic drugs to treat Alzheimer's disease need to pay close attention to curcumin.

The Link Between Diet and Cognitive Performance

It should not come as a surprise that eating a balanced diet with plenty of fruits, vegetables, grains, and dairy products that reduces your risk of heart attacks would also help with keeping your brain in top condition. A poor high-fat diet is linked with hypertension and the development of ministrokes, and these in turn have been shown to contribute to the deterioration of memory. Researchers have determined that those with a healthy diet are less likely to develop cognitive impairment.[35]

In a study of more than 1600 people older than seventy in Italy, researchers at the National Institute in Milan decided to formally examine the link between diet and memory function. Participants were asked about what they ate on a regular basis, and then their memory, attention, and language skills were checked in standard neuropsychological tests. Participants put their diet on a scale of 1 to 7, with 7 being the healthiest diet—consisting of low fat, low cholesterol, high fiber, and plenty of polyunsaturated omega-3 oils, vegetables, nuts, and fruits.[36]

Researchers classified the cognitive performance of the participants into either "no impairment," or mild, moderate, or severe impairment. The findings, reported in the *European Journal of Clinical Nutrition* (December 2001), were that most individuals who consumed a healthy diet had no or mild cognitive impairment. Those with a poor diet score were three times more likely to score poorly on their cognitive tests than those with a good diet score. The study confirmed what most Italian grandmothers would tell their children anyway: "Eat your vegetables!"

Alzheimer's and Antioxidant Vitamins

Vitamin E supplements are used for treatment of Alzheimer's disease. A recent study compared the levels of vitamin E in blood samples from 20 patients who suffered from Alzheimer's disease and 23 elderly healthy individuals. Patients with Alzheimer's had a significantly lower level of vitamin E in their blood. This may have been due to excess free radicals and inflammation in their brains consuming the available vitamin E and leading to the lower levels.[37]

Other studies have shown that Alzheimer's patients have lower levels of vitamin E and folate in the fluid that normally surrounds the brain (the cerebrospinal fluid, or CSF). And still other research has shown that giving vitamin E and C supplements to patients with Alzheimer's disease does lead to higher levels both in their blood and CSF.[38]

In short, there is an overwhelming amount of research suggesting that a vitamin deficiency may contribute to memory loss and the development of symptoms in Alzheimer's disease.

Vitamin E Lowers the Risk of Alzheimer's

Two recent studies published in the *Journal of the American Medical Association* (June 26, 2002) provided further evidence that dietary intake of antioxidant vitamins are linked with a lower risk of Alzheimer's disease.[39] In one longitudinal study in Rotterdam, Netherlands, Monique Breteler, M.D., Ph.D., and her colleagues at Erasmus Medical Center interviewed 5395 subjects who were fifty-five or older.[40] Detailed information was gathered from the participants concerning their daily food intake, education, smoking habits, and use of antioxidant supplements. From published charts, the researchers calculated the exact amount of vitamins in the participants' diets, then monitored them over a six-year period.

Of the 197 participants who developed dementia, 146 were diagnosed with Alzheimer's disease. Examining the dietary habits of the demented individuals, it turned out they were consuming the least amount of vitamin E. Those consuming the highest amount of vitamin E were 43 percent less likely to develop Alzheimer's disease.

Martha Clare Morris, Sc.D., and her colleagues at Rush Institute for Healthy Aging performed a similar longitudinal study in Chicago.[41] For four years they monitored 815 subjects who were older than sixty-five. Participants taking the highest amount of vitamin E had a 70 percent less chance of developing Alzheimer's disease, compared to those taking the least amounts. Other groups of scientists presented studies showing a similar protective effect of vitamin E at the Eighth International Alzheimer's Conference in July 2002 in Stockholm.[42] These scientists studying separate populations of subjects in different countries arrived at the same conclusion: Those who take vitamin E do indeed have a lower risk of cognitive decline and dementia.

One interesting finding in two of the studies was that eating a diet rich with vitamin E was more effective than taking vitamin E supplements. The other three groups did not find the same results. Also, the evidence for the effectiveness of vitamin C and beta-carotene was not convincing in all these studies. To establish exactly how much vitamin E is beneficial to improve cognition and lower the risk of dementia, and to determine if other vitamins are as important, scientists need to carry out a careful placebo-controlled double-blind clinical trial consisting of thousands of volunteers in different areas for five to ten years. Several such trials are currently underway.

For now, vitamin E appears to be effective in delaying the onset and progression of Alzheimer's disease. Many of the healthy Alzheimer's researchers and clinicians take vitamin E themselves. They know that this vitamin, at doses of 400 to 1000 IU a day, is safe and has the great potential to slow the oxidation process that comes with aging in the body. Some patients attribute all their good health to vitamin E.

Mrs. Dover was a healthy and happy eighty-five-year-old woman who had decided to participate in the Alzheimer's research study at Johns Hopkins Hospital. She had no memory problems and also performed very well in our formal memory tests. Her only medication was vitamin E. She felt the reason for her overall good health and her good memory was vitamin E. She had not missed a single dose since she was fifty years old. She may have been right, though she had a lot of other things that worked in her favor. Her blood pressure, cholesterol, homocysteine, B12, and thyroid levels were normal, and she enjoyed eating well, exercising, doing crossword puzzles, and socializing.

Does Drinking Wine Lower the Risk of Memory Loss?

In a recent study published in the prestigious journal *Lancet* (January 26, 2002), Dr. Monique Breteler and her colleagues found that drinking one to three glasses of alcohol per day significantly reduces the risk of developing dementia.[43] The source of their data was from the same 5395 elderly volunteers who had enrolled in the long-term research study on aging in Rotterdam between 1990 and 1993 and were examined regularly for six years. Those who consumed one to three drinks a day had a 42 percent lower risk of developing dementia. The protective effects of alcohol were noticeable, whether people drank wine or other forms of alcohol.

Other studies have shown beneficial effects of drinking one or two glasses of wine against stroke and heart attacks. How drinking a small amount of alcohol would have so many positive health effects remains a mystery. It may be related to blood thinning or the cholesterol-lowering properties of alcohol, or to the fact that it can increase your HDL.

On a cautionary note, the adverse effects of alcohol should not be forgotten. Here are a few things to consider:

- Heavy drinking damages the brain directly. In the above study, those who had more than four drinks a day were 1.5 times more likely to develop dementia. Heavy drinkers lose their memory and develop alcoholic dementia, which is just as debilitating as Alzheimer's disease.
- When you drink alcohol, your memory may not function quite as sharply for a few hours. If you need to pay attention and learn something important at a dinner party, drinking alcohol would not be a good idea.
- Excessive alcohol consumption damages your stomach and liver. Many alcoholics have problems with bleeding from their stomach, which in some cases can cause death.
- If drinking is against your family or religious teachings, then you should focus on other factors that can help you ward off dementia.

One or two drinks per day is only one of the many things you can do to prevent memory loss with aging—not the only thing.

Diets That Help Prevent Memory Loss

We've been over this, but it can't be emphasized enough: A diet rich in a variety of fruits and vegetables and low in fat and cholesterol is associated with better memory and cognition in animal studies and with a lower risk of strokes, heart attacks, and cognitive decline in humans. Antioxidants, either in the form of vitamin E supplements or in vegetables and herbs, may directly prevent the free radicals that damage the brain in aging and in Alzheimer's disease. B12 and folate keep the homocysteine levels from rising and reduce the risk of dementia. What's more, a healthy diet is good not only for your brain, but also for your heart and skin. The same process of aging that damages your skin and joints affects the brain too, and any intervention would reduce the damage in all organs.

So a diet that contains plenty of fruits, vegetables, bread, fish, and some meat may protect your skin, heart, and brain from the negative aspects of aging—and perhaps from Alzheimer's disease as well. Taking vitamin supplements is optional and depends on your personal preferences. Many physicians taking care of Alzheimer patients recommend vitamin E—especially those physicians who take it themselves!

One cautionary note: **Vitamin E at high doses can lead to bleeding in people who have blood clotting problems or in patients who take blood thinning medications like coumadin. As with all other over-the-counter medications, you should start taking vitamin E supplements only under the care of your physician.**

Here are some suggestions for eating a better diet for your memory:

- Eat five or six fruits a day. As long as you eat different fruits, you're more than likely to acquire sufficient vitamins.
- Include dairy products, bread, and vegetables in your diet every day.
- Try taking vitamin E supplements—at a suggested dose of 400 to 1000 IU a day—if you feel you don't have enough fruits and vegetables in your diet.
- Eat fish at least twice a week.
- Consider drinking one to two glasses of wine with dinner. Avoid drinking during the day, as it may slow your thinking. Never drink if you have to drive.

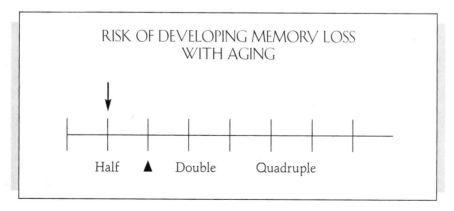

RISK OF DEVELOPING MEMORY LOSS
WITH AGING

Half ▲ Double Quadruple

A DIET RICH WITH ANTIOXIDANT VITAMINS, ESPECIALLY VITAMIN E, LOWERS YOUR RISK OF DEVELOPING ALZHEIMER'S DISEASE.

FOODS FOR BETTER MEMORY

SOURCES OF B12:
Milk products
Meat
Poultry
Fish

SOURCES OF FOLATE:
Leafy green vegetables (like spinach)
Dry beans and peas
Fortified cereals
Grain products
Tomatoes
Oranges
Chickpeas
Beets
Soybeans
Fish
Eggs

SOURCES OF VITAMIN E:
Vegetable oil
Whole grain
Green leafy vegetables
Sweet potatoes
Avocados

OTHER SOURCES OF ANTIOXIDANTS:
Blueberries
Sweet potatoes
Pomegranates
Carrots

SOURCES OF POLYUNSATURATED OMEGA-3 OILS:
Fish
Walnuts
Flaxseed
Canola

STEP 5:
PROTECT YOUR BRAIN FROM INJURY

Your brain is the best protected part of your body. The skull is thick and durable, while the brain itself is soft and mushy. A sudden blow to the head can jolt the brain inside the skull and lead to negative long-term consequences. According to several recent studies, head trauma severe enough to cause loss of consciousness for hours is considered a risk factor for depression or memory loss decades later.[44]

Evidence Links Head Trauma with Alzheimer's

Brenda Plassman, Ph.D., of Duke University and her colleagues at the National Institute of Aging in Baltimore reviewed medical records from World War II and identified 548 veterans who were hospitalized for head trauma between 1944 and 1945.[45] Their average age at that time was twenty-one. Some had mild head trauma with loss of consciousness for less than half an hour, while others were in a coma for more than twenty-four hours after their injury. When these individuals were interviewed between 1996 and 1997, those with severe head trauma fifty years earlier were 4.5 times more likely to have developed Alzheimer's disease. The more severe the injury, the more likely was their risk of dementia.

There is no evidence that a head trauma causes Alzheimer's disease by itself; millions of people who have had severe head trauma never develop Alzheimer's disease. However, there is overwhelming evidence that a severe blow to the head—one that leads to a coma, for instance—means a higher likelihood of poor cognition decades later. Such a trauma appears to lower the brain's ability to fight back if the Alzheimer's process does set in. If it's combined with five other risk factors for memory loss, it can bring a person's cognitive ability down below the threshold for showing symptoms of Alzheimer's disease.

What Happens After Severe Head Trauma?

There are many hypotheses as to what happens to your brain after you bang your head in an accident such as a car crash. The brain cells have long branches that cross the brain from one side to the other and also reach to the spinal cord. A head injury severe enough to make a person lose consciousness for hours can tear some of these long branches and impair the ability of neurons to communicate with one another. Multiple traumas, causing multiple jitters to the brain, can lead to hundreds or thousands of tears. This in turn would mean the loss of some neurons or synapses, and perhaps a smaller "brain reserve." Immediately after the injury, a person may have no symptoms, but years later he or she may be more prone to develop memory loss.

Some scientists believe that head trauma may directly increase the amount of amyloid plaques in the brain. John Trojanowski, Ph.D., and his colleagues at the University of Pennsylvania performed an experiment on mice to test this hypothesis.[46] They anesthetized a group of genetically engineered mice that usually develop Alzheimer's plaques in their brains when they get older. They discovered that mice who had two traumatic brain injuries had four- to tenfold more plaques in their brains, compared to the mice who either had no head injury or only one injury. Their findings support the idea that multiple traumatic brain injuries may lead to damage in the brain that is usually associated with memory loss.

Could Head Trauma Result from Alzheimer's?

In some cases, a person with early signs of dementia may get confused while getting around her house or her streets and fall. She would then continue to show more symptoms, and the family might think that the fall was the cause of her worsening memory and thinking problems.

Richard Mayeux, M.D., and researchers at Columbia University in New York studied a group of elderly in Manhattan. They too discovered that people with prior history of head trauma were more likely to develop Alzheimer's disease. However, this association was most impressive for people with a fall within five years of diagnosis. Since it takes several years for the Alzheimer's process in the brain to grow before a person is symptomatic enough to be diagnosed, these researchers did not believe the falls triggered Alzheimer's disease, but that the early Alzheimer's may have put the head trauma victims at a higher risk of falling.[47]

There is another way a head trauma can cause confusion or memory loss. The elderly are more likely to develop a small bleed on the surface of their brains after they fall. It can grow slowly over weeks to months, and when it grows to be the size of an eggplant, it pushes on the brain, which can lead to depression, memory loss, or even strange behaviors. Since it gets larger gradually, people around such a person may not immediately link the symptoms with the fall. A brain scan in the E.R. would show this kind of bleed in a few minutes. Fortunately, surgeons can easily scoop out the blood clot from the surface of the brain.

Some Cautions to Follow

To protect your brain against trauma, and a higher likelihood of memory loss in the future:

- Wear a helmet when you bike or play contact sports like football or hockey.
- Buckle up every time. Make sure that your family members do the same.
- If you or someone in your family develops sudden difficulty with memory and thinking following a head trauma, go to the hospital; it may be caused by a small bleeding in the brain that could be surgically treated.

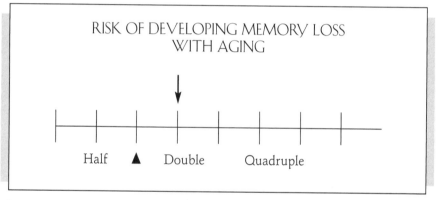

RISK OF DEVELOPING MEMORY LOSS
WITH AGING

Half   ▲   Double   Quadruple

INCREASED RISK OF MEMORY LOSS FOLLOWING MULTIPLE SEVERE HEAD TRAUMA ASSOCIATED WITH COMA.

STEP 6:
CHECK YOUR EYES AND EARS; SHARPEN YOUR SENSES

For you to remember something you read, or to recall someone's name, you first need to register that information in your brain (and especially your hippocampus) clearly and firmly. You then need a systematic approach to retrieve that information. For this to happen, you need to be mentally alert, awake, and interested. This may sound obvious, but in fact most people don't appreciate it.

With advancing age, people's hearing and vision are not as crisp as they once were. Cataracts and mild hearing loss are common among the elderly and interfere with their ability to acquire new information from the world around them. Many of the elderly are also on multiple medications, some of which may dull their senses. These factors, especially if combined with fatigue, anxiety, or insomnia, can prevent them from remembering names and events around them.

Poor Vision and Hearing Affect Memory

Imagine looking in front of you at a sign with large letters that says "HIPPOCAMPUS." Now imagine looking at a crumbled piece of paper with a word written on it with a pale pencil and in small letters that reads "entorhinal cortex." Which one do you think you'd remember better? The large word will make a stronger impression in your brain and is registered more firmly because you can see it more clearly. If you haven't had your eyes or your eyeglasses checked in a while, you may not be seeing the world as sharply as you can, and as a result, your brain might not be registering the information.

Needless to say, if you simply look at something and don't pay attention to what you see, you again fail to register the information in your hippocampus. If you're looking at a book but thinking about your plans for the weekend, you can't expect to remember what you read. In short, poor vision, especially if accompanied by poor attention, interferes with the "acquisition" step of good memory.

Poor hearing also interferes with memory acquisition. If you're at a crowded party and someone introduces himself, chances are you may not remember his name as well as you would if you were listening to the same information in a calm and quiet room. As a part of our routine cognitive tests, we ask our patients to try and remember a list of three to five words. We usually ask them to first repeat it after us. If they can't do this, we need to make sure their hearing works well. Not infrequently, we find that they need a hearing aid.

Medication Side Effects and Memory

If a drug makes you groggy, your memory won't work well. In this case, you may have registered certain information in your brain well before, but now have difficulty mostly with "retrieval" of that information. Fortunately, memory problems associated with new medications go away soon after you stop taking them.

Fatigue and Memory Acquisition and Retrieval

Sometimes you hear something but you don't pay attention because you're too tired. When you're exhausted from too much work, your brain cannot absorb new information. On days when you have too many things going on at once, you shouldn't blame yourself for being unable to remember all that happens around you. If the data does not get registered in your brain firmly, it would be difficult to retrieve it at a later time.

If you don't get an adequate amount of sleep, your memory will not work well the next day. Now a group of researchers in Germany has provided scientific evidence for this common observation.[48] In the evening, they gave fifty-two healthy volunteers a sequence of finger-tapping movements to remember. These involved tapping the left-hand thumb on the index, ring, and other fingers in a specific sequence; for example, 4-1-3-2-4. Then one group slept for eight hours while the other group stayed awake all night. As expected, the rested group performed much better in the morning. They were 33.5 percent faster and 30.1 percent more accurate than the groggy group.

Poor vision, limited hearing, medication side effects, and lack of adequate sleep may each contribute to a small degree to your memory problems. If a number of these factors work against you simultaneously, you may find that the cumulative effect is adding up to a significant memory loss. Therefore, the best way to protect your brain against memory loss over years is to make it a habit to ensure that the new information gets registered in your brain well; that the information can get access to your hippocampus fully—better vision and hearing; and that you're rested enough to readily retrieve the information stored in your cortex.

Here are some specific suggestions to sharpen your senses:

- If you find that the words on the newspaper or the street signs are blurry, have your vision checked.
- If you find yourself asking people to repeat what they just said, or that your spouse complains that you turn the sound on the radio or television set too high, have your primary physician check your hearing or order a hearing test.
- If you take multiple medications, ask your pharmacist to check and see which of them may cause sedation, grogginess, or lethargy, especially if you think your memory has declined since you started a new medication.
- If you cannot fall sleep, or you wake up numerous times during the night, or you don't feel rested in the morning, ask your physician to evaluate your sleeping pattern. You may need to avoid taking naps during the day, avoid eating before going to sleep, put on fresh bed sheets, and wear comfortable clothing at night (to improve your sleep hygiene).

- Make getting an adequate and uninterrupted sleep every night a priority. "Adequate" for some people means only five hours and for others nine hours.
- If you are obese, you may need evaluation for sleep apnea (periods of not breathing during sleep at night and a tendency to fall asleep frequently during the day—sometimes while driving!).
- Some people feel an urge to keep moving their legs all night. They feel better when they get up and walk. This condition is called Restless Legs Syndrome. If moving your legs all night prevents you from getting a restful sleep, discuss it with your physician. There are medications that can help.

STEP 7:
EXERCISE

An article in the *New England Journal of Medicine* in March 2002 showed that people who exercise more live longer.[49] Researchers looked at the 6213 men who were referred for an exercise tolerance test. They measured how long each person was capable of running on the treadmill. Over six years, 1256 of these individuals died of various causes. More of these patients were from the group who could not run for a long time. For each extra minute they could run, their risk of dying was 12 percent less.

Hundreds of other studies have established the positive link between exercise capability and better overall health. Regular physical activity improves your blood circulation, heart function, sexual performance, and mood. It also lowers blood pressure, reduces tension, and helps you lose weight. Now researchers are discovering that exercise improves your memory and reduces your risk of dementia later in life.

The Link Between Low Physical Fitness and Memory Loss

Richard Camicioli, M.D., from the University of Alberta, and his colleagues at the University of Oregon recently monitored a group of 108 healthy men and women from sixty-eight to one hundred years old, over a six-year period, by obtaining brain MRIs, performing cognitive tests, and measuring how fast they could walk thirty feet.[50]

As expected, they found that those who had shown a smaller hippocampus on their MRI or those who had a great deal of difficulty with their memory at baseline were more likely to develop cognitive decline over the period of the research study. Surprisingly, however, they also discovered that those who walked slower at baseline were more prone to memory loss; for every second that they were slower, their risk was 1.14 times higher. Using physical fitness as a prediction for a person's risk of mental decline is a new concept.

Physical Fitness Leads to Better Memory

In the "Canadian Study of Health and Aging," involving 4615 elderly men and women over the age of sixty-five, Kenneth Rockwood, M.D., and others in several provinces in Canada discovered that people who did more exercise were less likely to develop Alzheimer's disease. They monitored these individuals over five years, from 1991–92 to 1996–97, and noted that 436 of them developed mild cognitive impairment and 285 developed dementia. Those with the highest level of regular physical activity had cut their likelihood of having cognitive impairment or dementia by half.[51]

In a similar long-term study of 6000 elderly women in California, Kristine Yaffe, M.D., and her colleagues at UCLA found an impressive correlation between more walking and better memory performance. Over six to eight years, these researchers monitored the level of physical activity and memory performance in this group and discovered that the more miles a woman walked on a daily basis, the lower her risk of becoming demented. For each daily extra mile, there was a 13 percent improvement in memory compared to women who walked less.[52]

Jeffrey Kaye, M.D., at Oregon Health & Science University, reported at the American Academy of Neurology meeting in Denver in 2002 that even those in their seventies and eighties lower their risk of developing dementia if they exercise. He and his researchers studied a group of 147 healthy men and women for approximately six years and found that those who exercised vigorously were more likely to ward off dementia.[53]

How Does Physical Activity Lead to Better Memory?

A few new discoveries are providing exciting clues to answer this question. In an article in the June 2002 issue of *Trends in Neuroscience*, a group of scientists from the University of California reported the possible link between exercise and better memory. They focused their attention on a protein called *brain-derived neurotrophic factor*, or BDNF. This natural protein improves neuronal health and survival. It makes neurons more resistant to injury caused by a stroke and helps with synthesis of new synapses.[54]

The scientists measured the levels of BDNF in the brains of mice who were sedentary, and in the brains of those that had a wheel in their cage and voluntarily exercised for many hours each night. The results were that the more miles the mice ran, the higher the level of BDNF in the hippocampus. Animals unable to make an adequate amount of BDNF had memory problems, which improved once BDNF was injected directly into their brains. In short, BDNF may be one of the key players in mediating the effects of exercise for improved memory. The levels of another protein, called *nerve growth factor*, have also been shown to increase with exercise.

These findings may explain why people who are more physically fit seem to have a better memory and stave off dementia. It encourages people to use exercise not only as a way of living longer, but also to keep the mind sharp during the last decades of their lives. The findings also provide hope for individuals who already have Alzheimer's disease. It may sound like science fiction, but scientists are considering surgically implanting these growth-factor proteins in the brains of patients with Alzheimer's disease to see if they'll get better.

How Much Exercise Is Enough?

No one has established an exact number of hours of exercise that will protect the brain against memory loss. The data seem to show that the more, the better. In all the published studies, there's a linear relationship between the level of daily activity and the benefits of exercise for improved memory. The current recommendation of the American Heart Association is for people to engage in moderately intense physical activity for at least thirty minutes on most—and preferably all—days of the week. In a recent study of 73,743 women between the ages of fifty and seventy-nine, researchers from Harvard Medical School found that even two and a half hours of brisk walking a week on a regular basis can lower vascular heart disease by 30 percent.[55]

Walking has been shown to lower blood pressure, increase the level of good (HDL) cholesterol, reduce the risk of stroke by half, delay the onset of diabetes in overweight people, reduce the risk of osteoporosis in women by 30 percent, increase gastrointestinal mobility, increase relaxation, reduce stress, and improve memory.

One way to implement physical activity into daily life is to incorporate it into your interactions with other people around you. For example, instead of meeting for tea with your friend, plan to get together for a walk in the park. Instead of having a lunch with family, you could invite everyone for a hike and a picnic. You need to make physical activity a priority in your life since everyone agrees that regular exercise is absolutely beneficial to your overall health in the long run.

Here are some specific suggestions. **Please discuss your physical fitness and ways to improve it with your doctor first; it is never a good idea to start a rigorous exercise program if you haven't increased your heart rate for months.**

- Make exercise a priority in your life.
- Start with a low level of daily exercise.
- Increase your exercise routine gradually.
- Set reasonable goals.
- Make it fun to exercise; do the sport you enjoy.
- Take the stairs every day.
- Park your car farther away and walk to your office.
- Sign up for "walks," such as for Alzheimer's or a breast cancer walk.
- Join a team in a club or team at your work.
- Go for hikes, bike rides, or long swims.
- Remind yourself that exercise is essential for you to live longer and helps ward off many illnesses, including cognitive decline.

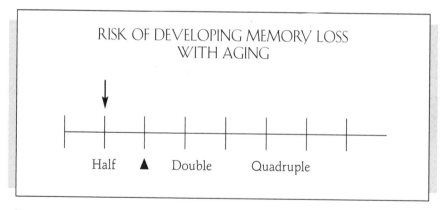

RISK OF DEVELOPING MEMORY LOSS WITH AGING

Half ▲ Double Quadruple

DECREASED RISK OF MEMORY LOSS WITH REGULAR EXERCISE.

Sedentary lifestyle is one more risk factor for developing memory loss in the last decades of your life, but it is not the only one. Hypertension, high cholesterol or homocysteine levels, and head trauma can lead to cognitive impairment too. There are millions of people who are obese and have no memory problems. If you have been overweight, it does not mean you will automatically develop Alzheimer's disease when you turn sixty-five. It takes multiple risk factors to lower your brain function below an accepted normal threshold. However, by exercising and losing weight, you have the opportunity to tilt the balance of having a better memory in your favor. In the process, you will also look better, feel better, and live longer.

STEP 8:
JOG YOUR BRAIN; USE IT OR LOSE IT

The concept of the protective effects of education against memory decline with aging was first noted in second-century biblical commentary: "Scholars grow wiser as they age, but the noneducated become foolish." Since the 1980s dozens of studies involving tens of thousands of subjects around the world have pointed to the fact that those who lack early education are more likely to develop Alzheimer's disease.

Robert Katzman, M.D., and his colleagues at the University of California in San Diego surveyed 5055 men and women in Shanghai, China, in 1988. They discovered that illiterate individuals were almost five times more likely than high school graduates to develop Alzheimer's disease.[56]

Laura Fratiglioni, M.D., Ph.D., and her colleagues at the Karolinska Institute in Sweden monitored 1296 elderly volunteers over the age of seventy-five for five years. They obtained information about their early education and discovered that those who had less than eight years of education were 2.6 times more likely to develop Alzheimer's disease.[57]

Dr. Fratiglioni's team more recently evaluated 7935 individuals over the age of sixty in the Ravenna province in Italy. As presented at the Eighth International Conference on Alzheimer's Disease and Related Disorders, they discovered that those with no education were 11 times more likely to develop dementia compared to those who had at least five years of education. These findings that link high school education with development of Alzheimer's disease sixty to seventy years later are impressive. It means that at least one factor in the risk of getting Alzheimer's disease can be determined, across decades of life experiences, to what an individual did as a child and a teenager.

It means that high school education is surprisingly critical for protecting your brain against Alzheimer's disease. Along with other studies, it can be said that an attitude of being open to reading and learning throughout the first two-thirds of life decreases the risk of memory problems in the last third. However, this does not automatically imply that all of those who did not attend high school will go on to suffer from Alzheimer's disease. Again, there are a dozen other factors that also affect the brain including blood pressure, cholesterol and homocysteine levels, diet, exercise, and smoking, as well as being intellectually active, which we'll get to shortly.

In another study concerning the difference early education can make in later Alzheimer's risk, David Snowdon, Ph.D., and colleagues interviewed a group of nuns living in the Midwest and, with their permission, read the application letters the women had written after finishing high school and applying to join various convents. The letters reflected how clearly the nuns had been able to articulate why they wanted to become nuns. Years later, at the time of Dr. Snowdon's study, those who had written essays full of ideas were far less likely to develop Alzheimer's disease than those nuns who had written simple short notes. In fact, there was a direct correlation between the higher density of ideas per sentence and a lower chance of developing Alzheimer's disease.[58]

Why Education Protects the Brain against Memory Decline

A skeptical explanation as to the benefits of education for the aging is that people with early education are better test takers, and therefore perform well later in life when they have to take memory tests as part of the Alzheimer's disease evaluation process. But this most likely is not the case. As shown in the study by Dr. Katzman in Shanghai, China, illiterate people who were young could still successfully complete the memory tests.[59] If the problem was the ability to take the tests, illiterate people would have a diagnosis of Alzheimer's disease even when in their thirties. There is overwhelming support for a different hypothesis.

In animal studies, Gerald Kempermann, Ph.D., and his colleagues have shown that mice living in more stimulating and enriched environments during their middle age had far more neurons and synapses in their brains than mice living in the usual laboratory cages. The "enriched" three feet by three feet living area was equipped with a rearrangeable set of plastic tubes, a small running wheel, nesting material, and toys. The privileged mice performed better in all learning parameters, exploratory behavior, and locomotor activity tests. Interestingly, the brains of these animals showed fewer signs of degeneration with aging. Authors concluded that "in mice signs of neuronal aging can be diminished by a sustained active and challenging life, even if this stimulation started at medium age."[60]

In humans, those who read and continue to learn also may create more synapses between their brain cells in their hippocampus.[61] According to such a hypothesis, with more synapses and communication between their neurons, these people can handle the challenges of daily life even if parts of their brains are damaged by Alzheimer's disease.[62] Alternatively, educated people may also have better coping skills and can find ways around forgetting people's names, current affairs, or even the year. Sometimes their spouses may be the only ones who detect their initial problems.

> *Dr. Thompson was the president of a university in a southern state. At his wife's insistence, he agreed to come to Johns Hopkins for a memory evaluation. At first encounter, he was pleasant and charming. At closer examination, however, it was amazing that he could still maintain his job. He did not know the names of their grandchildren, the month of the year, or any of the current affairs in the news. He could not draw a clock. When he did not know the answer to questions, he would try to change the subject. Other times, he would look at his wife for help. He clearly had dementia. Like Ronald Reagan, he had managed to stay at a high-level job and to get around his symptoms of profound memory loss. He agreed to undergo further medical evaluation and to start taking one of the new Alzheimer's medications.*

David Bennett, M.D., at Rush Alzheimer's Disease Center in Chicago, and colleagues at the University of Pennsylvania, recently provided further exciting evidence for the observation that educated people resist the process of Alzheimer's disease in their brain and manifest signs of dementia much later than less educated people.

Among the 106 older Catholic clergy who were monitored with annual cognitive tests, some were demented while most others were functioning well. After these volunteers died, researchers examined their brains and counted the numbers of plaques and tangles. They discovered that the more educated clergy handled loads of plaques and tangles in their brains and showed no signs of memory loss at the time of their death. Those with less education showed symptoms of Alzheimer's disease with fewer plaques and tangles. Each additional year of education made a difference in how much longer the individuals could remain cognitively intact and withstand the deleterious effects of Alzheimer's disease in their brain. These results were presented at the Eighth International Conference on Alzheimer's Disease and Related Disorders in 2002.[63]

In some ways, highly educated people have a disadvantage in that their disease is not recognized until it has reached an advanced stage. By the time they lose their mental faculties, Alzheimer's has spread throughout their brain and they do not benefit as much from the new medications. They need family members who are vigilant and, like the example of Dr. Thomson's wife, urge the person involved to seek medical attention when they begin to show an unusual drop in their baseline level of cognition.

Cognitive Stimulation throughout Life
May Protect You against Alzheimer's

Continued interest in learning is crucial for protecting your brain against memory decline with aging. In an article published in the *Journal of the American Medical Association* in February 2002, Robert Wilson, Ph.D., of Rush Presbyterian-St Luke's Medical Center in Chicago reported the findings of a study he and his colleagues made on the link between intellectual activities and a reduced risk of Alzheimer's disease.[64] They interviewed 801 Catholic nuns, priests, and brothers over the age of sixty-five—men and women who had the same educational background—once a year over an average five-year period. They monitored how often they read books, played cards, solved crossword puzzles, or watched TV and discovered that those who enjoyed stimulating their brains with mental activities had better memory until the very last years of their life. In fact, those who devoted the most time to cognitively engaging leisure activities seemed to cut their risk of developing Alzheimer's disease by half. In other, similar studies, researchers are reaching the same conclusions.

Here are some suggestions about remaining intellectually active:

- Follow the political events not only in the United States, but elsewhere in the world. Read the news daily.
- Keep track of the scores and winning teams in your favorite professional sport.
- Try to do simple calculations in your head. For example, guess your grocery bill before the cashier tells you, figure out how much it would cost

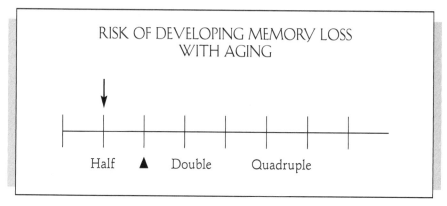

RISK OF DEVELOPING MEMORY LOSS
WITH AGING

Half ▲ Double Quadruple

DECREASED RISK OF MEMORY LOSS WITH A LIFELONG HABIT OF READING AND LEARNING.

to fill your tank with gas or how much time you would spend in the car if you traveled 10 miles an hour slower. Do it for the fun of it.

- Try to solve puzzles you hear on the radio or to answer questions on TV quiz shows.
- Try some crossword puzzles.
- Join a book club.
- Play bridge with your friends.

STEP 9:
SOCIALIZE; BECOME A MORE INTERESTING PERSON

While the importance of education in protecting your brain against dementia was established for twenty years, discoveries in the last two years show that a diverse set of leisure, productive, or social activities can also help ward off Alzheimer's disease. Those who participate in interesting and fun group engagements seem to preserve their mental capabilities better in their last decades of life than those with a habit of staying home and passively watching television.[65]

Yaakov Stern, Ph.D., and his colleagues at Columbia University College of Physicians and Surgeons in New York recently found a direct link between more leisure activity and less chance of developing dementia.[66] For up to seven years, 1772 volunteers who were older than sixty-five were asked if they engaged in a list of twelve leisure activities. The activities included knitting and other hobbies; walking for pleasure or excursion; visiting friends or relatives; going to movies, classes, restaurants, or sporting events; doing unpaid community volunteer work; playing cards or bingo; attending church or synagogue; and reading magazines and newspapers. They found that those who participated in multiple leisure activities on a regular basis had a 38 percent less risk of developing dementia. More specifically, there was 8 percent less risk of dementia for each additional leisure activity. Interestingly, those who preferred intellectual activities did better than those who enjoyed mainly physical or social options.

> Dr. Jones was a seventy-five-year-old scientist in Puerto Rico. She had hypertension, diabetes, heart failure, and high cholesterol. She was a happy person and loved to entertain people. She would often invite the members of her laboratory or other friends and relatives to her house for parties. She would laugh with them as they played group card games. Thanks to her stimulating career, social lifestyle, and positive attitude, she

had no sign of cognitive decline despite her multiple risk factors and living on a long list of medications.

In another study, in Cleveland, Ohio, researchers led by Robert Friedland, M.D., contacted the family members of 193 patients diagnosed with Alzheimer's disease who had lost their memories and could not accurately remember their hobbies and activities when they were younger. The researchers obtained information about the intellectual, physical, and passive activities of these patients when they were in early adulthood (twenties and thirties) and middle adulthood (forties and fifties). They also asked another group of men and women, with an average age of seventy-one, to complete the same questionnaires. It turned out that those with a lifelong habit of passive activities, such as watching TV, were 3.85 times more likely to develop Alzheimer's disease in their seventies. In contrast, individuals who participated in diverse intellectual activities in their early and middle adulthood were more likely to ward off Alzheimer's disease in late adulthood.[67]

Some individuals in this study had increased the percentage of time they spent on intellectual hobbies in their forties and fifties; others had become lazy after their thirties and spent more time in front of the TV. Researchers found that those who turned more active from early adulthood to middle adulthood minimized their probability of developing Alzheimer's disease in their seventies, while those who became more passive maximized this probability.

Productivity and Socialization Make a Difference

As part of the "Honolulu Asia Aging Study," Jennifer Balfour, Ph.D., and her colleagues at the National Institute of Aging in Bethesda, Maryland, examined the social lifestyle of 2486 Japanese-American men living in Hawaii and their risk of developing dementia. These men, who were seventy years old or older, were monitored for three years with regard to productive activities, such as helping others, volunteering, or doing paid work. Researchers also noted their social engagements with their spouses, contacts with friends, group membership, and "confidant reciprocity." They took into account their educational background and history of heart disease and depression.

At the end of the three-year period, they found that men with high productivity and an active social lifestyle were seven times less likely to develop dementia. There was a direct relationship between the number of productive or social activities and the protective effects against dementia.

For example, with each additional engagement in social activities, the risk of memory decline dropped by 17 percent. These important results, presented at the 2001 meeting of the American Academy of Neurology, show the protective aspects of productivity and social engagement against Alzheimer's disease or other forms of dementia.

In another study concerning the effects of social activity and Alzheimer's, Dr. Fratiglioni's team in Sweden analyzed information they obtained from 1375 elderly subjects in their longitudinal study in the Kungsholmen neighborhood of Stockholm. The subjects had been monitored since 1987. They had completed questionnaires at the beginning of the study, once more between 1991 and 1993, and a third time between 1994 and 1996. They answered questions about how often they would engage in:

- Productive activities: gardening, housekeeping, cooking, working for a salary, doing volunteer work, sewing, weaving, crocheting, knitting
- Mental activities: reading books or newspapers, writing, studying, painting, drawing, doing crossword puzzles
- Social activities: going to the theater, concerts, or exhibitions; traveling, playing cards, attending group meetings, joining organizations
- Physical activities: swimming, walking, gymnastics
- Recreational (passive) activities: watching television, listening to the radio

Those involved in a rich social network, who were active and productive on a daily basis, had cut their risk of Alzheimer's disease by half. Those who lived alone, watched TV, and avoided social ties were twice as likely to develop dementia in their eighties.

Why Does Socialization Help Ward Off Dementia?

Several studies have shown that elderly individuals who participate in a diverse set of leisure activities, remain involved with their family and community, and mingle with other people can preserve their mental capability in good working condition until they die. Whether it's volunteering in a hospital, participating in a bird-watching group, going to church, or playing bingo, a meaningful and fun lifestyle involving interactions with other people seems to prevent, or at least delay, memory decline.

It's not clear how these activities may protect your brain against dementia. One possibility is that they stimulate large areas of the brain. Frontal lobes need to be activated to organize appropriate speech, behavior, and action. Temporal lobes need to be engaged to remember people's names and backgrounds. Parietal lobes need be pulled to action to keep track of time and where things are. Motor areas need to be recruited to coordinate walking or speaking. Thus, participation in productive and intellectual leisure activities and social gatherings keep many of the brain regions active, ensuring that they remain in good functioning condition. Falling asleep in front of the television is a passive activity that often does not challenge the mind. Like muscles, many of the brain synapses get weaker when they're not used. The concept of "use it or lose it" does apply to both muscles and the brain.

In my evaluation of individuals who participate in the Alzheimer's Disease Research Center at Johns Hopkins Hospital, I always ask about their hobbies. I find that those who lead interesting lives filled with fun leisure and productive activities are less likely to develop Alzheimer's disease in the near future. I worry more about individuals who lack interest in the world around them and spend most of their time staying home and doing nothing.

It's never too late to start challenging your brain and becoming a more interesting person. Just as you can tone up your arm muscles and get into shape with physical exercise at any age, you can shape up your memory muscles and improve your brain function at any age. Engaging in stimulating leisure activities and exchanging ideas with friends will help you preserve your cognitive abilities. Though not proven in humans, exposure to thought-provoking environments and social gatherings may indeed increase the number of synapses in your brain and enhance your brain reserve. At a minimum, it slows down the loss of synapses that occur as part of the normal aging process.

I recommend that you take on leisure activities that you enjoy but have not had the time to do. The more you like them, the more likely it is that you'll continue with them. Here are some suggestions:

- Join a dance class.
- Work a few hours a week as a volunteer at an organization you like.
- Invite your friends for dinner more often; try new recipes.
- Become more involved with your local community.
- Visit an antique shop with a friend.
- Attend concerts of your choice.
- Take your family to an aquarium, museum, or a botanical garden near where you live.

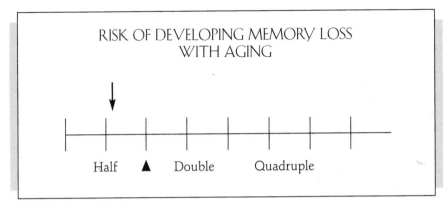

RISK OF DEVELOPING MEMORY LOSS
WITH AGING

Half   ▲   Double   Quadruple

DECREASED RISK OF COGNITIVE DECLINE WITH MORE LEISURE ACTIVITIES
AND LIVING IN A RICH SOCIAL NETWORK.

STEP 10:
BEWARE OF DEPRESSION AND STRESS, BE HAPPY

Chronic stress and depression impair memory. The majority of those who
complain about memory problems may be experiencing symptoms of
chronic stress, fatigue, and depression. Patients with Alzheimer's disease
often don't complain about their memory, since they have less insight into
their problem. Ronald Petersen, M.D., Ph.D., and colleagues at the Mayo
Clinic in Rochester, Minnesota, recently evaluated depression in 145
patients with mild cognitive impairment (MCI) and 1034 control subjects.
They found that the percentage of individuals with depressive symptoms
was four times higher in the MCI group than in the control group.[68]

Depression often crawls in so gradually that the person may not realize
when it started. Her symptoms may begin with lack of energy and apathy.
She may find herself dragging out of bed with no interest in going to work,
attending meetings, seeing friends, or participating in her usual hobbies.
She may feel guilty and blame herself for all that goes wrong around her at
the office and at home. She would feel stressed out and irritable, lose her
self-esteem, perhaps find herself to be ugly and fat, and not pay as much
attention to the way she dressed and presented herself. She would either
sleep too much or not enough. Her attention and memory would deteriorate and she would have difficulty making decisions and remembering the
phone numbers and names that she always knew by heart.

If this happened to a seventy-year-old woman, she and her family might
wonder if she had Alzheimer's disease. Unfortunately, some people are
misdiagnosed as having Alzheimer's disease when their main problem is

depression. Unlike Alzheimer's, depression can be treated successfully with medications. It's a tragedy when someone ends up in a nursing home with a label of Alzheimer's disease, when they could have been treated with antidepressive drugs and continued to enjoy their lives with their families at home.

As people grow older, they may lose friends and family members, develop disabling arthritis and be forced to limit their activities, and have new financial problems. These frustrations, and the realization that they may be near the end of life, can give rise to unbearable stress and depression. And with elderly couples, one person's depression often has a major impact on the other person's well-being.

> *Mr. and Mrs. Brown, educated professionals in their retirement years, came for their regular yearly visit. Mrs. Brown reported that her husband had become more forgetful, that he was often agitated, and that they had to stop seeing their friends because he would often lose his temper. She was concerned that he might be developing Alzheimer's disease. But he reported a different version of the situation. According to him, she had become more depressed.*
>
> *Mrs. Brown had severe scoliosis in her back that required a complicated back surgery. She was afraid of having any operations at her age and had decided to live with her disabling skeletal malformation. However, this abnormality had led to more recent problems, including shortness of breath when she walked short distances. As she became more frustrated, her husband could no longer handle her mood swings and in turn had lost his temper on some occasions. In fact, he had a serious kidney problem and was worried that he might not live more than two or three years himself.*
>
> *Finally, they both confessed to feeling hopeless regarding their medical conditions. They had many problems, but Alzheimer's disease was not one of them.*

Stress and Depression Cause Memory Loss

In the past five years, scientists have made a great deal of progress in understanding the biological basis for the link between stress, depression, and memory decline. It's all starting to make sense.

Stress is not necessarily bad; or not all stress, anyway. Mild stress improves your attention and strength. It triggers the release of the "fight or flight" hormones that helped our ancestors cope with danger. One of these hormones is cortisol.[69] Along with adrenaline, it increases the blood flow to your heart and leg muscles, raises your awareness of the world around you, and quickens your heartbeat. This overdrive system is meant to work for minutes to hours. When high levels of cortisol persist daily, however, as in a stressful job, it begins to damage all organs in your body, including your brain.

Robert Sapolsky, Ph.D., professor of neuroscience at Stanford University, has provided much of the evidence that points to the hippocampus as the major target of damage by excess cortisol. Dr. Sapolsky traveled to Africa and for months observed the behaviors of monkeys living freely in the jungle. He noted that dominant monkeys were less stressed than subordinate ones. He measured the levels of cortisol in their blood and discovered that stressed monkeys had much higher levels of cortisol. Later, he examined their brains and found that the hippocampus was smaller in the stressed monkeys. This smaller size, it turns out, is due to loss of neurons in the hippocampus in animals with a stressful life. In other words, the cortisol hormone, which for brief periods can stimulate the brain to improve memory and attention in stressful situations, kills the brain cells in the hippocampus when present at high levels for extended periods of time.[70]

Since the hippocampus is so important for memory and learning, it would make sense that a stressful lifestyle would increase the risk of Alzheimer's disease. However, it's been difficult to show this direct link in longitudinal studies because every person's response to a stressful situation varies. Some people get stressed when they're late for work, while others remain calm even in emergency circumstances. For now, it remains clear that both Alzheimer's disease and chronic stress injure the hippocampus. As such, it makes intuitive sense that if they happened together in a person, he or she would be more likely to lose his memory than someone who instead would only have mild Alzheimer's disease.

Depression may lead to memory loss in two ways. More than half the patients with depression have high cortisol levels in their blood. According to Dr. Sapolsky, it's possible that they are experiencing injury to their hippocampus, which may explain at least part of their memory problems.[71] Another explanation revolves around norepinephrine and serotonin, a set of messenger molecules in the brain. The brain cells that make these neurotransmitters sit at the base of the brain and send out millions of nerve endings to all areas of the cortex and hippocampus. Under normal circumstances these messenger molecules provide a background activity level for the cortex that helps it function well. Their levels rise with heightened attention, which in turn enable you to think and remember better. In depression, the levels of norepinephrine and serotonin are lower. With less stimulation, your cortex and hippocampus cannot function optimally. This may be the reason why melancholic patients have difficulty focusing and remembering well.

Depression is a common disease that needs immediate medical evaluation. It could be due to low thyroid, folate, or B12 levels; low levels of blood cells (anemia), infections, low blood circulation to the brain, head trauma, mini-strokes, or a dozen other causes. Patients often delay seeking psychiatric evaluation because they blame themselves for how they feel and don't realize that their symptoms are secondary to biological problems in their brain and that the imbalance in the levels of neurotransmitters can be corrected with medications.

Do Treatments for Depression Work?

Sometimes apathy and lack of interest in the usual hobbies may reflect early signs of Alzheimer's disease in an elderly person. In such cases, medications for depression improve behavior, though the person continues to lose his memory and cognition. In most other cases, drugs for depression work very well. Treated patients return to their previous level of functioning.

Mrs. Johnson was a sixty-five-year-old nurse. Her mother was diagnosed with Alzheimer's disease the previous year, and since then she had become more conscious of the fact that she was forgetting names. In addition, her husband had just had a heart attack. Mrs. Johnson was forced to quit her job to take care of her mother and her husband. She was overwhelmed and gradually found it difficult to cope with all her responsibilities. Her memory also seemed to fail her more often. Convinced she had Alzheimer's disease, she decided to come to our clinic for further evaluation.

When I spoke with her at length and tested her memory, I found out that she could remember well—if she paid more attention. Most of her neuropsychological test results were normal. Her sad mood was contagious; she made me feel gloomy too.

Mrs. Johnson's primary problem was depression, not Alzheimer's disease. Realizing that her symptoms would improve once her depression was treated calmed her fear of Alzheimer's and made her smile a lit-

tle. She agreed to take antidepressive medications, look for a new job, and seek help from her family to care for her mother. When she returned for a follow-up visit four months later, she'd lost some weight, found a new job, appeared happy, and was in control of her life again.

Patients with depression often feel horrible, overwhelmed with their responsibilities, and think that life is not worth living. After a few months on antidepressive medications, they see the light again. In the majority of cases, they regain their energy, look forward to the future, and can't believe how much better they feel. Patients with mild depression may get better even without medications.

Ms. Dalson was a pleasant and energetic eighty-five-year-old woman. I asked her if she was ever depressed. She explained that two years earlier she used to be fatigued, had no energy to get out of bed, did not wish to see her friends, and had gained weight due to overeating. Then one day she saw an advertisement on TV that said if you have such symptoms, you have clinical depression. "I realized that I had all the symptoms of depression," she told me. "Just knowing what the problem was made me snap out of it."

If you've had signs of depression for more than three months, discuss it with your primary physician. The signs may include a combination of any of the following:

- Lack of interest in the usual hobbies, in seeing friends, or in sex
- Excessive or inadequate sleep
- Loss of energy
- Feeling of sadness, guilt, helplessness, or an unexplained anxious mood
- Thoughts of or attempts at harming yourself
- Overeating or loss of appetite
- Unusual slowness in performing your usual activities
- Irritability and restlessness

To be happy, you need a strategy to reduce and manage stress. One solution for lowering stress and daily anxiety is better time management and better planning. Successful people who are free of stress set priorities and decline responsibilities that are of minor importance to them. Stress management requires a problem-solving analysis of your life in order to determine how the circumstances can be improved. It means understanding that life is not perfect and that you have to accept a certain degree of imperfection in yourself and in those around you—both at home and at work. A positive attitude will give you a sense of control, and brings with it a sense of inner peace—and memory improves when chronic stress is minimized.

It's possible to be happy even with a hectic schedule and many life problems. Meditation is another excellent option to calm anxiety and improve inner peace. Smile often and you'll remember better.

Here are some suggestions on how to reduce stress and be happy:

- Exercise daily.
- Be patient with people around you. Relax and take it easy.
- Plan your weeks and days ahead of time.
- Learn to say no when you have too much to do already.
- Once in a while, treat yourself to things you like to do but find too expensive.
- Buy flowers or gifts for your spouse or friends.

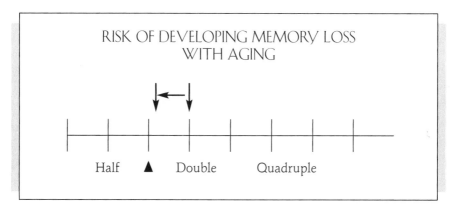

DECREASED RISK OF MEMORY LOSS WITH TREATMENT OF DEPRESSION AND REDUCING STRESS. UNCONTROLLED STRESS CAN DOUBLE YOUR RISK OF DEVELOPING COGNITIVE DECLINE (ARROW ON THE RIGHT). TAKING CONTROL OF STRESS CAN SIGNIFICANTLY LOWER THIS RISK (ARROW ON THE LEFT).

TAKING THE FIRST STEPS

Every person's lifestyle is different. As you identify your own risk factors, consider making gradual changes in your lifestyle. Set realistic short-term goals for yourself to make the necessary changes. I suggest starting with three changes. What are the three best things you can do realistically toward maintaining your cognitive abilities way into your nineties? You may choose to start walking three times a week, eating three to five pieces of fruit every day, adding fish to your diet, taking on some fun and intellectually challenging activities, or to stop smoking. Make a list for yourself now:

1. _____

2. _____

3. _____

After three months or after you achieve your initial goals, you can start to add more items to the list.

4. _____

5. _____

6. _____

By taking control of your health and reducing the risk factors in your life, you can dramatically reduce your chances of cognitive decline in your later years. This memory protection plan provides the tools to preserve your memory into your seventies, eighties, and beyond.

7

NEW MEDICATIONS FOR ALZHEIMER'S PREVENTION AND TREATMENT

Scientists around the world are trying to find medications that will successfully prevent and treat Alzheimer's disease. Work over two decades has shed light on what happens in the brain undergoing the normal aging process, and what goes awry for those who suffer from Alzheimer's.

With healthy aging, the dendritic branches of neurons lose some of their synapses, excess of amyloid protein in a few nerve endings aggregates into gumlike plaques, and a mild degree of inflammation forms around these plaques. Inside other neurons, some proteins tangle up into clumps. However, the synaptic loss, plaques, and tangles are not pronounced enough to interfere with the intricate network of millions of neurons that contribute to memory and cognition.

In a brain with Alzheimer's disease, however, too many synapses are lost, too much amyloid leads to excess inflammatory reactions and free radical oxidation, and too many tangles kill affected neurons. The dying neurons in the cortex trigger even more inflammation, and subsequently more neurons are destroyed. Even neurons in the base of the brain that make the acetylcholine neurotransmitter and provide positive stimulation for neurons in the cortex shrivel away.

Since the damage usually starts in areas of the brain around the hippocampus, the first signs of the disease are memory loss and confusion. As more neurons are destroyed, patients lose more of their cognitive abilities, such as reading, writing, and the ability to perform simple calculations and understand the news. The process of Alzheimer's disease begins and grows slowly; by the time a patient shows the first symptoms, a great deal of damage has already occurred.

With the number of potential Alzheimer's patients expected to almost quadruple by the year 2050, pharmaceutical companies and researchers in academic centers are in a race to find drugs that will block the formation of plaques and tangles or prevent acetylcholine-producing neurons from dying. Given the phenomenal potential for financial rewards, and the satisfaction of curing one of the most frustrating diseases of our time, the incentive is high to discover a miracle drug. In fact, a new, effective medication similar to those discovered to lower cholesterol may soon be on the market. There are more new drugs in various stages of clinical trials for Alzheimer's disease than for all other neurological conditions combined, including epilepsy, migraine, or Parkinson's disease. The sheer volume of clinical trials is reason to be optimistic.

PREVENTING ALZHEIMER'S WITH VITAMINS, DRUGS, HERBS, AND HORMONES

As we discussed in the last chapter, the best way to protect yourself against memory loss and Alzheimer's disease is to focus on your lifestyle and on modifying your risk factors. This approach is called "primary prevention," and it has proven to work well for other areas in medicine.

Doctors are researching how to treat people who already show the early signs of cognitive impairment. In the field of cardiology, they know that when a patient comes to the E.R. with mild chest pain due to partially blocked arteries (angina), he's likely to develop a heart attack in the future. Tests are performed to evaluate the degree of blockage in the arteries of the heart, and the patient is advised to quit smoking, improve his diet, lower his cholesterol, start taking an aspirin a day, and take good control of his blood pressure. These interventions, referred to as "secondary prevention," have proved successful in warding off catastrophic heart attacks.

Neurologists now view people who have significant memory problems in the same fashion. We want to establish measures to help these individuals minimize their risk of developing Alzheimer's disease, or at least to delay its onset. Secondary prevention would include consulting an Alzheimer's specialist for evaluation and testing. Memory loss, like chest pain, can serve as a warning sign to be used to the patient's advantage in preventing progressive cognitive decline.

A number of dietary supplements and drugs have shown promising results in delaying the onset of Alzheimer's disease. These include vitamin E, vitamin B12, ginkgo biloba, nonsteroidal anti-inflammatory drugs, sex hormones, and cholesterol-lowering statin medications. Scientists discovered the protective effects of many of these drugs against Alzheimer's when they were studying patients taking them for other purposes. Another exciting area of research is to find out if the new medications called cholinesterase inhibitors used for the treatment of Alzheimer's disease also could be used for its prevention. Currently, placebo-controlled double-blind studies are in progress to find the best drug, herb, or vitamin for preventing Alzheimer's disease. (Double-blind means that neither the subjects nor the experimenters know the makeup of the test or the control groups during the course of the experiment.) Until such studies prove a drug, herb, or vitamin to be successful in preventing Alzheimer's, doctors cannot rely on these medications the same way they can prescribe aspirin for patients with angina.

VITAMIN E

Vitamin E has emerged as significant in maintaining and improving brain function. There's overwhelming evidence that vitamin E can reduce the damage in the brain of an Alzheimer's patient by neutralizing some of the excess free radicals—the overactive oxygen molecules we discussed earlier. Many signs of aging are in part due to the formation of these free radicals, and the success of vitamin E in helping to prevent memory loss is attributed to its antioxidant properties.

In one study, 341 Alzheimer's patients received either vitamin E, Selegiline, or a placebo. On average, patients taking vitamin E remained independent for a longer period of time—670 days, compared to 440 days for patients who only took a placebo pill. Of the patients taking Selegiline, the figure was 655 days.[1] As a result of this study, vitamin E became a routine treatment for Alzheimer's disease. Veterinarians sometimes use Selegiline in older dogs with short-term memory problems.

In 2002, the results of five longitudinal studies observing volunteer subjects for three to ten years revealed that those taking vitamin E were less likely to develop Alzheimer's disease. Coming from groups of scientists in different parts of the world, these results are impressive, but they await confirmation in clinical trials specifically aimed at showing that long-term use of vitamin E will indeed curb the number of patients with Alzheimer's disease. The answers should become available in the next two years.

A *word of caution*: While taking vitamin E supplements may have beneficial effects for your skin, joints, heart, as well as your brain, you should discuss its use with your physician first.

VITAMIN B12 AND FOLATE

Elderly individuals with low levels of vitamin B12 and folate are twice as likely to develop Alzheimer's disease as those with normal levels.[2] In fact, measuring blood levels of B12 and folate is a routine part of evaluating patients with dementia. If you have a poor diet or difficulty with the absorption of vitamins in your gastrointestinal tract, your levels of B12 will be lower than normal. Since B12 and folate are necessary to convert homocysteine to another amino acid, Methionine, their low levels mean higher levels of homocysteine.

Several studies are now in the works to see if vitamin supplements that lower homocysteine levels will prevent or delay Alzheimer's disease. Initial reports from clinical practice at the Eighth International Alzheimer's Conference in Stockholm in 2002 were promising, indicating that vitamin supplements may reduce cognitive decline. Final results from these studies should be available within the next two years.

B vitamins are abundant in leafy dark green vegetables, milk products, fish, and fruits. You should eat these foods in abundance. As we discussed in the last chapter, taking daily vitamin B12 and folate tablets can supplement your diet. If your levels are too low (as determined by a blood test your physician can administer), your physician may prescribe monthly vitamin B12 injections.

GINKGO BILOBA

Ginkgo biloba, an herbal medicine, enhances the blood circulation and has antioxidant properties. Its active ingredients include flavonoid glycosides and ginkgolides. Ginkgo has been used in China and Europe for treating a wide range of diseases from high altitude mountain sickness to Alzheimer's disease. In the United States, it has been a subject of dozens of research studies. Although there have been anecdotal reports of its effectiveness in treating Alzheimer's, we do not yet have convincing standard studies. Some studies have shown treatment with ginkgo biloba was effective, while others failed to note any meaningful improvements in patients with Alzheimer's disease.

In a study published in the *Journal of the American Medical Association* (August 2002), Paul Solomon, Ph.D., and his colleagues at the Bronfman Science Center in Williams College, Massachusetts, carried out a random, double-blind, placebo-controlled trial on 330 healthy volunteers to see if ginkgo improved memory.[3] The subjects were sixty years old or older and had no cognitive or memory problems at baseline. Over the six-week period of study, there was no difference between the ginkgo and placebo group with regard to learning, memory, attention, or verbal fluency. Their spouses, relatives, and friends also felt there was no improvement in the cognitive function of the subjects taking ginkgo. The decision to take ginkgo remains a personal choice. Some people focus on the fact that it's natural, that millions of people have used it for centuries, and that it may improve your memory or lower your risk of developing Alzheimer's disease, if even by a very small amount. Others point out that ginkgo has failed to show significant benefit in a formal scientific research study in the United States, that the preparations in some nutrition stores may not be pure, and that it does have side effects: It has been shown to potentially increase the risk of bleeding in some people, and it can interact with other medications. In any case, **if you do choose to take ginkgo, you must inform your physician first.**

MOTRIN OR ALEVE

Patients with arthritis who take anti-inflammatory drugs seem to have fewer cases of Alzheimer's disease. A longitudinal study published in the *New England Journal of Medicine* in 2001,[4] involving almost 7000 volunteers in Rotterdam, Netherlands, confirmed this observation. Researchers interviewed volunteers who were fifty-five or older and were taking nonsteroidal anti-inflammatory medications (NSAIDs) for various reasons and for various amounts of time. They discovered that those who had taken these drugs for more than two years were 80 percent less likely to develop Alzheimer's disease.

These findings supported many similar but smaller studies that were carried out in different parts of the world. It also raised the possibility that anti-inflammatory drugs may be helpful in reducing the risk of Alzheimer's disease by mechanisms other than stopping inflammation.[5] Some patients who showed benefit from them were taking very low doses of Motrin, levels too low to reduce inflammation in the brain.

Should patients with Alzheimer's disease start taking Motrin or Aleve? The answer is "no." In a clinical trial, presented at the Alzheimer's conference in Stockholm in 2002, the anti-inflammatory drug rofecoxib was not effective in slowing the progression of Alzheimer's disease.[6] Perhaps by the time a patient has Alzheimer's disease too much damage has ravaged the brain and the treatment with anti-inflammatory drugs will not reverse the process.

Should you start taking these drugs to lower your risk of developing Alzheimer's disease? The answer is "not yet." More research is needed to more definitively answer this question. Only when the benefits are absolutely confirmed in clinical trials using placebo would it be advisable to start taking them on a regular basis. If you have arthritis and have to take NSAIDs anyway, your risk of getting Alzheimer's disease may be less than your friends who don't have arthritis pain in their knees and wrists. If you don't have arthritis and can't wait until the results of clinical trials become available in the next two years, you can discuss taking low doses of NSAIDs with your physician. You need to know that daily use of NSAIDs can cause gastrointestinal bleeding.

SEX HORMONES

The use of estrogen in hormone replacement therapy to prevent the onset of Alzheimer's disease is controversial. In one clinical trial, women taking estrogen were just as likely to develop Alzheimer's as women who were not taking any hormones.[7] In a survey of 200,000 women, David Drachman, M.D., and researchers at New England Medical Center in Boston found that Alzheimer's was just as common in women who were taking estrogen hormones as in those who were not.[8]

However, Sanjay Asthana, M.D., of the University of Wisconsin School of Medicine, found that high doses of estrogen, delivered by a skin patch, appear to improve memory and attention skills in women with Alzheimer's disease. Women on estrogen performed better on memory tests and were able to name more items in formal object recognition tests.[9]

More research is needed to determine the role of estrogen in cognitive function and in the prevention of Alzheimer's disease. While estrogen may show some improvement in cognition, like many other possible answers, there are increased risks that accompany the potential benefits. Estrogen increases the risk of breast and ovarian cancer, for instance, and at the moment is not recommended for treatment or prevention of Alzheimer's disease.

The same applies to testosterone in men. Testosterone augments muscle bulk, enhances energy levels, and improves memory.[10] But it also increases the risk of prostate cancer. No formal research study has shown that it prevents or treats Alzheimer's disease. If you're a man with some degree of impotence and decreased libido, as well as some memory problems, you may benefit from treatment with a testosterone patch. Of course, you would need to discuss this with your physician.

CHOLESTEROL-LOWERING MEDICATIONS

A subtype of cholesterol-lowering medications collectively referred to as "statins" (because their names ends with -*statin*, such as Lovastatin), may be more promising than vitamin E or NSAIDs for prevention of Alzheimer's disease. A half-dozen research studies have shown that these medications lower your risk of developing dementia by 50 to 70 percent.[11] They may soon become a routine part of preventive therapy for people who want to protect their brain against loss of cognitive function, even if they do not have very high cholesterol.

Statins lower the cholesterol in your blood and have been proven to reduce the risk of heart attack and stroke. Now it's becoming apparent that they may also have antioxidant properties or a direct effect on the aging process in the brain. If you have high cholesterol, you must consider taking statins. If your cholesterol level is normal, then you would have to wait until the results of all the clinical trials are available before you can decide to take these medications. It may turn out that people with normal cholesterol would benefit more from vitamin E, ginkgo biloba, cholinesterase inhibitors, or Motrin, or some combination of them.

DRUGS FOR TREATING ALZHEIMER'S DISEASE

CHOLINESTERASE INHIBITORS

Cholinesterase inhibitors increase the amount of acetylcholine in the brain, in an effort to compensate for loss of neurons that normally produce this messenger molecule. Clinical trials have shown they are safe and moderately effective. They do not stop the progression of Alzheimer's disease, but they can delay the symptoms of cognitive decline.[12]

If a patient takes one of these medications and two years later hasn't declined further, this is considered a success. Patients who do not take the same medication would get worse more rapidly and become completely dependent on others sooner. Thanks to these medications, patients can stay with their families for one to two years longer before needing additional care.

In a recent study at the University of Pittsburgh School of Medicine, scientists compared data in 135 patients with Alzheimer's disease who had taken cholinesterase inhibitors for an average of three years with those who never took any of these medications. Their report in the *Journal of Neurology, Neurosurgery, and Psychiatry* in March 2002 noted that the rate of decline was significantly lower in treated patients.[13] More than 40 percent of untreated patients were admitted to a nursing home during the three-year period of the study, compared with 6 percent of those taking cholinesterase inhibitors.

The discovery of these drugs has been a small but promising step forward. While they may cause side effects such as nausea and gastrointestinal upset, the newer versions—including Aricept, Exelon, and Reminyl—have fewer side effects. Some patients gain benefits for much longer than two to three years. It also appears that those who get treatment sooner do better in the long run. These cholinesterase inhibitors are now the only medications approved by the FDA for treatment of Alzheimer's disease. The most recent studies show that they can be used for treatment of other forms of dementia as well. Now physicians are anxiously waiting for the results of ongoing clinical trials to see if these medications can be used for treatment of mild cognitive impairment and for prevention of Alzheimer's disease.

Choosing among the new drugs is not always easy for physicians, especially since newer drugs come to the market every two to three years. Each of the three available drugs has features that may appeal to certain patients. For example, some patients prefer Aricept because they need to take this medication only once a day. Other patients respond better to Exelon or Reminyl, even though they need to take these medications twice a day. Physicians and their patients have several options to choose from and can switch from one drug to another, as needed.

Jeffrey Cummings, M.D., a leading authority in the field of Alzheimer's treatment, presented an update on these medications at the American Academy of Neurology meeting in April 2002. He stated that cholinesterase inhibitors produce the most benefit by helping patients with their behavioral problems and attention. He noted that patients who lack interest in participating in fun activities with their grandchildren start playing with them again. Those who become easily agitated and lose their temper manage to smile more and get along better with their caregivers. Those who develop strange behaviors, such as undressing themselves in public, may become more conscious of their behavior among other people.[14]

Sometimes these medications, by themselves, are not enough to reduce the many behavioral problems in Alzheimer's patients. In such cases, physicians fall back to using medications that are normally prescribed for patients with depression, anxiety, hallucinations, or insomnia. A calm and peaceful environment with some soft music in the background is also a great complement to drug therapy.

MEMANTINE

This is the newest drug on the market, available only in Europe. Physicians there give Memantine to patients who have moderate to severe Alzheimer's disease.[15] This drug may become available in the United States within the next couple of years.

Memantine works by blocking the flow of information transmission along a specific set of neurons. Glutamate is a neurotransmitter that binds to its receptors on neurons and causes them to become excited and more active. Sometimes it can serve as a toxin and overexcite a neuron to death (excitotoxicity). Some degree of glutamate excitotoxicity may contribute to the damage in the brains of patients with Alzheimer's disease. Memantine blocks a subset of these glutamate receptors and limits their damage.

FUTURE TREATMENT OF ALZHEIMER'S

SURGICAL OPTIONS

There is no tumor or large mass to be removed in the brains of patients who suffer from Alzheimer's disease. However, surgeons may still have a role in helping Alzheimer's patients. This discovery started with a chance observation.

Neurologists on occasion drain some of the cerebrospinal fluid, or CSF, that normally bathes the brain. They can test this fluid and try to find out what disease their patients may be suffering from. This drainage also helps some patients who have hydrocephalus, or too much fluid in their brain. Neurologists do this by a simple procedure called a *spinal tap*, in which a long needle is inserted in the patient's lower back to drain a few spoonfuls of spinal fluid. At any rate, some neurologists taking care of dementia patients noted that a patient's memory occasionally improved after the spinal fluid was drained for other purposes.

A study was initiated to see if this drainage of fluid might help Alzheimer's patients too. It began with just fifteen patients. Instead of taking a small amount only once, surgeons placed a shunt in patients with mild to moderate Alzheimer's disease that constantly drained the spinal fluid. The majority of patients who received a shunt did slightly better on memory tests than those who did not receive a shunt. Surgeons did not notice any long-term complications in patients with the shunt. There is now a larger clinical trial under way, COGNIShunt, to evaluate the effectiveness of such a shunt in a larger sample of patients.

SCIENCE FICTION

Another surgical option, too futuristic for now, is to implant nerve growth factor directly inside the brains of patients with Alzheimer's disease. In animal models this growth factor helps neurons that make acetylcholine live longer. It may work in humans too.[16] It is also conceivable that surgeons can place pumps and continuously feed the brain with various other brain growth factors.

Brad Hyman, M.D., Ph.D., professor of neurology at Massachusetts General Hospital, and his colleagues have shown that surgical injection of antibodies into the brain can make plaques dissolve. Scientists had thought that once the amyloid plaques were formed, they could not be cleared. Dr. Hyman directly planted the antiamyloid antibodies into the brains of animals that were genetically engineered to develop Alzheimer's plaques. After the treatment, the amyloid plaques had dissolved. The idea that plaques can be cleared from the brain is both exciting and encouraging. However, injecting antibodies into the brains of patients with Alzheimer's disease remains science fiction—for now.

EXPERIMENTAL VACCINES

Immunization against amyloid protein is one of the most exciting areas of Alzheimer's research.[17] Like the measles vaccine, AN-1752 promotes the production of antibodies in the blood. After passing several trials for safety and efficacy in animals, it was given to human volunteers with Alzheimer's disease. The first stage of the clinical trials showed that people taking this medication did not have significant side effects. Unfortunately, when it was given to a larger number of patients, some of them developed an inflammation in the brain and the trial had to stop. Another group of scientists, at Cornell University, have made a different vaccine and showed that it is effective in animals. Their vaccine is now advancing in clinical trials.

The vaccines that can prove successful in such trials involving humans may prove to be the long-awaited solution for Alzheimer's disease. If everyone gets vaccinated against plaques and tangles, people may never develop dementia. Vaccines for polio helped eradicate it from much of the world; it would be ideal if new vaccines can clear Alzheimer's disease from the planet as well.

Because newer techniques and drugs are being developed for this disease every few months, it's possible an effective treatment for Alzheimer's, or even a cure, may be just around the corner. But for now, the only proven medications for treatment of Alzheimer's disease are cholinesterase inhibitors and vitamin E.

PART III

ON THE HORIZON

8

DIAGNOSING ALZHEIMER'S DISEASE

If someone you love is experiencing memory loss and is unable to carry out daily functions, he or she should see his or her physician and undergo formal evaluation. Though some age-related memory loss is normal, when there's a significant change in a person's normal level of activity and cognition—his or her baseline—it might be because of Alzheimer's disease.

Difficulty reading a newspaper might be a sign of Alzheimer's, but not for someone who never attended school. Inability and confusion when directing meetings would be of concern if it happens to the CEO of a large company, but not for a poet. A decline in a person's level of mental functioning may turn out to be a combination of stress, anxiety, insomnia, or depression, but regardless, it should be evaluated.

In the majority of cases, neurologists and other brain specialists find that their elderly patients who complain of memory problems have age-associated memory impairment (AAMI). Such patients occasionally forget where they left their keys, the names of some acquaintances, or a doctor's appointment. They don't have difficulty performing their jobs, balancing checkbooks, or following current affairs, and they can usually take notes to remind themselves of important appointments. Only in about 10 percent of the cases we face does a patient indeed have Alzheimer's disease.

Mr. and Mrs. Kotsios were married for more than forty years. He was still madly in love with her and adored her daily. For the past year, she had been more forgetful. She attributed this to getting older and to mild depression. She also complained that it took her longer to read the daily newspaper. He brought her to our hospital for evaluation. Mrs. Kotsios, who appeared well-dressed and sophisticated, kept saying that she was fine and that he was overreacting. But as we talked, it became apparent that she could not write a simple sentence or draw a clock. She did not know the year, the name of the president, or her address. These neuropsychological tests, and the fact that her brain MRI and all her blood tests were normal, established that she most likely had Alzheimer's disease.

Peter Rabins, M.D., M.P.H., professor of psychiatry at Johns Hopkins Hospital and author of *The 36-Hour Day*, says that families sometimes avoid seeking medical help for a loved one who seems to be experiencing memory loss.[1] They choose not to put that person "through the ordeal of an evaluation." Dr. Rabins and other experts in this field believe that every person with memory problems or cloudy thinking should be fully evaluated. The evaluation process is not necessarily an unpleasant ordeal. Staff who work with forgetful patients are aware of their special needs and take particular care to be gentle and caring. It's important to see a doctor in order to find the cause of any dementia, since it may turn out to be a reversible or treatable condition, as we discussed in Chapter 5.

WHO SHOULD DO AN EVALUATION?

When seeking a doctor who can diagnose Alzheimer's, you can start with your primary physician. Ask if he has experience in the field and how he would go about making a diagnosis. He may perform a preliminary evaluation—with a screening cognitive test and routine blood tests—and then, if necessary, refer you to a memory clinic. You can also ask your local hospital about any local physicians with particular interest in memory and dementia. Other good resources are academic centers and teaching hospitals with memory disorder clinics. And your local Alzheimer's association may be able to refer you to memory specialists as well.

You need to feel comfortable with the physician who performs this very important evaluation. You need to trust his judgment and understand that making a diagnosis of Alzheimer's disease is not a simple task. If you're not confident about the final diagnosis, you should discuss your concerns with him frankly and seek a second opinion.

MEMORY LAPSES OR ALZHEIMER'S DISEASE?

Most age-associated memory impairment consists of *memory lapses*; a person may forget the name of a movie he saw last weekend or an old colleague's name he met at a party, but he can remember them with prompting or later when he is doing something else. Patients with Alzheimer's disease experience complete *memory loss*; they have no recollection of ever seeing that movie or having ever met that colleague. Another feature favoring a diagnosis of Alzheimer's is to determine if the patient has experienced a significant decline from a prior level of functioning. A pattern of confusion with time and familiar places, and difficulties performing the routine activities of daily living, is of far more concern than a few episodes of memory lapses. Accurate answers from people who know the patient well and see him on a daily basis for years can help doctors determine if he has Alzheimer's disease or other forms of dementia.

Another consideration comes from a person's insight into his difficulty with memory. Many Alzheimer's patients are not aware of their dementia. They may think the year is 1978 and laugh when you tell them they're wrong.

Based on my experience, most people who are aware and concerned about their memory problems do not have Alzheimer's disease. They often have normal age-associated memory impairment or mild to moderate depression. Moreover, the memory skills of most patients with Alzheimer's deteriorate over a period of one to five years, so if they've been complaining about difficulty with remembering names for the past twenty years, they most likely do not have the disease.

SPECIFIC STEPS IN MAKING A DIAGNOSIS

At Johns Hopkins Hospital, I often see patients who have been referred to us from primary physicians or other local hospitals. I perform the same routine for all my patients—an evaluation that involves the following steps:

OBTAINING:

- An account of the memory problems
- Information about the patient's life history, including prior education and occupational achievements
- Information about other medical illnesses, medications, and family members with Alzheimer's disease
- Information about living situation, diet, exercise, and family dynamics

PERFORMING:

- A physical and neurological examination, including checking blood pressure, visual acuity, and making a hearing evaluation
- A neuropsychological battery of tests

REVIEWING:

- Patient's prior laboratory tests, brain scans, or notes from other physicians

The goal of my interview is to determine the nature and severity of the problem. I usually begin by making the patients feel comfortable. I ask about their hobbies and about their knowledge of current affairs—to see how they've kept up with the news. If patients say they have no memory problems, and family members raise their eyebrows in surprise, I'm concerned. If the patients provide detailed accounts of the few occasions they forgot something, I'm reassured that they most likely do not have Alzheimer's disease.

My questions also cover their education, their accomplishments in life, and why they retired. I try to discern if their memory problems are new or if they have a lifelong history of difficulty remembering things. I ask about their daily routines and try to judge if they no longer do some of their hobbies because they found it more difficult. I look for evidence of depression as I ask them about their appetite, sleep, sex life, exercise, and interactions with family and friends.

An important part of my evaluation is to obtain a full medical history— if they experienced heart, kidney, joint, liver, head trauma, depression, high cholesterol, or psychiatric problems in the past. I review their medication lists and see if the start date for any of them coincided with the onset of their memory problems. I ask if they take cholesterol-lowering medications, vitamin E, or estrogen for hormone replacement therapy.

Then we discuss the possibility of other family members who might have had Alzheimer's disease. Sometimes their parents were not formally diagnosed with this disease but were considered to be "senile." I inquire about their smoking and drinking habits, if they've gained or lost weight, and if they have vision or hearing problems.

The information from family members who know the patient well is critical for making a diagnosis of dementia. Here are examples of questions I may ask them:

- How long has he had problems with his memory?
- Did the problems start abruptly (over a day) or gradually (over several months/years)?
- Can he remember important dates like his birthday?
- Does he ask the same questions several times during the same conversation?
- Can he still drive a car?
- Does he get lost in his own neighborhood?
- Has he stopped his hobbies due to any trouble thinking?
- Does he need help to get dressed?
- Has he been unusually suspicious of others?
- Has he had trouble balancing his checkbook?
- Has he acted inappropriately in public?

After talking with the patient and the family in detail, I perform a complete physical and neurological examination that involves looking for evidence of heart disease, breathing problems, or blocked arteries in their neck. I check their blood pressure, vision, hearing and other senses, as well as their strength, muscle reflexes, and the ability to walk. I try to find out if they've had mild strokes by searching for subtle findings. For example, a patient may have a mild weakness in his right arm that he does not know about, but it becomes apparent with formal testing of muscle strength in both arms simultaneously.

I then check their language, memory, attention, calculation skills, and other cognitive functions. For example, I may ask them to write a sentence, draw a clock, name as many fruits as they can in one minute, name the months of the year backward, and remember four things. These are called *neuropsychological* tests, and they're done with paper and pencil.[2] You'll read more about these later in this chapter.

I review all blood and imaging tests. I then evaluate all the clinical and laboratory information and determine if the patient has memory problems related to depression, mini-strokes, other neurological or medical disorders, or medication side effects. He may have age-associated memory problems, mild cognitive impairment, or Alzheimer's disease or another form of dementia.

WHO MAKES THE FINAL DIAGNOSIS

Again, a definitive diagnosis of Alzheimer's disease can only be made after a person dies; this is the reason we know less about the disease than we know about conditions that can be examined while those who experience them are alive. In autopsy, pathologists look for evidence of abundant plaques and tangles. In some cases even the pathologists cannot be 100 percent sure if the patient met the criteria for Alzheimer's.

Barbara Crain, M.D., a professor of brain pathology at Johns Hopkins Hospital, has examined the brains of hundreds of people who died with a possible diagnosis of Alzheimer's disease. She agrees that even diagnosing Alzheimer's on pathological grounds can be challenging. "It is not always a black and white situation," she says. Some patients may have many plaques and tangles in their brain but not enough to formally call it Alzheimer's disease. More puzzling is when a person has no dementia but his or her brain shows many plaques and tangles. A great deal of exciting research is now under way to develop a uniform and definite diagnostic test that can determine Alzheimer's disease while a person is still alive.

NEUROPSYCHOLOGICAL TESTS

A clinical diagnosis with the help of neuropsychological, paper-and-pencil, tests can be 80 to 90 percent accurate.[3] Based on current concepts of how the frontal, parietal, and temporal lobes of the brain work, and how these are affected in patients with Alzheimer's disease, each subset of tests focuses on evaluation of a specific region of the cortex. Some require the ability to organize a set of symbols in order—a function attributed to the frontal lobes. Others require the ability to draw a clock—a function attributed to the parietal lobes. Still other tests require the ability to understand language and learn new things—a function attributed to the temporal lobes. These tests can point to the primary areas of malfunction in the brain of a patient with memory problems.

When administered and interpreted accurately, paper-and-pencil tests can determine if a person has dementia; that is, if he has problems with memory *plus* one or two other areas of cognition, such as understanding language, orientation for the location of things, or difficulties with judgment. Brain specialists then use more advanced questions to determine if a person's dementia is due to Alzheimer's disease—as it is in 60 to 70 percent of dementia cases—or to less common causes, such as alcoholism, frontotemporal dementia, diffuse Lewy body disease, or vascular dementia.

The Challenge of Neuropsychological Tests

Imagine you are offered $100,000 to establish a standard test to measure normal physical strength among the elderly. Your test will be used to determine if a person who complains of weakness has a real disease or is experiencing the effects of aging. How would you go about developing this test? Would you expect an eighty-five-year-old woman to have the same strength as a sixty-five-year-old man? Can you set limits by age? Should all seventy-year-old men and women have the strength to lift a thirty-pound bag? I'm sure you can understand the challenge, especially since results of the test you create would have a major impact on the lives of the elderly and their families.

Perhaps the best approach would be to ask a person how much they could usually lift in the past, and then establish if there's been a significant change in their strength over several years. This method would allow each individual to serve as his or her own control. However, some acceptable lower limits would have to be established: for example, every person should be able to carry ten books and walk up ten steps—even if they're one hundred years old.

The challenges for designing neuropsychological tests to determine a diagnosis of Alzheimer's disease in the elderly play out the same scenario as above. Diagnosing mild cognitive impairment or Alzheimer's disease depends heavily on a person's prior level of intellectual function. The same criteria cannot be used to evaluate a fifty-year-old active professor and an eighty-year-old retired boxer. Memory specialists have to adjust for the patient's age, level of education, and past experiences. A simple score on any single test does not constitute a diagnosis, and there are very few absolute cut-off "passing scores." A person's scores do, however, serve as a baseline for future comparisons when the same subject is retested.

A Typical Test

Dozens of neuropsychological tests are available to test your short- and long-term memory, as well as your attention span and language and problem-solving abilities. Different sets of tests are preferred at different academic institutions. They often require an hour or more to complete. The subject sits comfortably in a quiet room while the examiner asks the questions and keeps a record of the answers.

Here are some typical questions you might see on some of these tests:

1. Who is the president? Please describe some of the current affairs in the news this week.

2. What are the names of your grandchildren?

3. What is today's date? What time do you think it is?

4. How would you go from your house to the nearest grocery store?

5. Spell the word *castle* backward.

6. Name the letters of the alphabet backward, starting from the letter J.

7. Name as many fruits as you can, in one minute.

8. Repeat these four words after me. Try to remember them. You will be asked about them again later.
   a. Car
   b. Red
   c. February
   d. Sky

9. Draw a clock. Put the hands of the clock so that it shows the time to be twenty-five minutes past seven.

10. What were the four words you were asked to remember?

11. How many dimes are there in one dollar and forty cents?

12. Write down what you see in this picture (see page 151) of a farm

INTERPRETING THE TEST RESULTS

These tests need to be evaluated and analyzed by memory experts: doctors who have spent many years specializing in neurology, psychiatry, or psychology. They see patients with Alzheimer's disease or other forms of memory problems on a daily basis. Like dermatologists, who have seen thousands of different skin lesions and can recognize a skin cancer at a glance, these experts review thousands of cases and can determine if you have dementia by analyzing your test results.

Here are some generalizations of what each of the questions may reflect about the brain of the person taking the test. I have briefly mentioned the test results that would be of concern for a healthy person:

1 and 2. *Fund of knowledge.* These questions test the functioning of the frontal and temporal lobes. Most people maintain their ability to know the major events in their family, home, and country. They should be able to describe their house, name the president, and know the major news of the week. It would be a concern if they could not recall the names of their grandchildren (assuming they see them regularly).

3. *Orientation to time.* This tests the functioning of the parietal and frontal lobes. Most people can answer it easily. They may not know the exact date or day of the week, but they should know the year and the month well. It would be of concern if a person did not know the year.

4. *Orientation to place.* This tests the functioning of the parietal lobes. Most people know where they are in a building with respect to the main entrance and the elevators. They should be able to provide some details of how they would get around their neighborhood. It would be of concern if a person could not count (from memory) the number of rooms in their house.

5 and 6. *Spelling.* This calls upon the functioning of temporal, parietal, and frontal lobes. It's not as easy as it sounds. Many normal people find it challenging, depending on their degree of education, fatigue, and stress. Some simply refuse to make the effort to pay attention to do the test correctly, especially if they're depressed.

7. *Naming.* This mainly requires the functioning of temporal and frontal lobes. Most elderly can name at least eight fruits in one minute. Therefore, it would be a concern if a person could generate only four.

8. *Repetition.* This mainly requires the functioning of temporal and frontal lobes. It's important that patients pay close attention when the words are read. They should be able to repeat the words at least once before they attempt to remember them. It would be a concern if the person could not repeat the items after three or four trials, or if he or she asked, "What list?" The test requires both attention and short-term memory. Hearing should be checked to make sure the subject can hear and understand the instructions.

9. *Clock drawing.* This mainly requires the functioning of parietal and frontal lobes. You may think that drawing a clock is simple, but in fact it's a fairly complicated task. Some patients with early Alzheimer's disease get confused with drawing the long hand of the clock to show twenty-five minutes past seven; instead of pointing the long hand toward 5, they draw two hands, one to point to 2 and another to 5, so their clock ends up having three hands (7-2-5). It would of course be a concern if a person could not draw a clock at all.

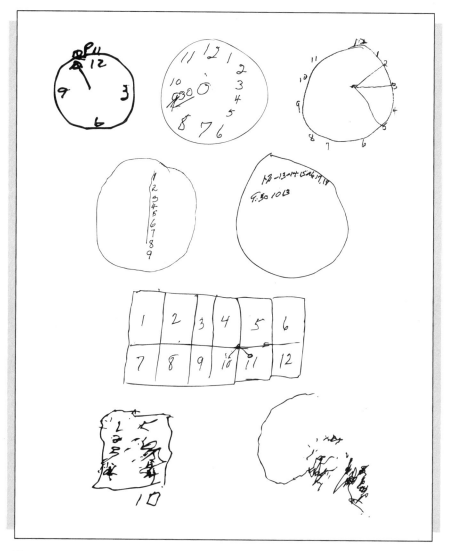

THESE EXAMPLES OF CLOCKS ILLUSTRATE THE PROGRESSION OF ALZHEIMER'S DISEASE IN PARIETAL LOBES.

10. *Recall.* This mainly requires the functioning of temporal lobes. Normal people may remember only two or three of the four items. It creates concern if the person does not remember any of the four items. If this is the only point they miss, they may have "memory only" problems. Their diagnosis may turn out to be mild cognitive impairment.

11. *Calculation.* This mainly requires the functioning of parietal and frontal lobes. The test needs to be made more difficult for an engineer or an accountant. If a person is a mathematician, he should be able to multiply 11 times 12 in his head. It would be a concern if a person could not add 20 plus 3.

12. *Writing to describe a scene.* This requires the functioning of the temporal, parietal, and frontal lobes. The level of detail in a patient's description is often judged with special consideration to his or her prior education. The paragraph they write can be compared with a letter they wrote in the past, and can serve as the baseline for future tests.

In any case, people do not lose their ability to write. It would be a concern if a person could not write a simple sentence. The same is true with reading a simple sentence. It's important to make sure that the patient can see clearly. They should wear their glasses, if they usually do. Patients with poor vision may not be able to read or write simply because they cannot see.

If a person has a low score on these tests, it does not necessarily mean he has Alzheimer's disease. In the same way that a person with chest pain may be experiencing either an upset stomach, panic attack, or heart attack, a person with poor scores can have a simple problem such as being nervous, fatigued, or stressed. A more accurate analysis requires consultation with a memory specialist, since not even your general physician can interpret them with confidence. Since many of these tests are subject to various interpretations, there is no one passing score.

WHY THERE'S NO DEFINITIVE TEST

Heart doctors have special blood tests to see if someone has had a heart attack. Liver doctors have reliable blood tests that can show if their patient has liver problems. Kidney and diabetes doctors also use blood tests to find out more about the severity of diseases in their patients. Skin doctors can just look at the lesions on their patients and determine what disease they have. Oncologists can use blood tests and X-ray images to see if a patient has cancer or if a tumor has metastasized. But brain doctors are still working to come up with one single, definitive test for Alzheimer's disease. Instead, they have to rely on neuropsychological tests, along with examining the results of blood tests and MRI or other brain imaging scans.

Why, you might ask, is there no definitive test?

First, your brain is far more complex than your heart, liver, kidney, and skin combined. Unlike your liver, your brain has thousands of different types of cells, each of which makes different combinations of chemical messengers. If all your brain cells made the same chemical, it would be easy to measure the levels of that chemical as a sign of brain disease. However, it is nearly impossible to try to measure all the messenger molecules, which are routinely present in minute amounts in everyone.

Second, people's hearts, livers, and kidneys are similar to one another. Your heart, for one, is not that different from your spouse's or your neighbor's heart. This similarity makes heart, liver, and kidney transplants possible. Your brain, on the other hand, is very different from your spouse's or your neighbor's. Many factors contribute to shape your brain, and the number of synapses in it. These include your childhood education, life experiences, occupational achievements, habits and hobbies, as well as your age and physical health. Therefore, it's difficult to make a test that can apply to all brains equally.

Third, Alzheimer's disease starts gradually and deterioration takes place slowly over years. It's not as if you possess normal memory skills on Monday and have Alzheimer's on Tuesday. As a consequence, it's possible to make a diagnosis of Alzheimer's disease in someone who is clearly affected, but not in someone during the very early stages.

NONCOGNITIVE TESTS: BLOOD, URINE, OR SMELL

Many private companies have tried to invent blood, urine, or smell tests to help diagnose Alzheimer's disease. These tests came about after researchers discovered that some patients with Alzheimer's disease had high levels of amyloid in their blood or urine, or that they could not smell things as well as those who weren't affected. It should be noted that these tests are not 100 percent accurate and that they are not routinely used at Alzheimer's centers around the country. A person who does not have Alzheimer's disease, for instance, may have high amyloid levels in her urine, while a person with Alzheimer's disease may have normal amyloid levels, and so a test for this would not necessarily be definitive.

To caution people who buy their laboratory tests on the Internet, the manufacturers usually provide two reasonable disclaimers:

1. If your tests results are abnormal, there is a likelihood that you have Alzheimer's disease. However, these tests are not 100 percent specific, and you may not have Alzheimer's disease; please see your physician.

2. If your test results are normal but you have significant memory problems, you may or may not have Alzheimer's disease; please see your physician.

Either way, you need to see a physician. This is perhaps one reason these tests have not become popular in academic centers. If you have significant memory problems, you should go directly to your physician and let him or her decide what to do next.

Exciting Breakthroughs

Two groups of scientists, one in Italy and one in the United States, are making exciting breakthroughs toward developing a simple blood test for Alzheimer's disease.

At the third conference on Aging of the Brain and Dementia, held in Florence, Italy, in 2001, Alessandro Padovani, M.D., and his team at the Universita degli Studi di Brescia presented their findings on 183 patients in various stages of Alzheimer's disease or those who didn't have the disease. They discovered that the amyloid precursor protein (APP), which makes amyloid, comes in two slightly different forms in blood platelets. The ratio of these two forms, as detected by immunological assays, is lower in patients who suffer from Alzheimer's disease than in healthy individuals. Those with a more severe form of the disease have an even lower ratio.[4]

Another group of scientists, headed by David Holzman, M.D., at the Washington University School of Medicine in St. Louis, has tested an antibody to amyloid protein in laboratory mice and reported the findings in the prestigious journal *Science*.[5] The mice were genetically engineered to have the Alzheimer's amyloid plaques in their brains and to develop memory problems with aging. The antibody injected into their blood caused the amyloid to leak out of the brain and into the bloodstream. There was a direct correlation between the degree of amyloid "load" in their brains and the amount of amyloid collected in their blood—mice with more plaques showed higher amyloid in their blood.

While it may appear that there's a direct link between the number of amyloid plaques in the brain and the severity of the Alzheimer's disease, this is not necessarily the case for all patients.[6] Some people have great amounts of amyloid in their brains (as discovered after their death at autopsy) and yet manifested no symptoms of Alzheimer's before they died. Conversely, some people have very few plaques (and tangles) and yet have Alzheimer's disease. This puzzle keeps many thousands of scientists busy at work around the world.

BRAIN IMAGING SCANS

Advanced brain imaging techniques are beginning to detect subtle changes in the brains of patients with mild cognitive impairment or Alzheimer's disease. MRI pictures of the brain reveal the size and shape of different brain structures. In patients with Alzheimer's, MRIs show that the size of the hippocampus is smaller than normal.

Expensive SPECT (Single Photon Emission Tomography) and PET (Positron Emission Tomography) scans employ radioactive molecules to determine the level of blood flow and metabolic activity in your brain. They show how active different parts of your brain are at the moment you're lying in the machine. Scans of Alzheimer's patients show less activity in the temporal and parietal lobes.

The problem with these imaging tests is the same as for blood, urine, and smell tests: The results cannot determine with absolute certainty if a patient has Alzheimer's disease, especially for those in early stages of the disease. Researchers are trying hard (and competing with one another) to fine-tune these techniques.

Recently, Daniel Silverman, M.D., Ph.D., at UCLA, and his two dozen colleagues around the globe, studied a group of 284 elderly patients with memory impairment.[7] These patients underwent a memory test and a PET scan at the beginning of the study and again three years later. PET scans were able to predict who was going to develop Alzheimer's disease accurately in most—but not all—cases. If a person had a negative PET scan, there was a 90 percent chance that he or she would not develop Alzheimer's disease in three years.

The newest PET scans now under development are beginning to show the plaques and tangles in the brains of living people.[8] Though expensive, they have the potential to become a routine part of evaluation of patients suspected to have Alzheimer's. For now, though, the best practical way to determine a diagnosis of Alzheimer's disease remains an evaluation by a memory specialist.

9

HEREDITY AND ALZHEIMER'S

If you have a family member with Alzheimer's, you may have a higher like-lihood of developing it too. The reason for this lies in your genes—the molecular blueprints that dictate the production of proteins. Proteins in turn are the building blocks for the cells in your liver, skin, heart, kidney, eyes, and brain. You inherit your genes from your parents. They determine how tall you are, the color of your eyes, and if you have a higher likelihood of developing some forms of cancer.

The good news, however, is that for the common type of Alzheimer's the risk may not be as high as you think. There are two forms of inherited Alzheimer's: *late onset* and *early onset*. As we'll discuss below, the particular type that can be found in your family will determine your level of risk for developing the disease, which should give you some direction about how to make changes that can impact your future lifestyle or finances.

LATE ONSET ALZHEIMER'S

In late onset Alzheimer's, if you have a family member diagnosed with this disease after the age of sixty-five, you have a higher chance of developing the disease. The risk starts becoming significant only when you pass the age of sixty-five, not sooner. At the age of fifty, your risk of developing the disease is the same as anyone in families with no history of Alzheimer's

159

disease. This late onset form accounts for 95 percent of the patients with Alzheimer's.[1]

In a 2002 study, Robert Green, M.D., M.P.H., and his colleagues at Boston University School of Medicine studied the risk level for people who have relatives with Alzheimer's.[2] They reviewed questionnaires from 25,245 individuals interviewed at 17 different medical centers. The subjects included 2594 patients with Alzheimer's disease, their spouses, and 19,920 members of their families. Dr. Green and his team studied the spouses of these patients as controls, since these individuals often were from the same cultural and socioeconomic background but were not from the same families. Spouses and relatives had lived in similar environments, eaten similar foods, and had similar educational experiences.

Dr. Green's team found that on average most people developed Alzheimer's disease between the ages of seventy-seven and eighty-five. People aged sixty-five or younger who had blood relatives with late onset Alzheimer's had the same low risk (less than 1 percent) of developing the disease as their spouses who had no relatives with Alzheimer's. However, when someone with an affected family member reached their seventies or eighties, the risk seemed to increase. At the age of eighty-five, those with a genetic link to Alzheimer's had a 2.5 times higher chance of getting the disease than spouses who had no genetic link.

Put simply, if you have a genetic link to someone with late onset Alzheimer's disease, your chances of acquiring the disease yourself only increase when you reach your seventh and eighth decade of life, not any sooner. Moreover, being at this higher risk does not mean that you'll definitely get the disease. You can have affected family members and not develop Alzheimer's, or you may have no one with Alzheimer's disease in your family and still develop it in your eighties.

Mr. Stone was an eighty-nine-year-old retired physicist. He and his wife were worried that he was developing Alzheimer's disease, primarily because both his sisters were diagnosed with the disease in their eighties. He felt he was forgetting the names of acquaintances often. He was also frustrated that he couldn't read his technical physics journals as quickly as he had in the past. As we talked more, he mentioned that he'd recently redone the bathroom in their house; this had required installing a brand new toilet bowl, which he did without assistance. In addition, Mr. Stone had written articles in the local newspaper, and he had some complex ideas on how to use the ocean tides to generate electricity. He performed fairly well in his memory tests. Even though he was eighty-nine years old, he was functioning very well. I explained to him that he did not have Alzheimer's disease. He was so happy he hugged me and cried.

Lifestyle choices, such as those that increase your cholosterol, blood pressure, and weight—regardless of your genetic makeup—can increase your risk of Alzheimer's disease up to eight times. Therefore, even if you do have family members with late onset Alzheimer's, you can lower your risk through changes in your lifestyle. The memory protection plan presented in Chapter 6 gives you ways to protect your brain against the disease.

EARLY ONSET FAMILIAL ALZHEIMER'S

Early onset Alzheimer's, also known as familial Alzheimer's, is the less common form of the disease. While late onset Alzheimer's patients usually display symptoms in their seventies and beyond, early onset patients show symptoms in their forties and fifties. If you have parents with this form of the disease, you have a 50 percent chance of developing it too. Fortunately, this form is uncommon and accounts for only 5 percent of the Alzheimer's disease cases in North America.[3]

Mrs. Sarponi was a delightful forty-five-year-old Portuguese American woman. She spoke four languages and was a teacher at a college. Over a period of twelve months she lost her ability to speak foreign languages and could no longer teach. She gradually could not even speak fluently in Portuguese. She soon had to be supervised all the time, got lost in her neighborhood, and sometimes even got lost inside her own house. Her children took turns bathing and dressing her. Half of her family also has this uncommon form of familial Alzheimer's disease. They are all participating in a research study aimed at finding the gene responsible for their disease.

Scientists are in a race to identify the genes behind the development of early onset familial Alzheimer's disease. If they can discover the culprit genes, drugs can be produced that target those genes and the proteins they code for, thus preventing future generations from acquiring the disease. The hope is that new medications may prove helpful to those with late onset Alzheimer's too. A handful of genes that seem to be connected to the disease have been discovered so far, and most are linked with production of amyloid plaques. It is expected that many more genes will be identified within the next two years.

THE HEREDITY LINK TO ALZHEIMER'S

Scientists study large groups of people with a specific disease to determine if there's a link between any particular genes and that disease. In these studies, they have discovered a few of the genes that may increase your risk for Alzheimer's disease. One surprising example has been the gene for proteins that carry cholesterol in your blood.

These proteins are called *Apo-lipoproteins*. They come in different sizes and forms. The one with links to Alzheimer's disease is called Apo-lipoprotein E, or *Apo-E* for short. There are three different forms of Apo-E: Apo-E2 (called epsilon 2), Apo-E3, and Apo-E4. The genes for these proteins vary among different individuals. You inherit them from your parents, one from your mother and the other from your father. Some people have two copies of Apo-E2 (E2-E2), while others have one copy of Apo-E3 and one copy of Apo-E4 (E3-E4).

Dr. Green's Boston University group, and many other Alzheimer's researchers, have shown that people who have Apo-E4 are at higher risk for developing Alzheimer's disease than those who have the other forms of Apo-E. Having two copies of Apo-E4 means you're at an even greater risk. If you have a parent with Alzheimer's disease, and if you carry the E4-E4 combination, your risk is much higher than a sibling who might have inherited the E4-E2 combination. Fortunately, people with two copies of Apo-E4 are a small minority of the population—only 1 to 2 percent.[4]

It's important to remember that these genes, sometimes referred to as susceptibility genes, do not cause Alzheimer's disease; they are one more risk factor among a dozen possible factors. You cannot change your genetic makeup, but you can reduce your overall risk of developing Alzheimer's disease by making changes in your lifestyle and habits, as discussed in Chapter 6.

APO-E AND THE INCREASED RISK OF ALZHEIMER'S

The Apo-E story is complex and continues to be the subject of intense research around the world. There are more than 2000 articles published on this subject. Some scientists believe that Apo-E protein may be involved in the brain's healing process if something injures it. The E4 version seems to be less effective in repairing damage in your brain than E3 or E2. As such, people who have one or two copies of E4 are also more likely to develop memory problems after a head injury or after a stroke.

The most recent research from Johns Hopkins Hospital shows that men with Alzheimer's disease who have the E4 version of Apo-E may have a slightly shorter survival time compared to women with the same characteristics.[5] Other researchers have shown that men or women with the E4 version have a smaller hippocampus.[6] More research is underway to put all the pieces of the puzzle together.

GENETIC TESTING FOR ALZHEIMER'S

Should you undergo routine genetic testing for Apo-E if you have family members with late onset Alzheimer's disease? For several reasons, most experts in this field would say no.[7]

For one, while the information about Apo-E genes would indicate whether you're at a higher risk of developing Alzheimer's disease, there is no one-to-one correlation between a positive E4 test and a definite likelihood of developing the disease. It would be difficult to make important long-term plans for your last decades of life based on such differences in probabilities. Also, you may spend many years of your life worrying about it. Every minor lapse of memory would make you think that you'd begun to experience Alzheimer's disease.

A second reason not to undergo genetic testing for Apo-E is that the E4 version may have beneficial effects in fighting other diseases. Margaret A. Pericak-Vance, M.D., of Duke University, and her colleagues examined the potential protective role of the Apo-E gene in macular degeneration, a form of eye disease that leads to blindness. They found that having an E4-E4 combination meant a 50 percent reduced risk of familial macular degeneration.[8] So even if the results of your genetic testing show an E4-E4 combination and a higher risk of developing memory problems, you might also be at a lower risk of developing other diseases.

Third, Apo-E is only one gene that has been discovered to increase the probability of developing late onset Alzheimer's disease. Many more genes may be discovered in the next two decades. As such, genetic testing for Apo-E would give only partial answers regarding the link between your genes and your risk for Alzheimer's disease.

Finally, there are a dozen other factors that can impact your risk of developing memory decline with aging. You're better off considering these factors, regardless of your genetic makeup. Interestingly, the presence of Apo-E often becomes more significant with the presence of other risk factors, such as high cholesterol or head trauma. Controlling those factors would reduce the impact of Apo-E as well.

QUESTIONS STILL TO BE ANSWERED

Despite attaining a great deal of success, researchers in the field of Alzheimer's disease are still working to answer some very basic questions:

What causes Alzheimer's disease?

How does Apo-E interact with amyloid protein within the plaques?

How are plaques and tangles related to each other?

How does alcohol exert its beneficial effects to reduce the risk of Alzheimer's disease?

How does high blood pressure in mid-life lead to a higher risk of Alzheimer's in late life?

Why is it that some patients who have many plaques in their brain do not develop the symptoms of Alzheimer's disease while others do?

How can patients with mild cognitive impairment prevent or delay the onset of Alzheimer's disease?

What is the best imaging technique to diagnose Alzheimer's with confidence?

How do high homocysteine levels increase the risk of Alzheimer's disease?

Should the same criteria be used to diagnose Alzheimer's in a fifty-year-old and an eighty-year-old person?

Studies like the ones mentioned in the book are being carried out on a daily basis, bringing us closer to solving the mysteries of the disease.

In practice, physicians order Apo-E testing when they're not sure if their patient with profound memory problems has Alzheimer's disease. If test results indicate one or two copies of E4, it's more likely that you'll develop Alzheimer's, though by itself does not establish the diagnosis. Some people occasionally get misdiagnosed with Alzheimer's disease because of a positive E4 testing.

Mr. Brown was a successful financial adviser in his sixties. He had decided to quit his job in order to take advantage of an excellent early retire-

ment package offered by his company. After retirement, he spent much of his time at home. Without the stimulating contacts with his coworkers and clients, he gradually became depressed. He was not interested in running errands around the house for his wife. She noticed that his memory had gotten worse and insisted that he see a physician.

Mr. Brown's formal neuropsychological testing showed borderline memory deficits. His blood test showed that he was Apo-E4 positive (E2-E4), and he was diagnosed with Alzheimer's disease. This was a shock to the Browns, and they came to Johns Hopkins for a second opinion. In my interview with him, I learned that he still took care of the finances for his family, had recently traveled abroad by himself for several months, and that he had signs of depression. He had mild memory problems, but was otherwise very coherent and capable of logical thinking. I felt that he probably had mild cognitive impairment with depression, but definitely not Alzheimer's disease. I explained to him and his wife that having an Apo-E gene does not automatically mean that a person has the disease. I encouraged him to look for business contracts to keep him busy and stimulated during the day, and to talk with his primary physician about taking antidepressants and vitamin E.

On the other hand, those researchers who favor Apo-E testing argue that knowing that you're likely to develop Alzheimer's may help you prepare for the future, both financially and emotionally.[9] This is especially the case for individuals who have family members with early onset familial Alzheimer's disease.[10] The issue of genetic testing for Alzheimer's disease is complex, controversial, and involves many ethical and cultural aspects. If you do have concerns, you should discuss them with your physician and your family members.

ALZHEIMER'S DISEASE AND WOMEN

According to Dr. Green at Boston University, Alzheimer's disease is slightly more common among older women than men.

Women in their seventies are 20 percent more likely to develop Alzheimer's than men in the same age group. Initially this was attributed to the fact that women tend to live longer than men, and thus were alive long enough to develop Alzheimer's disease. But as more men live into their eighties, they still have a lower incidence of Alzheimer's disease. In fact, the difference between the incidence rates between men and women becomes even more noticeable for people in their nineties.[11] This area of research remains controversial and more studies are needed before a conclusion can be reached.

HORMONE REPLACEMENT THERAPY

Should postmenopausal women undergo hormone replacement therapy to lower the risk of developing Alzheimer's disease?

For now the answer is "no." A recent study of 16,608 postmenopausal women for more than five years showed that hormone replacement therapy (estrogen plus progestin) increases the risks for heart disease, stroke, blood clots in the lungs, and breast cancer.[12] Clinical trials are now under way to find out if estrogen alone can ward off dementia.

▬▬▬

ALZHEIMER'S AND AFRICAN AMERICANS

Compared to Caucasians, African Americans may have a higher tendency to develop Alzheimer's disease in the last decades of their lives (not before age sixty-five). Dr. Green's team has provided detailed information about the differences in prevalence of Alzheimer's disease between African Americans and Caucasians: By the time they get to their eighties, African Americans have twice as many cases of Alzheimer's. Other investigators have confirmed similar higher numbers of Alzheimer's disease among older African Americans.

This higher rate among African Americans may in part be due to higher prevalence of hypertension, heart disease, and diabetes. This higher rate also may be attributed to the screening tests used to make the diagnosis. Vicki Lampley, Ph.D., assistant professor in the department of geriatric medicine at the University of Oklahoma, believes that the screening tests for dementia may contain inherent biases against African Americans. Though difficult to prove, Caucasians are more likely to have taken frequent paper-and-pencil tests in their lives than African Americans and may find the memory tests easier to complete. Other explanations include possible differences in early education and access to health care between African Americans and white Americans.

FROM INDIANAPOLIS TO NIGERIA

African men and women living in Africa have far fewer cases of Alzheimer's disease than African Americans living in the United States.[13]

Kathleen Hall, Ph.D., and her colleagues at Indiana University collaborated with Adesola Ogunniyi, M.D., in Nigeria to compare the lifestyle and medical history characteristics among the African American community living in Indiana and in Nigeria. They found that 1.4 percent of people over the age of sixty-five living in Nigeria develop Alzheimer's disease, compared to a much higher 6.2 percent of African Americans of the same age living in Indianapolis.

What's more, the researchers noted that Africans living in Nigeria had lower cholesterol levels, were less likely to be obese, and had fewer cases of hypertension and diabetes. It could be that differences between the commonplace diets in the United States and in Africa is part of the explanation. The differences could also be related to the social dynamics of the different cultures. Africans in Nigeria, for instance, live in large social groups (tribes), whereas Americans tend to live in smaller families. And increased opportunities to socialize and healthy social networks, as noted in Chapter 6, are likely factors in delaying the onset of symptoms, because such involvement and activity stimulates the brain.

A dozen research studies suggest that environmental factors such as diet or lifestyle make a difference in how frequently people within a certain race or culture develop Alzheimer's disease. Japanese people, for example, have a low incidence of Alzheimer's disease. However, those who move to Hawaii and adopt an American lifestyle more commonly develop Alzheimer's than their siblings in Japan.[14] For another example, Canadians living in rural parts of Manitoba have fewer cases of Alzheimer's than those who live in the province's largest city, Winnipeg.[15] Diet, stress, and exposure to hectic environments may be factors explaining the differences.

HOW COMMON IS ALZHEIMER'S DISEASE IN NORTH AMERICA?

According to Walter Rocca, M.D., professor of epidemiology and neurology at the Mayo Clinic in Rochester, Minnesota, "Alzheimer's disease is common, but not as common as people think it is." He and Laura Fratiglioni, M.D., Ph.D., professor of geriatric medicine at Karolinska Institute in Sweden, report the actual percentage of people with dementia in North America[16] to be 0.3 percent for people between the ages of sixty and sixty-four, 0.9 percent for those between sixty-five and sixty-nine, 2.0 percent for those between seventy and seventy-four, 4.1 percent for those between seventy-five and seventy-nine, and 11.7 percent for those between eighty and eighty-four. Only after the age of eighty-five do these numbers rise above 22.8 percent.

This means that if you are seventy years old and your genetic and racial background doubles your risk, your probability of developing Alzheimer's is 4 percent, instead of 2 percent for someone without those features. Lifestyle factors can multiply your risk by eight times or drop it by 80 percent. Thus, if you have a genetic susceptibility to Alzheimer's disease, you still have many opportunities to lower your risk of developing it, especially if you start modifying your risk factors in your mid-life. There are now more reasons than ever before for you to eat better, exercise more, lower your stress, engage in fun and stimulating activities, and have a positive outlook toward yourself and others.

AFTERWORD

EXCITING AND ENGAGING YOUR MEMORY

If you're walking in a park and looking around, several groups of neurons from different parts of the brain are activated simultaneously, some from vision parts, some from hearing parts, and some from arousal parts. The theory that the hippocampus is significant in the formation of memories would point to the indirect links all these neurons have with the hippocampus and the fact that they can activate it. If someone throws a tomato at you while you're walking in the park, the hearing, vision, emotion, and arousal parts of your brain will all be activated at once and will stimulate the hippocampus; as a result, you'll remember this experience for many years to come.

On the same day in the park, you may also hear birds, see dogs running about, and smell flowers. These experiences will stimulate your brain too, but to a milder degree, so your hippocampus may not register them as worth remembering. Events that lead to a significant activation of the hippocampus are more likely to be remembered.

The trick to enhancing memory is to increase your arousal and attention; put another way, to make an impression on your own hippocampus. When this occurs naturally, forming strong memories is effortless. A man who sees a woman and falls in love with her will always remember everything about that moment: the color of her eyes, her dress, her scent, and her voice. The excitement he feels at that moment revs up his arousal, attention, and, in turn, his memory. Only a few experiences in your daily life render such a high degree of brain activity. Sometimes you need to force your brain to become more engaged with mundane facts, such as names or phone numbers, so you can recall them later. You can accomplish this by *paying extra attention.*

There are different techniques for exciting and engaging the memory parts of the brain. You will need to try each technique to see which one works for you. One point to remember at the onset is that, just as building muscles requires effort, desire, and training, building memories requires *energy.* Some people assume they must remember things as effortlessly as when they see them. This is simply not the case.

Another point to keep in mind is the great degree of individual variability in regard to memory and learning. Just as people have different amounts of muscle mass, they have different capabilities when it comes to remembering things. You can improve your "memory muscles" by *dedication, passion,* and *persistence.* It's not realistic to expect yourself to remember every name you hear and every face you see. It is, however, realistic to expect yourself to remember the events and people who are important to you and your family, such as the name of your boss or the date of your anniversary. You can set reasonable goals for yourself and then try to beat your expectations by regular "memory workouts."[1]

EXERCISES TO HELP YOU REMEMBER

There are many ways you can enhance your memory,[2] and here are some suggestions. One way to remember them all later is to use a pneumonic tool: think of the word ATTENTION.

1. **A**ttention

2. **T**ake notes

3. **T**ry hard

4. **E**motions

5. **N**o fatigue, and no stress

6. **T**ease your brain

7. **I**magination

8. **O**rganization

9. **N**ever too late

ATTENTION

Paying attention is the single most important practice for attaining better memory skills. Attention is the process by which you focus all your senses on one issue. The more you pay attention, the more likely it is that the information you want to remember will be firmly registered in your hippocampus.

If you need to remember a person's name, pay extra attention when he introduces himself. Tune in. If you're at a party, for instance, try to phase out all the distractions around you. Listen carefully for the name. Repeat it once or twice, either silently or by calling his name for various reasons. Spell it out in your head. Pay attention to his eyes, his mouth, his chin, and his ears. Try to make an association between his name and his face. Become engaged with the name as if remembering him would bring you money and fame. Pretend this is a game, and if you don't remember his name and face you'll lose. Do all you can to etch an impression in your hippocampus.

Apply the same degree of concentration when you hear somebody speak. To remember what they say, focus on it. Bring all your attention to the words. The more you limit distractions around you and the harder you think as you listen, the easier it will be for you to remember it later.

When you read an article or a chapter in a book, does it often seem you can't remember any of it the next day? Try reading the same article and paying extra attention. Again, avoid distractions. When you finish, close the magazine or the book and think about what you just read. Thinking engages many areas of your brain. Understanding a concept makes a long-term impression on the hippocampus. If you pause after reading an article to think about it and ensure that you understand the main concept, you won't forget it for a long time.

TAKE NOTES

You don't always have to strain your brain to memorize unnecessary things around you—you can write them down. Taking notes is the most reliable way to remember things. Using color Post-it Notes is particularly helpful.

Society today is filled with information overload. You're bombarded with information daily, from e-mail and phone calls to twenty-four-hour news channels. There's no point trying to remember everything that happens around you every day. Instead, you can simply write down the things you need to do, the places you need to go, and the people you have to see.

Mrs. Mellar was a forty-five-year-old secretary who always impressed everyone with her memory. But in fact she did not have a photographic memory. Before driving to parties, she would review the names of people who were going to be there. She'd repeat them several times with her husband in the car. At the party, if she met some new people, she'd make a point to first memorize their names. She would then go to the bathroom and write down their names and some other information— such as their jobs, their hometowns, or the names of their children—on a piece of an index card. Writing down this information helped her remember their names better. She would keep this card and review it with her husband the next time they were expecting to meet these people at another party.

TRY HARD

Strengthening your muscles requires effort and discipline. In the same fashion, you can improve your memory skills by trying hard and working to consciously improve your memory. Again, you need to be realistic. Just as you don't expect to become a bodybuilder after a couple of push-ups, you can't expect to have a photographic memory overnight. But you can try to improve your current skills and impress yourself.

When you need to memorize a list, you can try different techniques:

1. Repeat it to yourself several times. Write it down. Repeat it with your eyes closed and try to remember as many items as you can. Then try again, and again, until you remember all the items on your list.

2. Group the items on the list into several categories, then memorize each category separately. After several rounds of practice, you'll know all the items in all the categories. For example, try to memorize your grocery shopping list by putting the items you need to buy in categories, such as bathroom, kitchen, or basement. It's easier to remember three items in each of three categories than to remember a list of nine items.

3. Make a word out of the first letters of each item. For example, Milk, Orange juice, Butter, and Sugar can be memorized as MOBS.

4. Try always to put your car keys, your glasses, your wallet, your shoes, and your briefcase in the same place in your house. "Forget-me-not spots" can help you find many items quickly.

5. Group numbers in sets of three or four. It's a lot easier to remember (104) 467–5318 than 1044675318. You can memorize your credit card number in this fashion and impress your spouse the next time you order something over the phone.

There's no magic in remembering things. Most people can memorize a short list if they really want to. Different techniques work for different people. The bottom line is that if you absolutely need to memorize something, you can. You may need more time and practice, but you can do it. Like most people, you probably underestimate how much you can commit to memory. To achieve your full potential, you simply need to try harder.

EMOTIONS

How does your brain remember the faces of high school friends you haven't seen for 20 years? The answer is both amazing and complex. New research suggests that you're more likely to remember events and names that had an emotional impact. You probably remember your high school sweetheart better than the classmates who sat in the back of the room. You remember your big career mistakes better than the small successes you made along the way. Day to day, you can put this property of emotions to good use in improving your ability to remember.

The amygdala is situated next to, and in front of, each hippocampus on the left and right sides of your brain. Along with a few other brain structures it connects to, the olive-size amygdala is an integral part of experiencing an emotion.[3] When you're afraid, for instance, or you experience intense sexual feelings, different parts of your amygdala may be activated.

Each amygdala has a direct and powerful impact on the hippocampus. Researchers believe that an event with inherent emotional significance to you activates your amygdala; your hippocampus is then flooded with activity and records that event as important. Considering this, one way to improve your memory is to link a nonsignificant object or list with something more exciting and dramatic.

Try and memorize the number 11047763226. Is it difficult?

Now pretend you were told secretly that these are the winning lottery numbers for tomorrow's drawing, and once again try to memorize these numbers. How did you do this time? Another example of the "amygdala" technique is to tell yourself that if you forget taking a book to work in the morning, you'll fall off a cliff as soon as you step out of your house. In the morning, as you leave, it could well be that you'll remember something about falling off a cliff and the fact that you need to take a book to work.

NO FATIGUE, AND NO STRESS

Fatigue dulls the memory. On days that you know you feel particularly tired, lower your memory expectations; make more lists and rely less on your ability to remember things. If you're not sleeping well and feel exhausted, don't expect to be able to remember all that you have to do that day. You may even blank out on your home phone number.

Mild to moderate levels of stress stimulate the arousal parts of your brain, quicken your heartbeat, and increase your blood pressure. Over the short term, these factors enhance your ability to remember things. However, high levels of stress, or chronic stress, damage the very organ that is needed for remembering: the hippocampus. Avoid excess stress as much as possible. If you're forced to do many things at the same time, chances are you'll forget several things. This is only normal. If you to wish to remember details, do one thing at a time.

When you "multitask," you're asking different parts of your brain to work on different projects at the same time. Your brain can do this, but not too well. If you talk on the phone with your friend, drink your tea, type an e-mail to someone else, and listen to music all at the same time, you might not remember the details of your conversation later. It would be unreasonable to expect your brain to take care of so many things at the same time, especially if you are tired. Relax and be reasonable.

TEASE YOUR BRAIN

Older individuals who maintain an intellectually challenging lifestyle seem to delay the memory problems that come with aging. This observation has led to the conclusion that to keep your memory in top condition, you should try learning new things. You can strengthen your memory with mental gymnastics just as you can strengthen your arm muscles with push-ups. Some memory specialists believe that cross training applies to your brain too: Just as doing weight lifting may improve your tennis, learning new dance steps may help you remember names better. Similarly, if you practice learning a new language, your ability to remember words in your own language may improve as well.

Here are some examples of memory workouts you can do to stimulate your brain:

- Take a dance class.
- Learn a new language.
- Join a book club.
- Solve a jigsaw or crossword puzzle.

Do these activities, or others you can think of, for the fun of it. In the process, you'll get better at keeping your hippocampus working. Chances are, you'll protect your brain from Alzheimer's disease too.

IMAGINATION

Vivid imagination is the key to effective memorization. If you can vividly see the items on a list in your mind, it's more likely that you'll remember them. If you can make them appear unusual and dramatic, it will have an even bigger impact on your hippocampus. The funnier and more ridiculous the picture, the easier it will be to remember it.

Give yourself three minutes and try to memorize the following grocery list:

Celery

Yogurt

Milk

Fish

Coke

Paper towels

Ice cream

Tea bags

Newspaper

Chocolate

How did you do? Now try to remember the same list by visualizing each item in a dramatic and funny way. Following is a suggestion for a story line. Let's see how many of the items you remember after reading the story.

As vividly as you can, picture a three-foot-long celery in front of the shopping mall. Then picture yourself carrying the huge celery into the supermarket and dipping it into a bucket of yogurt. Then add milk to the bucket, just for the fun of it. Then picture yourself throwing out the celery, because you see three red fish swimming in the milk. You're stunned with amazement. You decide that adding Coke would help save the fish, and you pour a gallon of Coke in the bucket. The bucket tips over and the whole floor of the supermarket is covered with milk, yogurt, fish, and Coke! You run to the cleaning aisle and find ten rolls of paper towels to clean the mess. The manager appreciates your efforts, smiles and offers you an ice cream cone the size of a football. You refuse and ask for tea instead. He cannot find where the tea bags are located and decides to check the newspaper for people who want to sell their secondhand tea bags. You get frustrated, steal some chocolate, and run out!

ORGANIZATION

The more organized you are, the less you need to strain your memory. Agendas, calendars, hand-held computers, index cards, or wall boards each work well for different people. Making a "to-do" list is a must for all busy people.

In the hospital, incoming new physicians are often overwhelmed with the huge load of patients who need to be seen and the dozens of things that need to happen in any single day. They learn quickly that they cannot rely on their memory alone. Small index cards become an essential part of their daily life. They devote one card for each patient and write down all the things that need to be done for him as a to-do list. They check each item as it gets done. By the end of their shift, which is sometimes 36 hours long, they know they haven't missed anything for any of their patients. They go home with peace of mind. It would be impossible to manage such stressful circumstances in any other way.

Take a few minutes every Sunday to decide what your priorities are for the week. Write them in your agenda book. Then allocate a general "things-to-do" list for each day. Each morning, make a new detailed list; you may use an index card, your hand-held computer, or a scrap of paper. This organization brings a sense of control and relieves stress; it allows your memory to function better. You can also take a few minutes the first day of each month to set priorities for each week and remind yourself of your goals for the whole year.

NEVER TOO LATE

The expression "You can't teach an old dog new tricks" is not true when it comes to memory. Older people can strengthen their memory muscles and benefit from organizing their work just as well as they can improve their physical strength. They simply need more time. Often, the elderly may feel they're too old, and as a result they give up easily. New research has shown that elderly individuals who forget where they left their car can be taught a system so they can find it each and every time.

Think positive. Give yourself positive reinforcements and compliments every time you do remember something, and do not dwell on the few occasions when your memory is not perfect.

APPENDIX A

RESOURCES

The information in this section was compiled from the publications and Web sites of the National Institute on Aging; the National Institute on Health—especially publication 01-738—the National Library of Medicine, and the Administration on Aging.

AGING

ADMINISTRATION ON AGING

Department of Health and Human Services (DHHS)

330 Independence Avenue SW

Washington, DC 20201

(202) 619-7501

(202) 619-0724

(800) 677-1116

Web site: www.aoa.dhhs.gov

A federal agency, the Administration on Aging develops policies affecting older Americans. Their services include

- Planning and delivery of home-based and community-based services to the elderly and their caregivers
- Educating the elderly about available benefits and services

ALLIANCE FOR AGING RESEARCH

2021 K Street NW, Suite 305

Washington, DC 20006

(202) 293-2856

(202) 785-8574

Web site: www.agingresearch.org

A citizen advocacy organization dedicated to the health and independence of older Americans, the Alliance for Aging Research

- Sponsors medical research and geriatric education

- Provides information on health-care options under Medicare

- Offers free publications on age-related issues (such as *Delaying the Disease of Aging*)

AMERICAN ASSOCIATION OF RETIRED PERSONS

601 E Street NW

Washington, DC 20049

(202) 434-2277

(800) 424-3410

Web site: www.aarp.org

A nonprofit organization, AARP advocates for health, rights, and well-being of older Americans. The group provides

- Extensive information about issues facing the elderly, such as crime prevention and consumer protection

- Publications on housing, health, exercise, and retirement planning, as well as money management, leisure, and travel

AMERICAN GERIATRIC SOCIETY

350 Fifth Avenue

New York, NY 10118

(212) 308-1414

Web site: www.americangeriatrics.org

E-mail: info.amger@americangeriatrics.org

A nonprofit organization for doctors and other health-care professionals taking care of the elderly, the society offers

- Information on issues such as long-term care and rehabilitation

- The publication *Complete Guide to Aging and Health* for information on healthy aging

AMERICAN SOCIETY ON AGING

833 Market Street, Suite 511

San Francisco, CA 94103

(415) 974-9600

(800) 537-9728

Web site: www.asaging.org

E-mail: info@asaging.org

Dedicated to improving the knowledge and skills of professionals who deal with older adults and their families, the ASA

- Provides information about issues related to the health of older people

- Publishes *Generations* and *Aging Today*

- Features a list of helpful books and other educational materials on their Web site

CHILDREN OF AGING PARENTS

1609 Woodbourne Road, Suite 302A

Levittown, PA 19057

(215) 945-6900

(800) 227-7294

This nonprofit organization

- Provides information and support to caregivers of older people

- Offers free publications on aging and information about support groups

GERONTOLOGICAL SOCIETY OF AMERICA

1030 Fifteenth Street NW, Suite 250

Washington, DC 20005

(202) 842-1275

Web site: www.geron.org

A professional organization for health-care professionals interested in aging, the GSA

- Provides referrals to researchers and specialists in gerontology
- Supports research in the field of aging
- Has publications on a variety of aging-related topics

NATIONAL ASSOCIATION OF STATE UNITS ON AGING

1225 I Street NW, Suite 725
Washington, DC 20005
(202) 898-2578
Web site: www.nasua.org
E-mail: info@nasua.org

Dedicated to advocacy on behalf of older Americans, this public-interest organization offers

- Information on rights of older people
- Referrals to lawyers specializing in elder law

NATIONAL COUNCIL ON AGING, INC.

409 Third Street SW, Suite 200
Washington, DC 20024
(800) 896-3650
Web site: www.ncog.org

The National Council on Aging is a private nonprofit organization that offers

- Information about senior center services, adult day care, financial issues, long-term care, and all other age-related issues
- Educational material on lifelong learning and intergenerational programs

ALZHEIMER'S DISEASE

ALZHEIMER'S ASSOCIATION

919 North Michigan Avenue, Suite 1100
Chicago, IL 60611
(312) 335-8700
(800) 272-3900

Web site: www.alz.org

E-mail: info@alz.org

A nonprofit organization, the Alzheimer's Association

- Offers up-to-date information about Alzheimer's disease and related disorders

- Provides information about support services, caregiver resources, new treatments, and clinical trials

- Sponsors research on the disease

- Has local chapters across the United States

- Has free educational publications in English and Spanish

ALZHEIMER'S DISEASE EDUCATION AND REFERRAL CENTER

P.O. Box 8250

Silver Spring, MD 20907

(800) 438-4380 (toll-free, in English and Spanish)

Web site: www.alzheimers.org/adear

E-mail: adear@alzheimers.org

ADEAR is a part of the National Institute on Aging (www.nih.gov/nia), which itself is a part of the National Institute of Health. It is a superb source of information about Alzheimer's disease and the research into possible causes and cures. You can call their toll-free 800 number or visit their Web site to

- Learn about new treatments

- Obtain information about the latest research

- Receive free publications about Alzheimer's disease

- Find additional services and resources

The following organizations outside the United States provide resources for Alzheimer's patients and their families, along with information about caregiver support groups and ongoing research. You can also check your telephone directory to look for an Alzheimer's-related organization in your city.

Alzheimer Europe

Luxembourg, France

Telephone: 352-29-79-70

Web site: www.alzheimer-europe.org

Alzheimer's International

London, England

Telephone: 44-171-620-3011

Web site: www.alzdisint.demon.co.uk

Canadian Alzheimer Association

20 Eglinton Avenue West, Suite 1200

Toronto, ON M4R 1KB

Canada

(416) 488-8772

(800) 616-8816

Web site: www.alzheimer.ca

AMERICAN HEALTH ASSISTANCE FOUNDATION

15825 Shady Grove Road, Suite 140

Rockville, MD 20850

(301) 948-3244

(800) 437-2423

Web site: www.ahaf.org

The American Health Assistance Foundation

- Has an Alzheimer's Family Relief Program that offers emergency grants of up to $500 to patients with Alzheimer's disease and their caregivers in need

- Provides free publications on Alzheimer's disease, glaucoma, heart disease, hypertension, and stroke

GENERAL HEALTH AND RELATED ORGANIZATIONS

AMERICAN ACADEMY OF FAMILY PHYSICIANS

11400 Tomahawk Creek Parkway

Leawood, KS 66211

(913) 906-6000

(913) 906-6094

(800) 274-2237

Web site: www.familydoctors.org

E-mail: fp@aafp.org

A national association of doctors in family practice, the American Academy of Family Physicians offers

- Referrals to certified family practice doctors
- Information on health care and disease prevention
- Publications on specific diseases, drug interactions, and sensible eating

AMERICAN COLLEGE OF PHYSICIANS–AMERICAN SOCIETY OF INTERNAL MEDICINE

190 North Independence Mall West

Philadelphia, PA 19106

(215) 351-2829

(800) 523-2400

Web site: www.acponline.org

E-mail: interpub@mail.acponline.org

The largest medical specialty society in the United States, the American College of Physicians–American Society of Internal Medicine provides lists of referrals for specialists in

- Internal medicine
- Cardiology
- Infectious diseases
- Rheumatology
- Gastroenterology
- Oncology

AMERICAN MEDICAL ASSOCIATION

515 North State Street

Chicago, IL 60610

(312) 464-5000

(800) 621-8335

Web site: www.ama-assn.org

For licensed physicians in the United States, the American Medical Association

- Sets standards on medical practice
- Provides referrals to qualified doctors
- Publishes the *Journal of the American Medical Association*, which features the latest discoveries in health and disease

American Pharmaceutical Association

2215 Constitution Avenue NW

Washington, DC 20037

(202) 628-4410

(800) 237-2742

Web sites: www.aphanet.org and www.pharmacyandyou.org (consumer information site)

E-mail: webmaster@mail.aphanet.org

This association of licensed pharmacists provides

- Public health information on issues related to medications
- Educational material such as *Managing Medicine as You Grow Older*, *National Medical Awareness Test*, and *Self-Medication Awareness Test*

National Council on Alcoholism and Drug Dependence

20 Exchange Place, Suite 2902

New York, NY 10005

(212) 269-7797

(800) 622-2255

Web site: www.ncadd.org

E-mail: national@ncadd.org

The NCADD is a nonprofit organization that provides

- Information and assistance on alcoholism and drug addiction
- Referrals for specialists
- A list of community resource centers
- Fact sheets about causes and treatments of alcoholism

NATIONAL COUNCIL ON PATIENT INFORMATION AND EDUCATION

4915 Saint Elmo Avenue, Suite 505

Bethesda, MD 20814

(301) 656-8565

Web site: www.talkaboutrx.org

The NCPIE offers

- Information on medications and their side effects
- Updates on the safety and efficacy of both prescription drugs and over-the-counter medicines
- Details about medications and manufacturers' recalls on its Web site

NATIONAL HEART, LUNG, AND BLOOD INSTITUTE INFORMATION CENTER

P.O. Box 30105

Bethesda, MD 20824

(301) 592-8573

(800) 575-9355

Web site: www.nhlbi.nih.gov

Part of the National Institute on Health, the NHLBI Information Center provides

- Referrals to doctors
- Important information on health-related issues, including high cholesterol, high blood pressure, heart disease, exercise, risk of and recovery from stroke, and sleep disorders
- The educational publications *HeartMemo* and *AsthmaMemo*

NATIONAL LIBRARY OF MEDICINE

National Institute of Health

Bethesda, MD 20894

(301) 496-6308

(888) 346-3656

Web site: www.nlm.nih.gov

E-mail: custserv@nlm.nih.gov

This is the world's largest medical library. It offers

- Access to medical information through a national network of libraries
- A comprehensive database of medical articles (MEDLINE)
- A Web site (www.clinicaltrials.gov) that provides up-to-date information about clinical trials in the United States

HEALTHY LIFESTYLE

AMERICAN HEALTH FOUNDATION

1 Dana Road

Valhalla, NY 10595

(914) 592-2600

Web site: www.ahf.org

An organization for research on health-related issues, the AHF

- Researches the effects of lifestyle, environment, and nutrition in preventing diseases
- Has publications on high cholesterol, hypertension, heart disease, cancer, and healthy living

CENTER FOR THE STUDY OF AGING/INTERNATIONAL ASSOCIATION OF PHYSICAL ACTIVITY, AGING, AND SPORTS

706 Madison Avenue

Albany, NY 12208

(518) 465-6927

E-mail: iapaas@acl.com

The Center for the Study of Aging/IAPAAS is a nonprofit organization that promotes research, education, and training in the field of aging, along with

- Providing educational material on health and fitness for the elderly
- Publishing a quarterly newsletter, *Lifelong Health and Fitness*

ELDER CRAFTSMEN

610 Lexington Avenue
New York, NY 10022
(212) 319-8128
Web site: www.eldercraftsmen.org
E-mail: eldercraftsmen@mindspring.com

Elder Craftsmen

- Offers programs and services to promote creativity in older adults
- Provides community and artist-in-residence services

NATIONAL ASSOCIATION FOR HEALTH & FITNESS

201 South Capital Avenue, Suite 560
Indianapolis, IN 46225
(317) 237-5630
Web site: www.physicalfitness.org

NAHF, a nonprofit organization,

- Promotes daily physical activity and healthy living
- Supports employee health and fitness programs
- Provides the interactive educational program encouraging daily exercise "Let's Get Physical"

NATIONAL SENIOR GAMES ASSOCIATION

3032 Old Forge Drive
Baton Rouge, LA 70808
(225) 925-5678
Web site: www.nsga.com

A nonprofit organization promoting fitness and sports for older people, the NSGA

- Runs the Summer National Senior Games, the Winter National Senior Games, and the Senior Olympics
- Networks with state and federal agencies to support healthy lifestyles for seniors

HEARING

AMERICAN SPEECH-LANGUAGE-HEARING ASSOCIATION

10801 Rockville Pike
Rockville, MD 20852
(800) 498-2071
(800) 638-8255
TTY (800) 638-8255
Web site: www.asha.org
E-mail: actioncenter@asha.org

An association for specialists in speech, language, and hearing sciences, the ASHA

- Works to help people with communication-related disorders
- Provides referral to specialists
- Has publications on hearing aids and other speech-related topics

BETTER HEARING INSTITUTE

5021-B Backlick Road
Annandale, VA 22003
(703) 684-3391
(800) 327-955 (800-EAR-WELL)
Web site: www.betterhearing.org
E-mail: mail@betterhearing.org

A nonprofit organization dedicated to helping patients with hearing loss, the Better Hearing Institute

- Provides information on medical, surgical, and rehabilitation options for improving hearing loss
- Has publications about hearing-related issues, such as hearing aids

INTERNATIONAL HEARING SOCIETY

16880 Middlebelt Road, Suite 4

Livonia, MI 48154

(734) 522-0200

(800) 521-5247 (Hearing Aid Helpline)

Web site: www.hearingihs.org

This professional organization

- Provides assistance in locating a hearing aid specialist and support and repair services
- Offers publications on how hearing works, types of hearing loss, and the design and use of hearing instruments

MENTAL HEALTH

AMERICAN ASSOCIATION FOR GERIATRIC PSYCHIATRY

7910 Woodmont Avenue, Suite 1050

Bethesda, MD 20814

(301) 654-7850

Web site: www.aagpgpa.org

E-mail: main@aagponline.org

This association of doctors who specialize in taking care of the mental health problems of older people provides

- Referrals to geriatric psychiatrists
- Publications such as *Growing Older, Growing Wiser: Coping with Expectations, Challenges, and Changes in Later Years*
- Free brochures on topics such as Alzheimer's disease and depression

AMERICAN PSYCHIATRIC ASSOCIATION

1400 K Street NW
Washington, DC 20005
(202) 682-6000
Web site: www.psych.org
E-mail: apa@psych.org

This association for doctors who take care of patients with mental and emotional disorders provides

- Information on medication use by older people, treatment of Alzheimer's disease, and nursing homes
- Referrals to local psychiatrists

AMERICAN PSYCHOLOGICAL ASSOCIATION

750 First Street NE
Washington, DC 20002
(202) 336-5500
(800) 374-2721
Web site: www.apa.org
E-mail: webmaster@apa.org

A professional organization for psychologists, the state and local chapters

- Give assistance and information on mental health issues
- Provide referrals to psychologists
- Have a quarterly subscription magazine called *Psychology and Aging* and publications for the elderly on topics such as dementia

NATIONAL INSTITUTE OF MENTAL HEALTH

National Institute of Health
Bethesda, MD 20892
(800) 421-4211
Web site: www.nimh.gov

The NIMH, a branch of the National Institute of Health, provides

- Funding for research in mental health, including aging and Alzheimer's disease
- Information on depression, dementia, anxiety disorders, and suicide

NEUROLOGICAL

AMERICAN ACADEMY OF NEUROLOGY

1080 Montreal Avenue

St. Paul, MN 55116

(651) 695-1940

Web sites: www.aan.com and www.neurology.org

This professional organization of neurologists in the United States and Canada offers

- Basic information and updates on neurological diseases, including Alzheimer's disease
- Referrals to accredited neurologists in the United States
- A *Patient Information Guide* on common disorders such as stroke

THE DANA ALLIANCE FOR BRAIN INITIATIVES

745 Fifth Avenue, Suite 700

New York, NY 10151

(212) 223-4040

Web site: www.dana.org

Dedicated to promoting more communication among public officials, researchers, and clinicians in the field of brain sciences, the Dana Alliance for Brain Initiatives

- Provides a forum for interactions among the public, press, policymakers, and experts in the field of neuroscience
- Hosts conferences to bring together specialists in basic science and the clinical aspects of brain disorders
- Publishes information on diagnosis, treatment, and research in brain diseases

NATIONAL INSTITUTE OF NEUROLOGICAL DISORDERS AND STROKE

P.O. Box 5801

Bethesda, MD 20824

(301) 496-5751

(800) 352-9424

Web site: www.ninds.nih.gov

E-mail: braininfo@ninds.nih.gov

A branch of the National Institute of Health, NINDS sponsors research about

- Alzheimer's disease
- Epilepsy
- Head and spinal injuries
- Huntington's disease
- Parkinson's disease
- Stroke

NATIONAL STROKE ASSOCIATION

9707 East Easter Lane

Englewood, CO 80112

(303) 754-0930

(800) 787-6537 (800-STROKES)

Web site: www.stroke.org

This national organization for improving prevention and treatment of stroke

- Offers referrals to support groups, care centers, and local resources for stroke patients and their families
- Sponsors research on the disease
- Provides educational material about the risk factors for stroke, improving acute care for stroke victims, and enhancing the quality of patient care

NUTRITIONAL WELL-BEING

AMERICAN DIETETIC ASSOCIATION

216 West Jackson Boulevard

Chicago, IL 60606

(312) 899-0040

(800) 366-1655 (Consumer Nutrition Hotline)

Web site: www.eatright.org

The ADA is a society for registered dieticians and other professionals in this field. It offers

- Information about nutrition and healthy lifestyle

- Referrals for registered dieticians in your local area

- A practice group on nutritional counseling and indirect assistance for older people through local meal programs

FOOD AND NUTRITION INFORMATION CENTER

Department of Agriculture

10301 Baltimore Avenue, Room 304

Beltsville, MD 20705

(301) 504-6856

Web site: www.nal.usda.gov

E-mail: fnic@nal.usda.gov

The FNIC, part of the Department of Agriculture, provides information about nutrition for older adults, including

- Educational material on diabetes, vegetarianism, food safety, and food labeling

- A resource guide on nutrition

NATIONAL ASSOCIATION OF NUTRITION AND AGING SERVICE PROGRAM

1101 Vermont Avenue NW, Suite 1001

Washington, DC 20005

(202) 682-6869

Web site: www.nanasp.org

A national organization for improving nutrition and well-being among the elderly, NANASP

- Supports nutrition and related services for older people
- Trains nutrition providers
- Works as an advocate for older Americans
- Provides free publications: *Legislative Action Manual* and *The Washington Bulletin*

SLEEP

NATIONAL SLEEP FOUNDATION

1522 K Street NW, Suite 500

Washington, DC 20005

(202) 347-3471

Web site: www.sleepfoundation.org

E-mail: nsf@sleepfoundation.org

This nonprofit organization provides

- Names of qualified sleep specialists
- Updates on sleep disorders
- Educational publications on sleep-related topics

SPECIFIC ILLNESSES

AMERICAN DIABETES ASSOCIATION

1701 North Beauregard Street

Alexandria, VA 22311

(703) 549-1500

(800) 232-3472 (800-DIABETES)

Web site: www.diabetes.org

Devoted to improving the lives of patients with diabetes, this organization provides

- Information on prevention and treatment of diabetes
- Information for health-care professionals taking care of patients with diabetes
- Specific outreach programs for minorities
- References to local chapters that offer support and referrals to community services
- Resources, research updates, and recipes on its Web site

AMERICAN HEART ASSOCIATION

7272 Greenville Avenue
Dallas, TX 75231
(800) 242-8721 (800-AHA-USA1)
(888) 478-7653 (888-4-STROKE)
Web site: www.americanheart.org

The nonprofit American Heart Association

- Works to increase the public's awareness about risk factors for stroke and heart attack
- Provides educational pamphlets, posters, and a Web site with information about heart disease, diabetes, hypertension, high cholesterol, as well as the latest treatments and research updates
- Has publications on heart attack treatment and improving diet and fitness

AMERICAN PARKINSON'S DISEASE ASSOCIATION

1250 Hylan Boulevard, Suite 4B
Staten Island, NY 10305
(800) 223-2732
Web site: www.apdaparkinson.org
E-mail: info@apdaparkinson.org

This nonprofit organization

- Sponsors research

- Provides referrals for specialists in Parkinson's disease
- Gives information on local community services
- Publishes educational material on Parkinson's disease, speech therapy, exercise, diet, and aids for daily living

RESTLESS LEGS SYNDROME FOUNDATION

819 Second Street SW

Rochester, MN 55902

(507) 287-6465

Web site: www.rls.org/foundation

E-mail: RLSFoundation@rls.org

The nonprofit Restless Legs Syndrome Foundation offers

- Information and updates about the syndrome
- Educational material about current research and treatment options

VISION CARE

AMERICAN ACADEMY OF OPHTHALMOLOGY

P.O. Box 7424

San Francisco, CA 94120

(415) 561-8500

(800) 222-3937

Web site: www.eyenet.org

An association of doctors specializing in eye diseases, the AAO offers

- Information about common diseases such as glaucoma and cataracts
- A list of ophthalmologists who provide free eye care for older Americans who have no health insurance and have not seen an eye doctor for at least three years

AMERICAN OPTOMETRIC ASSOCIATION

243 North Lindbergh Boulevard

St. Louis, MO 63141

(314) 991-4100

(800) 365-2219

Web site: www.aoanet.org

This national organization for optometrists

- Provides referrals to certified optometrists
- Offers VISION USA, a free eye-care program for older people with low income and/or no insurance
- Supports research and educational programs
- Provides information on floaters, macular degeneration, and glaucoma
- Issues publications such as *Driving Tips for Older Adults* and *Contact Lenses after 40*

BETTER VISION INSTITUTE

1655 North Fort Myer Drive

Arlington, VA 22209

(703) 243-1508

(800) 424-8422

Web site: www.visionsite.org

A nonprofit organization for helping patients with eye diseases, the Better Vision Institute provides

- Information on detection, prevention, and treatment of eye diseases
- Updates on issues related to vision health
- Publications on cataracts, nutrition, eyeglasses, diabetes, and vision care

NATIONAL EYE HEALTH EDUCATION PROGRAM

National Eye Institute (NEI)

2020 Vision Place

Bethesda, MD 20892

(301) 496-5248

Web site: www.nei.nih.gov

The program provides

- Referrals to eye doctors and other health-care professionals in this field

- Information on diabetic eye disease, glaucoma, and low vision

- Free educational material on how to protect your eyes and prevent vision loss

APPENDIX B

CLINICAL TRIALS

Clinical trials are the keys to determining risk factors for Alzheimer's disease, effective medications for preventing memory loss, and better treatments for patients who suffer from Alzheimer's. Some clinical trials are recruiting volunteers to test new medications, while others seek participants to find the best imaging techniques for detecting early indications of cognitive decline.

Clinical trials may be sponsored by governments or funded and conducted by the pharmaceutical industry. People who enroll in these studies receive a great deal of information before they give their consent to participate. They often feel a sense of personal satisfaction when they join a clinical trial, and enjoy contributing to the state of knowledge in this field, which in turn will help their children and grandchildren.

If you're considering joining a clinical trial, start by visiting the following Web sites.

WEB SITES

ALZHEIMER'S ASSOCIATION

Web site: www.alz.org

The research/clinical trial section of this Web site provides information about new treatments under investigation and a listing of the main clinical trials in the United States. It also provides links to the sites mentioned below.

ALZHEIMER'S DISEASE EDUCATION AND REFERRAL CENTER

Web site: www.alzheimers.org/trials/index.html

This site, prepared by the U.S. Food and Drug Administration and the National Institute on Aging, also provides a listing of the current clinical trials. You can leave your e-mail address for them and they will automatically inform you about new trials.

CenterWatch

Web site: www.centerwatch.com

Provided by research centers, the pharmaceutical industry, and service equipment vendors, this site lists all the small and large open trials in each state, as well as a link to studies by the National Institute of Health.

Clinicaltrials.gov

Web site: www. clinicaltrials.gov

This site provides a detailed list of the trials that are funded by the U.S. National Institute of Health agencies. For each clinical trial, you will learn about the goals of the trial, the eligibility criteria, and the contact numbers.

Veritas Medicine

Web site: www.veritasmedicine.com

This site helps you find the clinical trial that may be most appropriate for you. There is an anonymous search template that asks you questions and then provides information on trials for which you're eligible. The site gives names and contact numbers for each trial so you can obtain additional information from the trial coordinators.

EXAMPLES OF TRIALS

The following are examples of trials, described by the clinicaltrials.gov, that are currently under way in several cities in the United States.

Alzheimer's Disease Anti-inflammatory Prevention Trial (ADAPT)

The ADAPT trial is sponsored by the National Institute on Aging and can be contacted at (206) 277-6548.

Goal

Scientists believe inflammation plays an important role in the degeneration of neurons, which leads to memory loss and Alzheimer's disease. People with arthritis who take anti-inflammatory drugs appear to have a lower risk of developing Alzheimer's disease. This clinical trial is designed to determine if nonsteroidal anti-inflammatory medications can prevent or delay the onset of age-related cognitive decline or Alzheimer's in healthy individuals who have a family member with this disease.

Study Design

Randomized, double-blind method, and placebo-controlled. Volunteers will receive either of two active medications, naproxen sodium or celecoxib, or an inactive placebo. There is an initial medical evaluation, followed by visits to a center every six months and telephone interviews twice a year. The study will run for five to seven years.

Main Eligibility Criteria

Participants must

- Be seventy years or older
- Have a parent or siblings with serious age-related memory loss, senility, dementia, or Alzheimer's disease
- Have someone to provide additional information and assist with monitoring of the trial, if needed
- Have sufficient fluency in English to participate in neuropsychological testings and interviews
- Be willing to limit use of other medications such as vitamin E (to a dose of 400 IU per day), aspirin (at doses no greater than 81 mg per day), ibuprofen or other NSAIDs, histamine H_2-receptor antagonists (such as Tagamet or Zantac), corticosteroids, and ginkgo biloba extracts
- Be able to participate in the study regularly
- Give informed consent

Main Exclusion Criteria

Potential participants will be excluded if they
- Have a history of peptic ulcer disease, stomach bleeding, or obstruction
- Have clinically significant liver or kidney disease
- Are hypersensitive to aspirin, ibuprofen, celecoxib, naproxen, or other NSAIDs
- Are taking anticoagulation medications such as Coumadin

- Have cognitive impairment or dementia
- Are currently alcohol abusers or drug dependent

Participating Centers and Contact Information

Arizona
Sun Health Research Institute
Sun City, AZ 85351
(623) 876-5432

Florida
University of South Florida
Memory Disorder Clinic
Tampa, FL 33613
(813) 974-3100

Maryland
Johns Hopkins University
Baltimore, MD 21287
(410) 955-1535

Massachusetts
Boston University School of Medicine
Boston, MA 02118
(617) 638-5425

New York
University of Rochester
Rochester, NY 14620
(716) 760-6474

Washington
Veterans Affairs Puget Sound Health System
University of Washington
Seattle, WA 98108
(206) 277-6548

Related Publications

J. C. Anthony et al., "Reduced Prevalence of AD in Users of NSAIDs and H_2-Receptor Antagonists: The Cache County Study," *Neurology* 54 (11): 2066–2071 (2000).

J. C. Breitner, "The Role of Anti-inflammatory Drugs in the Prevention and Treatment of Alzheimer's Disease," *Annual Review of Medicine* 47: 401–411 (1996).

P. L. McGeer et al., "Arthritis and Anti-inflammatory Agents as Possible Protective Factors for Alzheimer's Disease: A Review of 17 Epidemiologic Studies," *Neurology* 47 (2): 425–432 (1996).

PREVENTION OF ALZHEIMER'S DISEASE BY VITAMIN E AND SELENIUM

The PREADVISE trial is sponsored by the National Institute on Aging and the National Cancer Institute, and can be contacted at (866) 846-1412.

Goal

A great deal of evidence suggests that antioxidants such as vitamin E have the potential to delay or prevent the onset of memory loss with aging and Alzheimer's disease. Several observational studies have shown that people on vitamin E have a lower risk of developing Alzheimer's disease. However, these results need to be confirmed in double-blind placebo-controlled studies. PREADVISE is an addition to an ongoing study examining the role of antioxidants in prevention of cancer. Investigators wish to find out if taking vitamin E and/or selenium (another antioxidant) can help prevent memory loss and dementia as well.

Study Design

Randomized, double-blind method, and placebo-controlled. Volunteers will take either an active medication (vitamin E or selenium) or an inactive placebo. They will undergo annual checkups that take less than 15 minutes.

Main Eligibility Criteria

- Eligible to men sixty-five years or older (sixty years or older if African American or Hispanic)

- Enrolled or enrolling in the Selenium and Vitamin E Cancer Prevention Trial (SELECT)
- In general good health with no neurological or psychiatric disorders

Participating Centers and Contact Information

Florida

Baptist Medical Center

Jacksonville, FL 32207

(904) 202-7073

Iowa

Bliss Cancer Center/McFarland Clinic/

Mary Greely Medical Center

Ames, IA 50010

(515) 239-2621

Kentucky

Louisville VA Medical Center

Louisville, KY 40206

(502) 895-3401

Our Lady of Bellefonte Hospital Inc.

Ashland, KY 41101

(606) 833-3253

Maryland

Anne Arundel Medical Center

Annapolis, MD 21401

(443) 481-5811

Montana

Montana Cancer Consortium CCOP

Billings, MT 59101

(406) 259-2245

Nebraska

Cancer Resource Center

Lincoln, NE 68510

(402) 483-2827

Missouri Valley Cancer Consortium CCOP/
    Creighton University

Omaha, NE 68131

(402) 280-5274

New York

Bassett Research Institute

Cooperstown, NY 13326

(607) 547-3399

Oklahoma

Muskogee Regional Medical Center

Muskogee, OK 74401

(918) 684-2387

Pennsylvania

Lehigh Valley Hospital

Allentown, PA 18103

(610) 402-0581

South Dakota

Sioux Community Cancer Consortium

Sioux Falls, SD 57105

(605) 331-3257

Tennessee

Methodist Regional Cancer Center

Oak Ridge, TN 37830

(865) 481-1664

Texas

Scott & White CCOP

Temple, TX 76508

(254) 724-8348

Washington

Northwest Hospital

Seattle, WA 98133

(206) 368-6591

Wisconsin

Marshfield Clinic

Marshfield, WI 54449

(715) 387-9521

Related Publications

M. A. Lovell et al., "Elevated Thiobarbituric Acid-reactive Substances and Anti-oxidant Enzyme in the Brain in Alzheimer's Disease," *Neurology* 45 (8): 1594–1601 (1995).

W. R. Markesbery and J. M. Carney, "Oxidative Alterations in Alzheimer's Disease," *Brain Pathology* 9 (1): 133–146 (1999).

M. Sano et al., "A Controlled Trial of Selegiline, Alpha-tocopherol, or Both as Treatment for Alzheimer's Disease. The Alzheimer's Cooperative Study," *New England Journal of Medicine* 336 (17): 1216–1222 (1997).

APPENDIX C

ALZHEIMER'S DISEASE CENTERS

The National Institute on Aging funds 29 Alzheimer's Disease Centers at major medical institutions in the United States. Each center consists of varying numbers of researchers, clinicians, and statisticians who work together to promote discovery of new medications and possibly a cure for Alzheimer's disease. For patients and families affected by Alzheimer's, many Alzheimer's disease centers provide

- Diagnosis and medical management
- Information about services and other resources
- Opportunities for volunteers to participate in drug trials, support groups, and clinical research projects

The following is a list of the Alzheimer's disease centers. You may contact individual centers to inquire about specific research and clinical trials in your area.

Alabama

University of Alabama at Birmingham

454 Sparks Center

Birmingham, AL 35294

(205) 934-2178

Arizona

Arizona Alzheimer's Disease Center

1111 East McDowell Road

Phoenix, AZ 85006

(602) 239-6999

Arkansas

University of Arkansas for Medical Sciences

4301 W. Markham, Slot 811

Little Rock, AR 72205

(501) 603-1294

Web site: www.alzheimer.uams.edu

California

Stanford/VA Alzheimer's Disease Center

Department of Psychiatry

3801 Miranda Avenue

Palo Alto, CA 94304

(650) 852-3287

Web site: www.alzheimer.stanford.edu

University of California, Davis

Department of Neurology

4860 Y Street, Suite 3900

Sacramento, CA 95817

(916) 734-5496

Web site: www.alzheimer.ucdavis.edu

University of California, Irvine

Institute for Brain Aging and Dementia

1113 Gillespie Neuroscience Research Facility

Irvine, CA 92697

(949) 824-5847

Web site: www.alz.uci.edu

University of California, Los Angeles

Department of Neurology

710 Westwood Plaza

Los Angeles, CA 90095

(310) 206-5238

Web site: www.adc.ucla.edu

University of California, San Diego
Department of Neurosciences
9500 Gilman Drive
La Jolla, CA 92093
(858) 534-4606
Web site: www.adrc.ucsd.edu

University of Southern California
Ethel Percy Andrus Gerontology Center
3715 McClintock Avenue
Los Angeles, CA 90089
(213) 740-7777
Web site: www.usc.edu/dept/gero/ADRC/

Georgia
Emory Alzheimer's Disease Center
1841 Clifton Road NE
Atlanta, GA 30329
(404) 728-6950
Web site: www.emory.edu/WHSC/MED/ADC

Illinois
Northwestern University
Cognitive Neurology and Alzheimer's Disease Center
320 East Superior Street, Searle 11-453
Chicago, IL 60611
(312) 908-9339
Web site: www.brain.nwu.edu

Rush-Presbyterian-St. Luke's Medical Center
Rush Institute for Healthy Aging
1645 West Jackson Boulevard, Suite 675
Chicago, IL 60612
(312) 942-4463
Web site: www.rush.edu/patients/radc/

Indiana

Indiana University

Indiana Alzheimer's Disease Center

635 Barnhill Drive, MS-A142

Indianapolis, IN 46202

(317) 278-2030

E-mail: iadc@iupui.edu

Kentucky

University of Kentucky

Sanders-Brown Research Center on Aging

Lexington, KY 40536

(859) 323-6040

Web site: www.coa.uky.edu/

Maryland

Johns Hopkins Medical Institutions

720 Rutland Avenue

Baltimore, MD 21205

(410) 955-5632

Web site: www.alzresearch.org

Massachusetts

Boston University

GRECC Program (182B)

200 Springs Road

Bedford, MA 01730

(781) 687-2632

Web site: www.xfaux.com/alzheimer/

Harvard Medical School/Massachusetts General Hospital

Department of Neurology

15 Parkman Street

Boston, MA 02114

(617) 726-1728

Web site: www.neuro-www.mgh.harvard.edu

Michigan

University of Michigan
Department of Neurology
1500 East Medical Center Drive
Ann Arbor, MI 48109
(734) 764-2190
Web site: www.med.umich.edu/madrc/

Minnesota

Mayo Clinic
200 First Street SW
Rochester, MN 55905
(507) 538-0487
Web site: www.mayo.edu/research/alzheimer_center/

Missouri

Washington University
4488 Forest Park Avenue, Suite 130
St. Louis, MO 63108
(314) 286-2881
E-mail: adrcdir@neuro.ewstl.edu

New York

Columbia University
630 West 168 Street
P&S Box 16
New York, NY 10032
(212) 305-1818
Web site: www.alzheimercenter.org

Mount Sinai School of Medicine/ Bronx VA Medical Center
Department of Psychiatry
P.O. Box 1230
New York, NY 10029
(212) 241-8329
Web site: www.mssm.edu/psychiatry/adrc

New York University
550 First Avenue, Room THN 310
New York, NY 10016
(212) 263-6991
Web site: aging.med.nyu.edu

University of Rochester
601 Elmwood Avenue
P.O. Box 645
Rochester, NY 14642
(716) 275-2581
Web site: www.urmc.rochester.edu/adc/index.html

North Carolina
Duke University
2200 West Main Street, Suite A-230
Durham, NC 27705
(919) 416-5380
Web site: adrc.mc.duke.edu/

Ohio
Case Western Reserve University
12200 Fairhill Road
Cleveland, OH 44120
(800) 252 5048
Web site: www.ohioalzcenter.org

Oregon
Oregon Health Sciences University
3181 SW Sam Jackson Park Road, CR 131
Portland, OR 97201
(503) 494-6976
Web site: www.ohsu.edu/som-alzheimers/

Pennsylvania

University of Pennsylvania

Maloney Building

3600 Spruce Street, Third Floor

Philadelphia, PA 19104

(215) 662-4708

Web site: www.med.upenn.edu/ADRC

University of Pittsburgh

200 Lothrop Street

Pittsburgh, PA 15213

(412) 692-2700

Web site: www.adrc.pitt.edu

Texas

Baylor College of Medicine

6550 Fannin Street

Smith Tower, Suite 1801

Houston, TX 77030

(713) 798-6660

Web site: www.bcm.tmc.edu/neurol/struct/adrc/adrc1.html

University of Texas

Southwestern Medical Center

5323 Harry Hines Boulevard

Dallas, TX 75390

(214) 648-7444

Web site: www2.swmed.edu/alzheimer/

Washington

University of Washington

Mental Health Service S116

1660 South Columbian Way

Seattle, WA 98108

(800) 317-5382

Web site: www.depts.washington.edu/adrcweb/

ENDNOTES

PART I

CHAPTER 1

1. E. R. Kandel, J. H. Schwartz, and T. M. Jessell, *Essentials of Neural Science and Behavior.* Norwalk, CT: Appleton & Lange, 1995; and A. Matynia, S. G. Anagnostaras, and A. J. Silva, "Weaving the Molecular and Cognitive Strands of Memory," *Neuron* 32 (4): 557–558 (2001).

2. E. S. Rosenzweig, C. A. Barnes, and B. L. McNaughton, "Making Room for New Memories," *Nature Neuroscience* 5 (1): 6–8 (2002).

3. C. G. Gross and J. Sergent, "Face Recognition," *Current Opinion in Neurobiology* 2 (2): 156–161 (1992).

4. G. Kempermann, "Why New Neurons? Possible Functions for Adult Hippocampal Neurogenesis," *Journal of Neuroscience* 22 (3): 635–638 (2002).

5. E. R. Kandel, J. H. Schwartz, and T. M. Jessell, *Essentials of Neural Science and Behavior.* Norwalk, CT: Appleton & Lange, 1995.

6. T. A. Salthouse, "Aging and Measures of Processing Speed," *Biological Psychology* 54 (1–3): 35–54 (2000).

7. G. J. McDougall, "Memory Improvement in Octogenarians," *Applied Nursing Research* 15 (1): 2–10 (2002).

8. B. Gordon, *Memory: Remembering and Forgetting in Everyday Life.* New York: Mastermedia Limited, 1995.

9. M. S. Albert and M. Moss, *Geriatric Neuropsychology.* New York: Guilford, 1988; and M. S. Albert, "Memory Decline: The Boundary between Aging and Age-Related Disease," *Annals of Neurology* 51 (3): 282–284 (2002).

10. M. S. Albert, "Memory Decline: The Boundary between Aging and Age-Related Disease," *Annals of Neurology* 51 (3): 282–284 (2002).

CHAPTER 2

1. R. Restak, *The Secret Life of the Brain.* New York: The Dana Press and Joseph Henry Press, 2001.

2. A. R. Damasio et al., "Subcortical and Cortical Brain Activity During the Feeling of Self-Generated Emotions," *Nature Neuroscience* 3 (10): 1049–1056 (2000).

3. N. R. Carlson, *Foundations of Physiological Psychology.* Boston: Allyn and Bacon, 1988.

4. D. H. Hubel, "The Brain," in *The Brain*. San Francisco, CA: W. H. Freeman, 1979, pp. 2–14.

5. G. Kempermann, H. D. Gast, and F. H. Gage, "Neuroplasticity in Old Age: Sustained Fivefold Induction of Hippocampal Neurogenesis by Long-Term Environmental Enrichment," *Annals of Neurology* 52 (2): 135–143 (2002).

6. R. Katzman, "Education and the Prevalence of Dementia and Alzheimer's Disease," *Neurology* 43 (1): 13–20 (1993); J. A. Mortimer, "Brain Reserve and the Clinical Expression of Alzheimer's Disease," *Geriatrics* 52 Suppl 2 (1997): S50–S53; and R. D. Terry and R. Katzman, "Life Span and Synapses: Will There Be a Primary Senile Dementia?" *Neurobiology of Aging* 22 (3): 347–348, discussion 353–354 (2001).

7. Ibid.

8. R. D. Terry and R. Katzman, "Life Span and Synapses: Will There Be a Primary Senile Dementia?" *Neurobiology of Aging* 22 (3): 347–348, discussion 353–354 (2001).

CHAPTER 3

1. D. J. Connor et al., "Subjective Memory Complaints in the Cognitively Intact Elderly" in *American Academy of Neurology*. Denver, CO: American Academy of Neurology Press, 2002.

2. D. A. Bennett et al., "Natural History of Mild Cognitive Impairment in Older Persons," *Neurology* 59 (2): 198–205 (2002); R. C. Petersen et al., "Current Concepts in Mild Cognitive Impairment," *Archives of Neurology* 58 (12): 1985–1992 (2001); F. Massoud et al., "Word-Reading Thresholds in Alzheimer Disease and Mild Memory Loss: A Pilot Study," *Alzheimer Disease and Associated Disorders* 16 (1): 31–39 (2002); and J. C. Morris et al., "Mild Cognitive Impairment Represents Early-Stage Alzheimer Disease," *Archives of Neurology* 58 (3): 397–405 (2001).

3. R. C. Petersen et al., "Current Concepts in Mild Cognitive Impairment," *Archives of Neurology* 58 (12): 1985–1992 (2001).

4. F. Massoud et al., "Word-Reading Thresholds in Alzheimer Disease and Mild Memory Loss: A Pilot Study," *Alzheimer Disease and Associated Disorders* 16 (1): 31–39 (2002).

CHAPTER 4

1. L. E. Hebert et al., "Annual Incidence of Alzheimer Disease in the United States Projected to the Years 2000 through 2050," *Alzheimer Disease and Associated Disorders* 15 (4): 169–173 (2001).

2. J. L. Price, D. W. McKeel, Jr., and J. C. Morris, "Synaptic Loss and Pathological Change in Older Adults—Aging versus Disease?" *Neurobiology of Aging* 22 (3): 351–352 (2001); and R. D. Terry, E. Masliah, and L. A. Hansen, "The Neuropathology of Alzheimer Disease and the Structural Basis of Its Cognitive Alterations," in *Alzheimer Disease*, 2d ed., R. D. Terry et al. (Eds.). Philadelphia, PA: Lippincott Williams & Wilkins, 1999, pp. 188–202.

3. R. D. Terry et al., "Physical Basis of Cognitive Alterations in Alzheimer's Disease: Synapse Loss Is the Major Correlate of Cognitive Impairment," *Annals of Neurology* 30 (4): 572–580 (1991); and R. D. Terry, E. Masliah, and L. A. Hansen, "The Neuropathology of Alzheimer Disease and the Structural Basis of Its Cognitive Alterations," in *Alzheimer Disease*, 2d ed., R. D. Terry et al. (Eds.). Philadelphia, PA: Lippincott Williams & Wilkins, 1999, pp. 188–202.

4. D. J. Callen et al., "Beyond the Hippocampus: MRI Volumetry Confirms Widespread Limbic Atrophy in AD," *Neurology* 57 (9): 1669–1674 (2001); and R. I. Scahill et al., "Mapping the Evolution of Regional Atrophy in Alzheimer's Disease: Unbiased Analysis of Fluid-Registered Serial MRI," *Proceedings of the National Academy of Sciences of the United States of America* 99 (7): 4703–4707 (2002).

CHAPTER 5

1. R. D. Adams and M. Victor, *Principles of Neurology*, 5th ed. New York: McGraw-Hill, 1993; and Walter G. Bradley et al., *Neurology in Clinical Practice*, vol. 2. Boston: Butterworth & Heinemann, 2000.

2. R. S. Wilson et al., "Depressive Symptoms, Cognitive Decline, and Risk of AD in Older Persons," *Neurology* 59 (3): 364–370 (2002).

PART II

CHAPTER 6

1. I. McDowell, "Alzheimer's Disease: Insights from Epidemiology," *Aging* 13 (3): 143–162 (2001); and R. Peters, "The Prevention of Dementia," *Journal of Cardiovascular Risk* 8 (5): 253–256 (2001).

2. D. A. Snowdon et al., "Linguistic Ability in Early Life and Cognitive Function and Alzheimer's Disease in Late Life. Findings from the Nun Study," *Journal of the American Medical Association* 275 (7): 528–532 (1996); D. A. Snowdon et al., "Brain Infarction and the Clinical Expression of Alzheimer Disease. The Nun Study," *Journal of the American Medical Association* 277 (10): 813–817 (1997); D. A. Snowdon, "Aging and Alzheimer's Disease: Lessons from the Nun Study," *Gerontologist* 37 (2): 150-156 (1997); and D. A. Snowdon, L. H. Greiner, and W. R. Markesbery, "Linguistic Ability in Early Life and the Neuropathology of Alzheimer's Disease and Cerebrovascular Disease. Findings from the Nun Study," *Annals of the New York Academy of Sciences* 903 (2000): 34–38.

3. J. He et al., "Factors Associated with Hypertension Control in the General Population of the United States," *Archives of Internal Medicine* 162 (9): 1051–1058 (2002).

4. L. Zhu et al., "Blood Pressure Reduction, Cardiovascular Diseases, and Cognitive Decline in the Mini-Mental State Examination in a Community Population of Normal Very Old People: A Three-Year Follow-Up," *Journal of Clinical Epidemiology* 51 (5): 385–391 (1998).

5. K. A. Jellinger, "Neuropathology and Clinical Relevance," *Neurobiology of Aging* 23S (2002): Abstract 535.

6. L. J. Launer et al., "The Association between Midlife Blood Pressure Levels and Late-Life Cognitive Function. The Honolulu-Asia Aging Study," *Journal of the American Medical Association* 274 (23): 1846–1851 (1995); L. J. Launer et al., "Midlife Blood Pressure and Dementia: The Honolulu-Asia Aging Study," *Neurobiology of Aging* 21 (1): 49–55 (2000); L. J. Launer, "Preventive Strategies in Dementia," *Neurobiology of Aging* 23S (2002): Abstract 538; S. Seshadri et al., "Elevated Midlife Blood Pressure Increases Stroke Risk in Elderly Persons: The Framingham Study," *Archives of Internal Medicine* 161 (19): 2343–2350 (2001); and I. Skoog et al., "15-Year Longitudinal Study of Blood Pressure and Dementia," *Lancet* 347 (9009): 1141–1145 (1996).

7. L. J. Launer et al., "Midlife Blood Pressure and Dementia: The Honolulu-Asia Aging Study," *Neurobiology of Aging* 21 (1): 49–55 (2000).

8. H. Petrovitch et al., "Midlife Blood Pressure and Neuritic Plaques, Neurofibrillary Tangles, and Brain Weight at Death: The HAAS. Honolulu-Asia Aging Study," *Neurobiology of Aging* 21 (1): 57–62 (2000).

9. M. Kivipelto et al., "Midlife Vascular Risk Factors and Alzheimer's Disease in Later Life: Longitudinal, Population Based Study," *British Medical Journal* 322 (7300): 1447–1451 (2001).

10. F. Forette et al., "Prevention of Dementia in Randomised Double-Blind Placebo-Controlled Systolic Hypertension in Europe (Syst-Eur) Trial," *Lancet* 352 (9137): 1347–1351 (1998).

11. C. Tzourio et al., "Cognitive Decline in Individuals with High Blood Pressure: A Longitudinal Study in the Elderly. Eva Study Group. Epidemiology of Vascular Aging," *Neurology* 53 (9): 1948–1952 (1999).

12. Sujuan Gao et al., "Antihypertensive Medicine and Cognitive Decline in Non-Demented Elderly African Americans," *Neurobiology of Aging* 23S (2002): Abstract 1074.

13. H. B. Posner et al., "The Relationship of Hypertension in the Elderly to AD, Vascular Dementia, and Cognitive Function," *Neurology* 58 (8): 1175–1181 (2002).

14. C. Bulpitt et al., "Hypertension in the Very Elderly Trial (HYVET): Protocol for the Main Trial," *Drugs and Aging* 18 (3). 151 164 (2001).

15. J. A. Panza, "High-Normal Blood Pressure—More 'High' Than 'Normal,'" *New England Journal of Medicine* 345 (18): 1337–1340 (2001).

16. J. Fiber, "Carotid Artery Stenosis—A Marker or Cause of Cognitive Dysfunction?" *Neurology Reviews* 9 (6): 35–36 (2001).

17. M. Kivipelto et al., "Midlife Vascular Risk Factors and Alzheimer's Disease in Later Life: Longitudinal, Population Based Study," *British Medical Journal* 322 (7300): 1447–1451(2001).

18. L. Bonetta, "Potential Neurological Value of Statins Increases," *Nature Medicine* 8 (6): 541(2002); J. Fiber, "Carotid Artery Stenosis –A Marker or Cause of Cognitive Dysfunction?" *Neurology Reviews* 9 (6): 35–36 (2001); and M. Simons

et al., "Cholesterol and Alzheimer's Disease: Is There a Link?" *Neurology* 57 (6): 1089–1093.

19. K. Yaffe et al., "Serum Lipoprotein Levels, Statin Use, and Cognitive Function in Older Women," *Archives of Neurology* 59 (3): 378–384 (2002).

20. C. Helmer et al., "Nutritional Factors and Risk of Incident Dementia in the Paquid Cohort," *Neurobiology of Aging* 23 (2002): Abstract 1022.

21. H. Jick et al., "Statins and the Risk of Dementia," *Lancet* 356 (9242): 1627–1631 (2000).

22. A. Goodman, "Statins Are Promising Therapeutic Tools for Alzheimer's Disease," *Neurology Today* 2 (3): 22–25 (2002).

23. R. C. Green et al., "Statin Use Is Associated with Reduced Risk of Alzheimer's Disease," *Neurology* 58 (2002): A81.

24. A. Goodman, "Statins Are Promising Therapeutic Tools for Alzheimer's Disease," *Neurology Today* 2 (3): 22–25 (2002).

25. S. Seshadri et al., "Plasma Homocysteine as a Risk Factor for Dementia and Alzheimer's Disease," *New England Journal of Medicine* 346 (7): 476–483 (2002).

26. B. Hultberg et al., "Markers for the Functional Availability of Cobalamin/Folate and Their Association with Neuropsychiatric Symptoms in the Elderly," *International Journal of Geriatric Psychiatry* 16 (9): 873–878 (2001).

27. I. I. Kruman et al., "Folic Acid Deficiency and Homocysteine Impair DNA Repair in Hippocampal Neurons and Sensitize Them to Amyloid Toxicity in Experimental Models of Alzheimer's Disease," *Journal of Neuroscience* 22 (5): 1752–1762 (2002); T. Matsui et al., "Elevated Plasma Homocysteine Levels and Risk of Silent Brain Infarction in Elderly People," *Stroke* 32 (5): 1116–1119 (2001); J. W. Miller et al., "Homocysteine, Vitamin B6, and Vascular Disease in AD Patients," *Neurology* 58 (10): 1471–1475 (2002); and S. E. Vermeer et al., "Homocysteine, Silent Brain Infarcts, and White Matter Lesions: The Rotterdam Scan Study," *Annals of Neurology* 51 (3): 285–289 (2002).

28. A. McCaddon et al., "Homocysteine and Cognitive Decline in Healthy Elderly," *Dementia and Geriatric Cognitive Disorders* 12 (5): 309-313 (2001); and E. H. Reynolds, "Folic Acid, Aging, Depression, and Dementia," *British Medical Journal* 324 (7352): 1512–1515 (2002).

29. S. Seshadri et al., "Plasma Homocysteine as a Risk Factor for Dementia and Alzheimer's Disease," *New England Journal of Medicine* 346 (7): 476–483 (2002).

30. K. Nilsson, L. Gustafson, and B. Hultberg, "Improvement of Cognitive Functions after Cobalamin/Folate Supplementation in Elderly Patients with Dementia and Elevated Plasma Homocysteine," *International Journal of Geriatric Psychiatry* 16 (6): 609–614 (2001).

31. J. F. Toole and C. R. Jack. "Food (and Vitamins) for Thought," *Neurology* 58 (10): 1449–1450 (2002); and H. X. Wang et al., "Vitamin B(12) and Folate in Relation to the Development of Alzheimer's Disease," *Neurology* 56 (9): 1188–1194 (2001).

32. R. L. Galli et al., "Fruit Polyphenolics and Brain Aging: Nutritional Interventions Targeting Age-Related Neuronal and Behavioral Deficits," *Annals of the New York Academy of Sciences* 959 (2002): 128–132.

33. M. C. Cartford, C. Gemma, and P. C. Bickford, "Eighteen-Month-Old Fischer 344 Rats Fed a Spinach-Enriched Diet Show Improved Delay Classical Eyeblink Conditioning and Reduced Expression of Tumor Necrosis Factor Alpha (TNFalpha) and TNFbeta in the Cerebellum," *Journal of Neuroscience* 22 (14): 5813-5816 (2002).

34. G. P. Lim et al., "The Curry Spice Curcumin Reduces Oxidative Damage and Amyloid Pathology in an Alzheimer Transgenic Mouse," *Journal of Neuroscience* 21 (21): 8370–8377 (2001).

35. M. Gonzalez-Gross, A. Marcos, and K. Pietrzik, "Nutrition and Cognitive Impairment in the Elderly," *British Journal of Nutrition* 86 (3): 313–321 (2001).

36. M. L. Correa Leite et al., "Nutrition and Cognitive Deficit in the Elderly: A Population Study," *European Journal of Clinical Nutrition* 55 (12): 1053–1058 (2001).

37. I. Bourdel-Marchasson et al., "Antioxidant Defences and Oxidative Stress Markers in Erythrocytes and Plasma from Normally Nourished Elderly Alzheimer Patients," *Age and Ageing* 30 (3): 235–241 (2001).

38. A. Kontush et al., "Influence of Vitamin E and C Supplementation on Lipoprotein Oxidation in Patients with Alzheimer's Disease," *Free Radical Biology and Medicine* 31 (3): 345–354 (2001).

39. D. J. Foley and L. R. White, "Dietary Intake of Antioxidants and Risk of Alzheimer Disease: Food for Thought," *Journal of the American Medical Association* 287 (24): 3261–3263 (2002).

40. M. J. Engelhart et al., "Dietary Intake of Antioxidants and Risk of Alzheimer Disease," *Journal of the American Medical Association* 287 (24): 3223-3229 (2002).

41. M. C. Morris et al., "Dietary Intake of Antioxidant Nutrients and the Risk of Incident Alzheimer Disease in a Biracial Community Study," *Journal of the American Medical Association* 287 (24): 3230-3237 (2002); and M. C. Morris et al., "Vitamin E and Cognitive Decline in Older Persons," *Archives of Neurology* 59 (7): 1125–1132 (2002).

42. J. C. Breitner et al., "Reduced Risk of Alzheimer's Disease in Users of Antioxidant Vitamin Supplements. The Cache County Study," *Neurobiology of Aging* 23S (2002): Abstract 1023; M. M. Corrada et al., "Reduced Risk of Alzheimer's Disease with Antioxidant Vitamin Intake: The Baltimore Longitudinal Study of Aging," *Neurobiology of Aging* 23S (2002): Abstract 1021; and M. C. Morris et al., "Dietary Fat Intake and the Risk of Incident Alzheimer's Disease," *Neurobiology of Aging* 23S (2002): Abstract 1112.

43. A. Ruitenberg et al., "Alcohol Consumption and Risk of Dementia: The Rotterdam Study," *Lancet* 359 (9303): 281–286 (2002).

44. Z. Guo et al., "Head Injury and the Risk of AD in the Mirage Study," *Neurology* 54 (6): 1316-1323 (2000); T. Holsinger et al., "Head Injury in Early Adulthood

and the Lifetime Risk of Depression," *Archives of General Psychiatry* 59 (1): 17–22 (2002).

45. B. L. Plassman et al., "Documented Head Injury in Early Adulthood and Risk of Alzheimer's Disease and Other Dementias," *Neurology* 55 (8): 1158–1166 (2000).

46. K. Uryu et al., "Repetitive Mild Brain Trauma Accelerates Abeta Deposition, Lipid Peroxidation, and Cognitive Impairment in a Transgenic Mouse Model of Alzheimer Amyloidosis," *Journal of Neuroscience* 22 (2): 446–454 (2002).

47. P. W. Schofield et al., "Alzheimer's Disease after Remote Head Injury: An Incidence Study," *Journal of Neurology, Neurosurgery and Psychiatry* 62 (2): 119–124 (1997).

48. S. Fischer et al., "Sleep Forms Memory for Finger Skills," *Proceedings of the National Academy of Sciences of the United States of America* 99 (18): 11987–11991 (2002).

49. J. Myers et al., "Exercise Capacity and Mortality among Men Referred for Exercise Testing," *New England Journal of Medicine* 346 (11): 793–801 (2002).

50. S. Marquis et al., "Independent Predictors of Cognitive Decline in Healthy Elderly Persons," *Archives of Neurology* 59 (4): 601–606 (2002).

51. D. Laurin et al., "Physical Activity and Risk of Cognitive Impairment and Dementia in Elderly Persons," *Archives of Neurology* 58 (3): 498–504 (2001).

52. K. Yaffe et al., "A Prospective Study of Physical Activity and Cognitive Decline in Elderly Women: Women Who Walk," *Archives of Internal Medicine* 161 (14): 1703–1708 (2001).

53. D. K. Friedman et al., "Use It or Lose It: A Prospective Evaluation of Intellectual Activity and the Development of Dementia," *Neurology* 58 (S3): A103 (2002).

54. C. W. Cotman and N. C. Berchtold, "Exercise: A Behavioral Intervention to Enhance Brain Health and Plasticity," *Trends in Neurosciences* 25 (6): 295–301 (2002).

55. J. E. Manson et al. "Walking Compared with Vigorous Exercise for the Prevention of Cardiovascular Events in Women," *New England Journal of Medicine* 347 (10): 716–725 (2002).

56. L. R. Hill et al., "Functional Status, Education, and the Diagnosis of Dementia in the Shanghai Survey," *Neurology* 43 (1): 138–145 (1993).

57. C. Qiu et al., "The Influence of Education on Clinically Diagnosed Dementia Incidence and Mortality Data from the Kungsholmen Project," *Archives of Neurology* 58 (12): 2034–2039 (2001).

58. D. A. Snowdon et al., "Linguistic Ability in Early Life and Cognitive Function and Alzheimer's Disease in Late Life. Findings from the Nun Study," *Journal of the American Medical Association* 275 (7): 528–532 (1996); and D. A. Snowdon, L. H. Greiner, and W. R. Markesbery, "Linguistic Ability in Early Life and the Neuropathology of Alzheimer's Disease and Cerebrovascular Disease.

Findings from the Nun Study," *Annals of the New York Academy of Sciences* 903 (2000): 34–38.

59. M. Zhang et al., "A Preliminary Analysis of Incidence of Dementia in Shanghai, China," *Psychiatry and Clinical Neuroscience* 52 (1998): S291–S294.

60. G. Kempermann, D. Gast, and F. H. Gage, "Neuroplasticity in Old Age: Sustained Fivefold Induction of Hippocampal Neurogenesis by Long-Term Environmental Enrichment," *Annals of Neurology* 52 (2): 135–143 (2002); and G. McKhann, "New Neurons for Aging Brains," *Annals of Neurology* 52 (2): 133–134 (2002).

61. R. Katzman, "Education and the Prevalence of Dementia and Alzheimer's Disease," *Neurology* 43 (1): 13–20 (1993).

62. R. D. Terry et al., "Physical Basis of Cognitive Alterations in Alzheimer's Disease: Synapse Loss Is the Major Correlate of Cognitive Impairment," *Annals of Neurology* 30 (4): 572–580 (1991).

63. D. A. Bennett et al., "Education, Neural Reserve, and the Clinical Expression of Alzheimer's Pathology," *Neurobiology of Aging* 23S (2002): Abstract 1087.

64. R. S. Wilson et al., "Participation in Cognitively Stimulating Activities and Risk of Incident Alzheimer Disease," *Journal of the American Medical Association* 287 (6): 742–748 (2002).

65. L. Fratiglioni et al., "Influence of Social Network on Occurrence of Dementia: A Community-Based Longitudinal Study," *Lancet* 355 (9212): 1315–1319 (2000); and H. X. Wang et al., "Late-Life Engagement in Social and Leisure Activities Is Associated with a Decreased Risk of Dementia: A Longitudinal Study from the Kungsholmen Project," *American Journal of Epidemiology* 155 (12): 1081–1087 (2002).

66. N. Scarmeas et al., "Influence of Leisure Activity on the Incidence of Alzheimer's Disease," *Neurology* 57 (12): 2236–2242 (2001).

67. R. P. Friedland et al., "Patients with Alzheimer's Disease Have Reduced Activities in Midlife Compared with Healthy Control-Group Members," *Proceedings of the National Academy of Sciences of the United States of America* 98 (6): 3440–3445 (2001).

68. Y. Geda et al., "The Neuropsychiatric Aspect of Mild Cognitive Impairment (MCI): Depression and MCI," *Neurobiology of Aging* 23S (2002). Abstract 571.

69. T. Esch et al., "Invited Nel Review. The Role of Stress in Neurodegenerative Diseases and Mental Disorders," *Neuroendocrinology Letters* 23 (3): 199–208 (2002).

70. A. L. Lee, W. O. Ogle, and R. M. Sapolsky, "Stress and Depression: Possible Links to Neuron Death in the Hippocampus," *Bipolar Disorders* 4 (2): 117–128 (2002).

71. R. M. Sapolsky, "Depression, Antidepressants, and the Shrinking Hippocampus," *Proceedings of the National Academy of Sciences of the United States of America* 98 (22): 12320–12322 (2001).

CHAPTER 7

1. M. Sano et al., "A Controlled Trial of Selegiline, Alpha-Tocopherol, or Both as Treatment for Alzheimer's Disease. The Alzheimer's Disease Cooperative Study," *New England Journal of Medicine* 336 (17): 1216–1222 (1997).

2. H. X. Wang et al., "Vitamin B(12) and Folate in Relation to the Development of Alzheimer's Disease," *Neurology* 56 (9): 1188–1194 (2001).

3. P. R. Solomon et al., "Ginkgo for Memory Enhancement: A Randomized Controlled Trial," *Journal of the American Medical Association* 288 (7): 835–840 (2002).

4. B. A. t' Veld et al., "Nonsteroidal Anti-inflammatory Drugs and the Risk of Alzheimer's Disease," *New England Journal of Medicine* 345 (21): 1515–1521 (2001).

5. S. Weggen et al., "A Subset of NSAIDs Lower Amyloidogenic Abeta42 Independently of Cyclooxygenase Activity," *Nature* 414 (6860): 212–216 (2001).

6. G. Block et al., "A Clinical Trial of Rofecoxib, a Selective Cox-2 Inhibitor, for the Treatment of Alzheimer's Disease," *Neurobiology of Aging* 23S (2002): Abstract 281.

7. R. A. Mulnard et al., "Estrogen Replacement Therapy for Treatment of Mild to Moderate Alzheimer Disease: A Randomized Controlled Trial. Alzheimer's Disease Cooperative Study," *Journal of the American Medical Association* 283 (8): 1007–1015 (2000).

8. S. Seshadri et al., "Postmenopausal Estrogen Replacement Therapy and the Risk of Alzheimer's Disease," *Archives of Neurology* 58 (3): 435–440 (2001).

9. S. Asthana et al., "High-Dose Estradiol Improves Cognition for Women with AD: Results of a Randomized Study," *Neurology* 57 (4): 605–612 (2001).

10. M. M. Cherrier et al., "Testosterone Supplementation Improves Spatial and Verbal Memory in Healthy Older Men," *Neurology* 57 (1): 80–88 (2001).

11. M. Simons et al., "Cholesterol and Alzheimer's Disease: Is There a Link?" *Neurology* 57 (6): 1089–1093 (2001).

12. R. Mayeux and M. Sano, "Treatment of Alzheimer's Disease," *New England Journal of Medicine* 341 (22): 1670–1679 (1999).

13. O. L. Lopez et al., "Cholinesterase Inhibitor Treatment Alters the Natural History of Alzheimer's Disease," *Journal of Neurology, Neurosurgery, and Psychiatry* 72 (3): 310–314 (2002).

14. J. L. Cummings and G. Cole, "Alzheimer Disease," *Journal of the American Medical Association* 287 (18): 2335–2338 (2002).

15. B. Reisberg et al., "Long-Term Treatment with Nmda Antagonist Memantine: Results of a 24-Week, Open-Label Extension Study in Moderately Severe to Severe Alzheimer's Disease," *Neurobiology of Aging* 23S (2002): Abstract 2039.

16. M. H. Tuszynski et al., "Nerve Growth Factor Gene Therapy for Alzheimer's Disease," *Journal of Molecular Neuroscience* 19 (1–2): 207 (2002).

17. E. M. Sigurdsson et al., "Immunization with a Nontoxic/Nonfibrillar Amyloid-Beta Homologous Peptide Reduces Alzheimer's Disease-Associated Pathology in Transgenic Mice," *American Journal of Pathology* 159 (2): 439–47 (2001).

PART III
CHAPTER 8

1. N. L. Mace and P. V. Rabins, *The 36-Hour Day*, 3d ed. Baltimore: Johns Hopkins Press, 1999.

2. M. Dennis et al., *Clinical Neuropsychology and Brain Function: Research, Measurement, and Practice*, T. Boll and B. K. Bryant (Eds.). Washington, DC: American Psychological Association, 1988; M. Freedman et al., *Clock Drawing*. New York: Oxford University Press, 1994; and L. C. Hartlage, M. J. Asken, and J. L. Hornsby, *Essentials of Neuropsychological Assessment*. New York: Springer, 1987.

3. M. S. Albert et al., "Preclinical Prediction of AD Using Neuropsychological Tests," *Journal of the International Neuropsychological Society* 7 (5): 631–639 (2001); P. Brooke and R. Bullock, "Validation of a 6 Item Cognitive Impairment Test with a View to Primary Care Usage," *International Journal of Geriatric Psychiatry* 14 (11): 936–940 (1999); and P. R. Solomon et al., "A 7 Minute Neurocognitive Screening Battery Highly Sensitive to Alzheimer's Disease," *Archives of Neurology* 55 (3): 349–355 (1998).

4. A. Padovani et al., "Amyloid Precursor Protein in Platelets: A Peripheral Marker for the Diagnosis of Sporadic AD," *Neurology* 57 (12): 2243–2248 (2001).

5. R. B. DeMattos et al., "Brain to Plasma Amyloid-Beta Efflux: A Measure of Brain Amyloid Burden in a Mouse Model of Alzheimer's Disease," *Science* 295 (5563): 2264–2267 (2002).

6. D. A. Snowdon, "Aging and Alzheimer's Disease: Lessons from the Nun Study," *Gerontologist* 37 (2): 150–156 (1997).

7. D. H. Silverman et al., "Positron Emission Tomography in Evaluation of Dementia: Regional Brain Metabolism and Long-Term Outcome," *Journal of the American Medical Association* 286 (17): 2120-2127 (2001).

8. G. W. Small, "Genetic Risk and Imaging," *Neurobiology of Aging* 23S (2002): Abstract 2061.

CHAPTER 9

1. J. L. Cummings and G. Cole, "Alzheimer Disease," *Journal of the American Medical Association* 287 (18): 2335–2338 (2002).

2. R. C. Green et al., "Risk of Dementia among White and African American Relatives of Patients with Alzheimer Disease," *Journal of the American Medical Association* 287 (3): 329–336 (2002).

3. J. L. Cummings and G. Cole, "Alzheimer Disease," *Journal of the American Medical Association* 287 (18): 2335–2338 (2002).

4. Ibid.

5. G. Dal Forno et al., "Apo-E Genotype and Survival in Men and Women with Alzheimer's Disease," *Neurology* 58 (7): 1045–1050 (2002).

6. M. Hashimoto et al., "Apolipoprotein E Epsilon 4 and the Pattern of Regional Brain Atrophy in Alzheimer's Disease," *Neurology* 57 (8): 1461–1466 (2001).

7. J. L. Cummings and G. Cole, "Alzheimer Disease," *Journal of the American Medical Association* 287 (18): 2335–2338 (2002).

8. S. Schmidt et al., "Association of the Apolipoprotein E Gene with Age-Related Macular Degeneration: Possible Effect Modification by Family History, Age, and Gender," *Molecular Vision* 6 (2000): 287–293.

9. R. C. Green, "Risk Assessment for Alzheimer's Disease with Genetic Susceptibility Testing: Has the Moment Arrived?" *Alzheimer's Quarterly* 3 (2002): 208–214.

10. E. J. Steinbart et al., "Impact of DNA Testing for Early-Onset Familial Alzheimer Disease and Frontotemporal Dementia," *Archives of Neurology* 58 (11): 1828–1831 (2001).

11. L. Fratiglioni and W. Rocca, "Epidemiology of Dementia," in *Handbook of Neuropsychology*, 2d ed., by F. Boller and S. Cappa (Eds.). Amsterdam: Elsevier, 2001, pp. 193–215.

12. "Risks and Benefits of Estrogen Plus Progestin in Healthy Postmenopausal Women: Principal Results from the Women's Health Initiative Randomized Controlled Trial," *Journal of the American Medical Association* 288 (3): 321–333 (2002); and J. V. Lacey, Jr., et al., "Menopausal Hormone Replacement Therapy and Risk of Ovarian Cancer," *Journal of the American Medical Association* 288 (3): 334–341 (2002).

13. H. C. Hendrie et al., "Incidence of Dementia and Alzheimer Disease in 2 Communities: Yoruba Residing in Ibadan, Nigeria, and African Americans Residing in Indianapolis, Indiana," *Journal of the American Medical Association* 285 (6): 739–747 (2001).

14. K. Kondo, M. Niino, and K. Shido, "A Case-Control Study of Alzheimer's Disease in Japan—Significance of Life-Styles," *Dementia* 5 (6): 314–326 (1994).

15. H. C. Hendrie et al., "Alzheimer's Disease Is Rare in Cree," *International Psychogeriatrics* 5 (1): 5–14 (1993).

16. L. Fratiglioni and W. Rocca, "Epidemiology of Dementia," in *Handbook of Neuropsychology*, 2d ed., by F. Boller and S. Cappa (Eds.). Amsterdam: Elsevier, 2001, pp. 193–215.

AFTERWORD

1. C. R. Green, *Total Memory Workout: 8 Easy Steps to Maximize Memory Fitness.* New York: Bantam, 1999.

2. B. Gordon, *Memory: Remembering and Forgetting in Everyday Life.* New York: Mastermedia Limited, 1995; and C. R. Green, *Total Memory Workout: 8 Easy Steps to Maximize Memory Fitness.* New York: Bantam, 1999.

3. E. R. Kandel, J. H. Schwartz, and T. M. Jessell, *Essentials of Neural Science and Behavior.* Norwalk, CT: Appleton & Lange, 1995.

ABOUT THE AUTHOR

Majid Fotuhi, M.D., Ph.D., has the unique distinction of being both a faculty member in neurology at Harvard Medical School and a neurology consultant at the Alzheimer's Disease Research Center at Johns Hopkins Hospital. He received his M.D. (cum laude) from the Harvard-MIT Division of Health Sciences and Technology in Boston and his Ph.D. in neuroscience and neurology residency training at Johns Hopkins Medical Institutions in Baltimore. Dr. Fotuhi has published a dozen scientific articles and has received numerous awards for his work in neurobiology, including a prestigious teaching award from the American Academy of Neurology.

INDEX

Note: An *i* following a page number indicates an illustration.